NO MORE H(

Written by

Omar Schartz

2014

DEDICATION

Dedicated to my wife Jewel, who passed away in 2007. I was crushed. But we had watched our kids grow into wonderful people and great parents. And really what more can a couple desire out of life? We had marched through life shoulder to shoulder, merely shoving aside any obstacles in our way. Every person should be so lucky.

ACKNOWLEDGEMENTS, APOLOGIES AND OMISSIONS

When my good friend, Jack Manion, suggested I write the story of my life, I laughed at him and explained that most of the stories would only point out that while I was occasionally thick-headed, I was also very lucky. At least I had been surrounded by great people who convinced me that life was hard, but it was also an incredible and rewarding journey. When Jack passed away my kids began pressing me to write my story. Apparently Jack had planted some very robust seeds in the minds of Jewels' and my kids. I tried all of the arguments that held Jack at bay, but the kids had the one thing that Jack didn't possess and that was youth and the inability to understand what "no" meant. When I told Jack that I had no idea how to begin he said he would gladly proof read anything I wrote down and he would get his editor and publisher to assist me on the path to becoming an author. I got the same rebuttal from my kids. Slowly they convinced me that there was no back door that offered escape. All of our kids knew exactly where to prod me to start and keep me writing. Carolyn, our youngest daughter, who has a degree in journalism, told me to just write as the memories came flooding back and she would organize and make them readable. Cindy waited eagerly as I filled notebook after notebook with my scribbled thoughts and went about typing every page before passing the stories on to Carolyn. Susan, and Sharon along with their brothers Jim and Tony became proof readers and constant reminders of stories they wanted included.

Each of the stories in the book was written exactly as I remembered. The primary thing that might be in error will be in the dates. I never had any ability to reference dates as I never kept any journals or notes. Dates seemed to flow together owing to our large and vibrant family's many birthdates and other milestones, and time seemed to simply morph together to form the tapestry of our lives. If any of my friends or associates are not mentioned in the book, it does not mean that I considered them irrelevant or unimportant. It only meant that I wanted to keep it as short and readable as possible. I can only hope that the reader enjoys our adventures through the middle and last part of the 20th century. Any mistakes found in this book are entirely my own.

TABLE OF CONTENTS

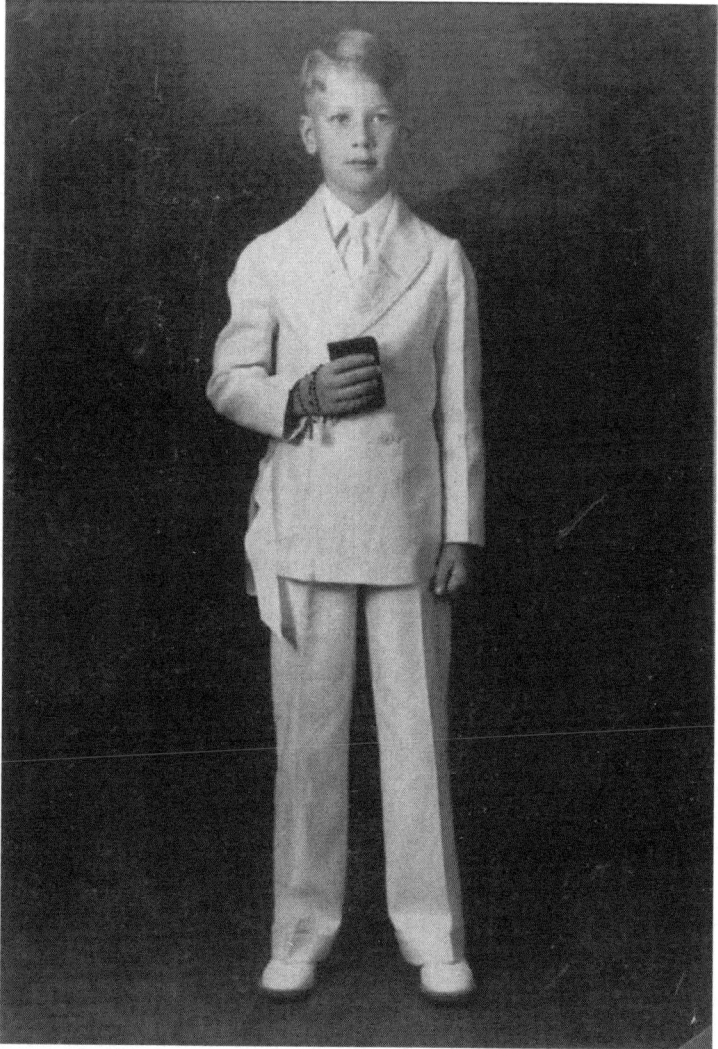

Omar First Communion, 1937

Corrine, Omar and Carol Jean

Zook High School Basketball

Omar, Jim Pfister, John Kirchgassner, Herb Bowman, 1948

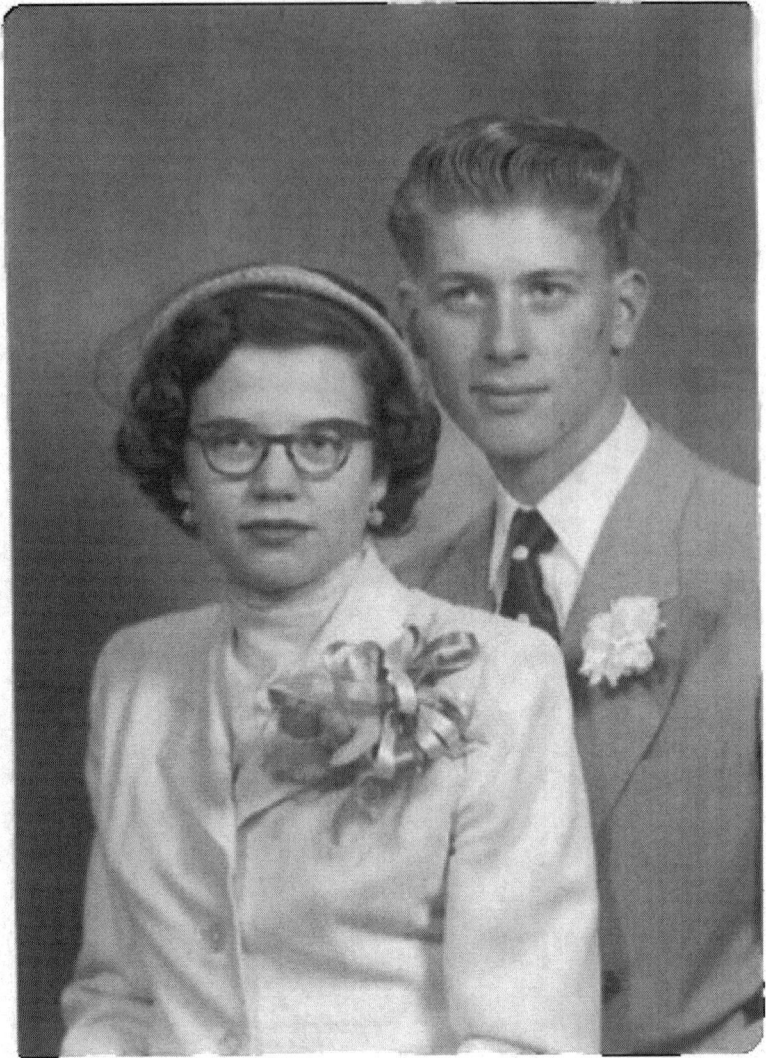

Omar and Jewel Wedding Portrait, 1951

Omar and Jewel at Wedding Reception, 1951

Vernon Schartz, Omar, Jewel and Corrine 1951

Omar, Jewel, Tony, Sharon, Susan and Cindy, 1956

Jewel, Carolyn, Omar, Cindy, Susan, Sharon, Tony, 1957

Behlen Dryer similar to one used at the Co-op

GREAT BEND, KANSAS,

SWIMMING'S A FAMILY AFFAIR with Mrs. Omar Schartz, rt. 2, Larned. When she decides to spend an afternoon at the pool, she not only takes her five children at right but usually stops by for her brother-in-law, six-year-old Gordon Schartz, at left. Her children are from left, Carolyn, 2; Susan, 5; Tony, 7; Sharon, 6, and Cindy, four. The children are teaching themselves to swim and their attractive mother is learning right along with them. They all make it a point to head for the pool once or twice every week.

Gordon, Jewel, Carolyn, Susan, Tony, Sharon, Cindy, 1958

Omar and Jewel on the Farm, 1968

Omar with Valley Water Drive, 1972

Singing Schartz Sisters (Susan, Carolyn, Cindy, Sharon)

Carolyn, Susan, Tony, Sharon, Cindy, Jim, Jewel, Omar – 1972

Acrylic painting of Tandem Tractor

Jim with Monkey Wheel, 1973

Pawnee Beefbuilders

12.26 '97

Omar and Jewel's Farmstead, 1997

KANSAS AG INNOVATOR

On-farm needs turn to off-farm income

Omar Schartz, Larned, describes himself as a blacksmith at heart. His touch is everywhere around the farm, from irrigation equipment to fertilizer and pesticide application components. As he learned that his needs were the needs of others, too, he went commercial. In 1980, he formed Pickle Creek Manufacturing, holder of numerous ag patents. Schartz will receive the first Kansas Ag Innovator award at the Farm Show.

TEXT AND PHOTOS BY HANK ERNST

Ag Innovator of the Year Article

Omar's family 1970: Omar, Gordon, Greg, Dora, Charlie, Corrine

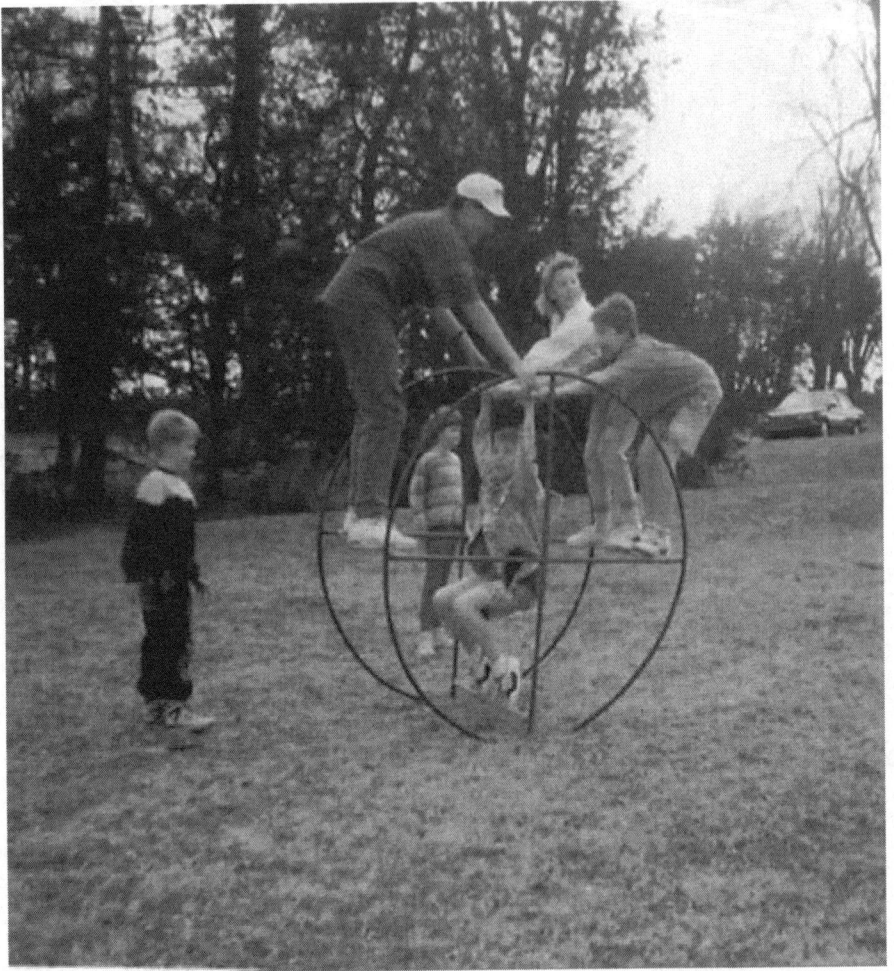

Grandkids playing on the Monkey Wheel

Farm Sale 1991

Gathering Storm (painted by Omar 1996)

Omar and Jewel 2005

The Hill Gang, 2005

Building model airplanes in Larned.

Jack Manion

Jewel at the Larned Methodist Church Organ

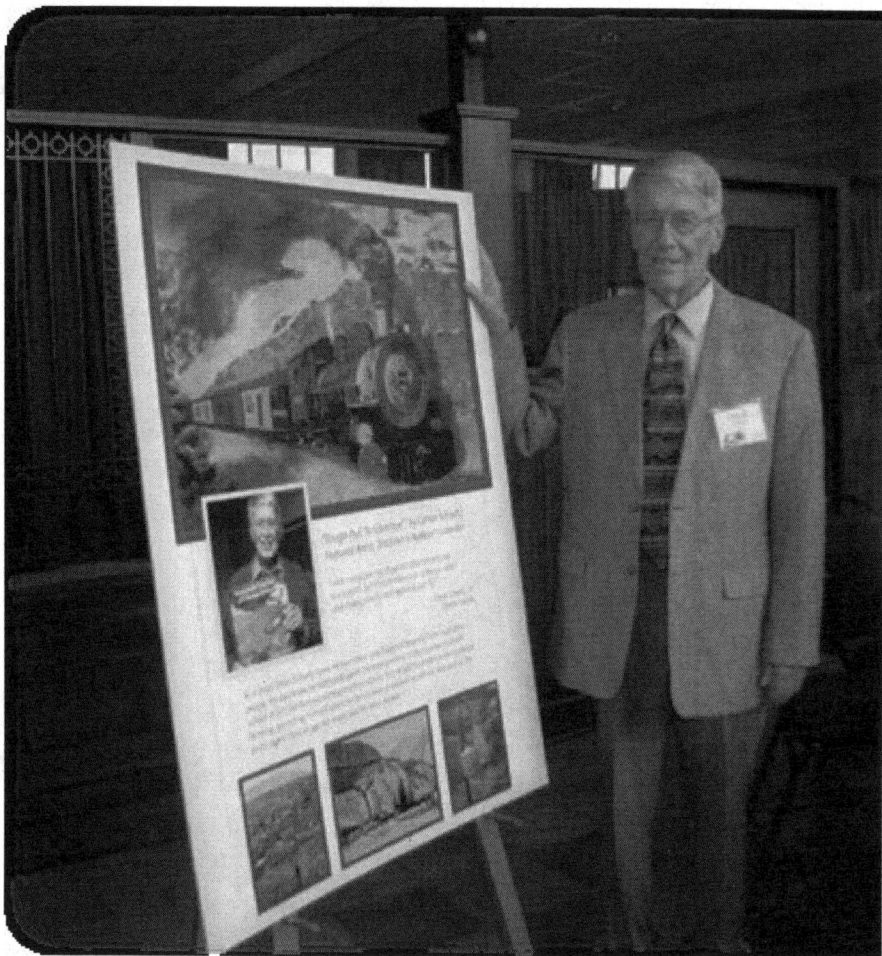

Kansas Governor's Art is Ageless Award, 2012

Dinner with the family at Aberdeen

Surfing the web on iPad 2014

CHARLIE AND DORA

My father, Charlie Schartz, was one of ten children, five boys and five girls, and grew up on a farm just outside of Ellinwood, Kansas. Their father P.J. lost his wife Amelia (Schaffer) when she was only 34 years old, and the oldest, Aunt Flora, was only seventeen. The youngest, Uncle Edward, was eight months old. Family history reveals that my grandfather was a land speculator and gone from home much of the time, leaving Flora in charge of raising the family. The kids walked a mile to school in Ellinwood. Aunt Flora took her responsibility very seriously, and under the circumstances, did an admirable job of raising her eight siblings (nine year old Aunt Anna, who was an invalid, died within months of Grandma).

I wish I knew more of the history of my grandfather's land trading enterprise but sadly I don't. The only thing I do know is that in his later life his land purchases were dictated by his desire to leave each of his kids a farm. When he died each of his kids inherited a farm complete with a farmstead. The Zook area must have been attractive to grandpa as many of the farms surrounded or were close to Zook, Kansas. The farm inherited by Lawrence, dad's older brother, was a half mile northwest of Zook. Dad's farm adjoined Lawrence's farm and the two farmsteads were only one-third mile apart. Uncle Albert's farm adjoined the Zook townsite to the east. Uncle Julius's was two miles northwest, while Aunt Lucy's was three miles south. Aunt Helen's farm was three miles northeast of Zook. Uncle Eddie's farm was four miles north and two miles east of Zook. Aunt Mathilda's farm was east of Spearville, Kansas and the only farm not in the Zook community along with Aunt Flora's who inherited the homeplace at Ellinwood.

My mother was the youngest child of Henry and Lena Sewing. Mom had three brothers, Henry, George and Herman and older sisters, Clara Reed, Lydia Winkelman, and Mayme Schartz. I believe Grandpa and Grandma were both born of German immigrants who came to this country from Germany. Their surname Sewing was always pronounced as 'Saving' which was the German pronunciation. It wasn't until I got older that my mother's relationship with her family seemed strange. I only remember Grandpa and Grandma Sewing visiting us on two occasions and our visits to them were only a few times more.

Grandpa and Grandma Sewing lived on a farm about 10 miles northeast of Ellinwood. I doubt that his farm was more than 160 acres because he was a carpenter as well as a blacksmith. Grandpa Sewing built the Lutheran Church, along with many of the homes in Ellinwood. It would end up that my dad and Uncle Lawrence married two of the Sewing sisters, Dora and Mayme.

According to family lore, the Sewing family were all staunch Lutherans and lost no love on Catholics. Both mom and Mayme converted to Catholicism, which could only have added to Grandpa and Grandma Sewing's dislike of Catholics. Family members have described Grandpa Sewing as having many of the traits of the men of German ancestry; they were the head of the family and what they said was the law. Having two daughters joining the enemy was reason enough to be a bit distrustful of their choice of husbands. Since my mother was the youngest in her family most of my cousins on her side of the family were several years older than I. Being younger plus seldom seeing them we never got to know each other very well.

After Grandfather Sewing passed away and Grandma was no longer able to live alone, Grandma was passed around among most of the siblings. When it was Mom's turn to take care of Grandma, Mom and Dad moved their bedroom upstairs and Grandma took their bedroom on the ground floor. Grandma lived with us several years until Aunt Clara and Uncle Fred Reed decided Grandma should join them in their home in Sioux City, Iowa. She spent the rest of her life in Sioux City.

Grandpa Schartz was very hard of hearing due to being knocked off a wheat stack by lightning as a young man. When we visited them as a youngster my sisters and I were glad to leave because of all the yelling and shouting. The family had grown up with grandpa's hearing problem and had compensated by shouting so grandpa could hear what was being said. All of the younger kids were loud talkers throughout their lives. As I have aged I don't doubt that my grandfather was struck by a bolt of lightning but I think that poor hearing was primarily a genetic problem. As most of dad's siblings aged their hearing deteriorated as well. Both my sister Corrine and I have poor hearing as do several of my kids. So for historical purposes I won't attribute my poor hearing to anything but genetics.

My extended family had a unique marriage history, at least I have never heard of any other family having a similar set of circumstances. As stated earlier, Uncle Lawrence and Dad married sisters Mayme and Dora Sewing. Dad's sisters, Helen and Lucy Schartz married brothers Arthur and Leonard Wurm. Dad's brother, Eddy and sister Flora, married Helen and George Birzer who were sister and brother. The only fact that I am aware of that could possibly have resulted in such a unique set of circumstances was religion as everyone but Uncle Leonard and Arthur were from large families. There are few families that produced as many double cousins as my immediate family.

GROWING UP

Dad was born in 1900 in their farmhouse near Ellinwood and Mom was born in 1910 in their farmhouse outside Ellinwood. They were married in 1928 at Sacred Heart Catholic church in Larned. There were five of us born to the marriage. I was the oldest, born in 1931, Corrine in 1932, Carol Jean in 1936, Greg in 1946 and finally Gordon in 1952. We were all born in the hospital in Larned, and we were mom's only pregnancies, as far as I know. We all grew up on the family farm northwest of Zook given to dad by Grandpa Schartz.

Growing up, our family ate very well and we did not want for anything. The day always started with doing chores right after we got up. Water had to be carried to the chicken house. We usually milked about five or six cows for the kitchen, separated the cream from the milk with a cream separator in the barn's milk room which also included an area for washing the pails, separator and the milking machine. After separating the cream from the milk the skim milk was fed to the bucket calves and hogs. Then the cow herd was fed silage and hay. In the thirties and early forties we burned coal for heat and cooking.

When we heard our parents stoking the stoves to start the day we knew it was time to get up. When we were small, Mom always helped Dad with the chores. Corrine, Carol and I would get dressed for school and go to the kitchen. The cook stove stood on legs that kept the bottom of the oven about a foot off the floor. We would lie on our bellies and slide under the stove to complete any unfinished homework. The warm floor under the stove guaranteed it would be a good place to start the day.

After the chores were done Mom always fixed breakfast. Beef, pork or chicken was on every menu except Fridays when our Catholic religion only allowed fish for the meat dishes. Breakfast on Friday was generally hot cereal or scrambled eggs and toast and sometimes a fruit salad and of course coffee. Other mornings of the week the breakfast consisted of meat, generally pork but occasionally beef, fried eggs, bread, or toast, and fried potatoes.

As I look back on growing up on a farm, I am ashamed that I didn't recognize how hard my mother and sisters had to work to keep the family clothed and fed. With a houseful of kids there seemed someone was always sick and the youngest always added diapers to the wash load. The laundry for a large family would have kept a person busy full time. There were no automatic washing machines or dryers, so the laundry was done mostly by hand. When the laundry was removed from the clothes line it was brought inside where it was sprinkled, rolled up, placed in a basket and then ironed the following day. Pants, shirts, dresses, and bedding were always ironed. Before electricity the irons were heated on the kitchen stove.

Mom had one day of the week when she baked. When we were small she always made our bread along with pies and cakes. On Saturdays she scrubbed the floors and cleaned the house. Until I left home after high school we never ate a meal in a restaurant. In her first thirty years of married life there had to be days when she felt bad and wondered how she could go on, but I never saw her in bed once she was up. When we got electricity in the late thirties my parents bought electric appliances that helped lessen the workload but they continued doing many of the things as they always had. When us kids were small my parents hired a young woman to help mom during harvest time as the cooking and extra laundry for the harvest help were more than she could do by herself.

Mom had a treadle powered sewing machine that she used to make dresses for herself and my sisters. She had a big box of dress patterns that she used when she sewed. The chicken feed that we bought in town was bagged in printed cotton sacks which mom used to make clothes. When buying feed we had to be sure the sacks all matched so there was enough material for mom's sewing projects.

All during grade school I wore denim overalls. Overalls were worn by all the boys and a few of the girls in grade school. Our family wore long stockings in the winter that were held up by garter belts. I don't know why but I always hated those garter belts and mom always checked to make sure I had put them on. During and after the second world war, clothes and styles rapidly changed. I remember the first pair of slacks that replaced my denim overalls. My farm shoes, which were lace up boots, were replaced by the loafer style which had become popular during the war. Our clothes fashion had changed from the farm clothing that had served as our identity to the more casual style that became popular after the war. Girls' styles changed as well. Skirts and blouses replaced the home made dresses. Heavy shoes and long stockings were replaced by loafers and bobby socks. However, hand me downs were still worn by kids who had older siblings at home.

There was a service station about a mile south of our house. The name of the family who operated the service station was Posey. Dudley Posey had a daughter who shared my birth date and, in fact, Mrs. Posey shared a hospital room with my mother when we were born. A few days before my sixth birthday I received a card requesting that I attend a birthday party to celebrate Eva Marie Posey's and my shared birthday. It wasn't until I just now wrote it down did I realize what a wonderful gesture this was. At the birthday party each of us received a small silver spoon that was smaller by a fourth than a regular teaspoon and on the end of the handle was a small image of Pinocchio. I took it home and placed it in the drawer with our silverware. That small spoon became the spoon that all of our kids learned to eat solid food out of. During one of our moves the spoon disappeared. I sometimes wish I could hold that spoon once more. Maybe it would help me recall some forgotten memories of the past.

THE MEDICINE CABINET

Our medicine cabinet on the farm always held the following: a pint of Castor Oil, a small bottle of Mercurochrome, a small bottle of Iodine, a jar of Vicks, and a roll of tape. As a young boy I developed a chronic sinus problem. My sinus flare-ups were always preceded by a migraine headache, so I had ample warning before my sinus attacks stated. As the attacks worsened Mom would take me to the doctor. The only treatment in the late thirties and early forties was a procedure known as sinus irrigation. Warm pressurized water was squirted into the sinuses and the mucosa was sucked out by a powerful vacuum machine. This was a very risky procedure as there was always the danger of puncturing a hole in the thin bone that covered the underside of the brain. When the suction was applied the brain could be suctioned out with the mucus. The first time this was used on me it only took one nurse and my mother to hold me down while Dr. Brenner manned the fire hose and suction line. As I got older more nurses were added to the hold down crew. I began to realize that in order to not be subjected to medical torture, the answer lay in not telling anyone that I was ill. I had begun to realize that most of the time the cure was always worse than the disease. It became a very fine line between being too sick to go to school and being ill enough that a trip to the doctor was called for. I was sick often enough that in twelve years of school I was never a candidate for having perfect attendance.

In the practice of farm home medicine all illnesses began or settled in the digestive tract. It was believed that a huge dose of Castor Oil was God's answer to any disease involving the inside of the body. To a six year old, a dose of Castor Oil is the vilest tasting and most disgusting thing that was required of them up until that age. If the compound that makes Castor Oil so distasteful could be isolated and the gene inserted into the recreational drugs that are becoming the scourge of society today, the drug problem would be solved overnight.

Mercurochrome was used on the small kids' cuts and scrapes. It had no medicinal or curative benefits at all, but a small cut and the area around the cut that were stained red by the Mercurochrome was a badge of proof that an injury had been inflicted on its victim. As the victims got older iodine replaced the medicine of choice by mothers. Iodine on a cut or scrape is another matter altogether. Iodine's main ingredient is liquefied red hot coals. When the trip to the medicine cabinet brought out the iodine the kid usually had a spontaneous healing and rushed from the house and resumed playing. Today, kids' medicines come in all colors and tastes so it's no wonder their mothers dash to the medicine cabinet when the kids suffer a cut or scrape. Spontaneous healing, in my opinion, is always preferable to healing brought on by a good tasting, pretty medicine.

RAISING CHICKENS/BUTCHERING HOGS

I found hog butchering time to be one of the highlights of my grade school years. It always occurred shortly after the first of the year when all of my aunts, uncles, and a few neighbors would get together and butcher the coming year's pork. This gathering always took place on our farm. My mother told me that the reason it was at our farm was because of our garage. It was about 24 feet square and had a concrete floor which made it easy to keep clean while processing the meat.

The process looked a little something like this: on Monday morning families would bring the hogs that were to be butchered to our farm and unload them into the barn while the men started a fire under the vat that the hogs would be scalded in after they were shot and bled. The women would be setting up tables with tubs used to hold meat as the hogs were being butchered. As the hogs were shot they were quickly drug to the windmill where a hoist was fashioned so they could be hung. Their throats were cut and some of the women would catch the blood in buckets to be processed later. After they bled out the women would take the blood inside where it would be stirred until it cooled. Once cooled, it wouldn't coagulate and would keep until it was used to make sausage. The hogs were then lowered into the vat with the boiling water. Once the hogs were scalded, the men used scrapers to remove the hair from the hide. The carcass was then taken into the garage where some of the men and several of the women would start cutting it up. The heart, liver, and brains were all removed and were given to whoever wanted them.

The intestines were saved, cleaned, and prepared to serve as sausage casings. It seemed that each hog's intestines would hold all the sausage that the carcass produced. After the intestines had been evacuated of the hogs' last meal, the intestines were washed and turned inside out. The inside of the gut, which was now on the outside, was coated with a kind of mucosa which could be easily removed by scraping with a kitchen knife. When cleaned, the casings were nearly transparent and went into a bucket of water to await being filled with sausage.

The meat was taken off of the bones and went into tubs waiting to be ground into sausage. In the meantime, the killing and scalding crew were getting more hogs ready for the butchering tables. By the time the first dozen hogs were killed a fire was built under my parents' cast iron fifty gallon kettle. The hides with scraps of fat and the fat trimmed from the meat went into the kettle and fat was rendered from the skins and meat. After rendering, the meat scraps were all saved and were made into mush. The rendered lard was used to pack the meat and most of the sausages into canning jars. After working together for a few years this group could butcher and process 24 hogs in six days.

I mentioned earlier that the blood was saved and was made into sausage. When it was time to make the blood sausage it always seemed an argument would break out amongst sausage makers as to the spice content of the sausage. The blood was mixed with sausage meat and was highly seasoned. No recipe was ever written down so everyone remembered something different. The blood sausage was the prize of the butchering festival and everyone made sure they got their share. About 35 years after the last butchering episode at our farm, one of my aunts found out that a butcher in a small town near where she lived was making small batches of blood sausage and was quietly selling it out of the back door of his butcher shop. She notified all of the farmer neighbors and friends who had taken part in the butchering events at our farm. They were able to once again enjoy the sausage that they had when they all assembled at our farm to prepare their pork for the following year. Because the state inspected all butcher shops, the state forbid him of making and selling his black-market sausage and we haven't had any since.

All of our pork except the sausage was salt cured. Most of the sausage was smoke cured while some were canned but the main cuts of pork were salt cured. The hams, shoulders, loins, and bacon were rubbed with rock salt right after butchering. These cuts continued to be hand rubbed with salt for a few weeks after butchering and placed in gunny sacks and hung in the barn until needed for the table. I remember Dad injecting salt brine into the shoulders and hams with a huge syringe but I don't know if they had been hand rubbed with salt or not.

Unlike pork we never butchered beef on the farm. We always bought our beef from the local slaughter house where it was processed and packaged and placed in their locker plant. The best way to preserve beef was to freeze it or to consume it as soon as possible after butchering. Most towns had butcher shops where meat could be purchased. Until refrigeration became available in the thirties the butcher shops butchered beef and pork only as fast as they could sell it. With the advent of refrigeration most of the butcher shops built refrigerated locker plants where customers could rent storage for processed meat that was purchased from the butcher. This allowed customers who rented locker space from the butcher to pick up their processed meat at any time. It also allowed butchers to process meat ahead of demand. When home freezers were introduced in the early forties, housewives had at their disposal a whole new way of food preservation and cooking options. When my parents, relatives, and friends bought home freezers, home butchering finally became a thing of the past.

Shortly after the holidays was always an exciting time because it meant we would soon be picking up the baby chickens which would be our main meat through the summer. Generally our parents would order about 250 baby chicks. We had a brooder house about 15' square that had an oil fired brooder stove in the middle of the building. The stove had a hood shaped like an umbrella which was about a foot off the floor. The chicks would huddle under the hood where it was always warm for the first week or so and only left their warm place to feed or drink. The floor was covered with peanut shells or peat moss that was purchased at the local feed store. After a couple of months Mom would start checking to see how soon they would be ready to eat. I always looked forward to the first fried chicken of the season because we had been eating salt cured pork all winter.

Generally the young chickens were ready to butcher about wheat harvest time and it became a daily chore for mom and my sisters. Since the roosters always grew faster than the hens the rooster numbers went down first. My mother looked forward to getting a home freezer so she could freeze dressed chickens, but when we had frozen chicken no one in the family liked it so she never stored any dressed chickens in the freezer after that. My mother, if she were alive today, would not believe the way poultry is processed and consumed. It is unbelievable that a whole generation has never tasted fresh home grown, pan fried chicken and gravy on new potatoes fresh from the garden.

Dad always hired summer harvest workers who were fed three meals a day plus a lunch in the middle of the afternoon which Mom and my sisters brought to the field. By the time the harvest hands went back home we had nearly depleted the chickens. (We kids always looked forward with excitement to harvest time when dad hired men from the Missouri Ozark hill country for harvest help. Their skills at making toys from everyday things always amazed me. They spoke with a southern drawl that required several days of intense listening before we could understand them.)

By the end of the summer, the chickens that were left had gotten too big to butcher and went into the chickenhouse where they began to lay eggs for the kitchen.

One of the things that make butchering hogs so valuable was the lard that the hogs produced. Lard was a staple that was used by farm wives when shortening was called for in their recipes. In our home used lard was never thrown out but was kept by my mother and used to make lye soap for laundry and dishes. Making soap was another yearly affair that usually occurred in the summer since it was warm enough to be outside. Several days were needed to make a year's supply of soap. Making soap is a skill that has gone the way of many of the things that farm families did to make it possible to survive the rigors of life on the farm.

RECREATION

I am amazed at just what the term recreation means and the changes in recreation that have occurred in my lifetime. I have always said that growing up during the depression of the thirties was one of the greatest legacies that my generation could have inherited. Unfortunately being told about the experience can never pass on the lessons that we learned by living them. As a parent you were responsible for not only your family but any and everything that contributed to your family and the herds and flocks that put the food on the table. I am also sure that our city cousins faced the same problems and dangers but our dangers were more immediate and obvious since most of our families and friends still lived on farms.

I remember as a child about five or six years old that we would all get in the car and make a drive around the section to check the crops. My father always would take the 22 caliber rifle along to shoot the chicken hawks or maybe a coyote or rabbit if we were lucky. Any bird bigger than a crow was always a chicken hawk and represented a danger to our chickens, and coyotes always were a threat to young calves or so we thought. I now know that none of that generation had ever witnessed a hawk taking a farmer's chicken for a meal or a coyote killing a calf. But they were perceived as a potential threat and needed to be eradicated.

Most of our recreational activities were centered around our hobbies and were enjoyed only when chores or school work allowed us the spare time. As for my father, I never knew of him having any interest outside of his farming. My mother seemed to enjoy sewing for my two sisters and herself. In her later years she enjoyed knitting and crocheting. She made beautiful afghans for us kids and her grandchildren.

PARTNERSHIP

When dad and his brother Lawrence started farming they formed a loose partnership and farmed together. They shared hay and later silage cutting equipment. Since Lawrence's buildings included a shop building, all of the equipment repair was done at his place. They maintained separate livestock herds however. As their herds and families grew they purchased grass lands just south of the Arkansas river. The cow herds were moved to these sand hill pastures in the spring and back to the farms in the fall. This procedure required that several times a week the pastures be checked to count the cattle and make sure the windmills were pumping water for the cattle.

The partnership, though rocky at times, survived for about fifteen years. When Lawrence's son Vernon and I were old enough to operate tractors, the partnership was dissolved. Most of the shop work consisted of changing the horse drawn equipment they owned so it could be pulled by a tractor.

In the early forties they decided to construct a large roundtop shed on Lawrence's farm. They hired local farm boys to help with construction. The buildings were so popular they would construct eight more in the course of the next two years. As of today, 2013, all of them stand except dads, which I burned down with a homemade stove in the early seventies. Most of the round tops were used to house harvesting equipment and tractors; however dad made the front end of his shed into kind of a blacksmith shop where he and I modified and repaired his equipment. After school and on weekends we were always busy with one project or another.

RELIGION

When my dad and his brothers settled in the area, it must have seemed like the whole Schartz clan descended and plopped themselves right in the center of Zook, a fiercely protestant neighborhood. In the early thirties the glue that held many communities together was a common religion. I'm sure that most of the families felt that they were being invaded by a bunch of Catholics. Suspicions and distrust had to be rampant on both sides. This distrust in the Schartz family was instigated by Uncle Lawrence who recognized danger behind every door and word. I suppose the perceived dangers were also recognized by the most devout Baptists and Methodists in the community. This distrust persisted for nearly thirty years until my cousins and I had become members of the community.

An example of this distrust is an incident that occurred sometime in the late thirties or early forties. Uncle Lawrence told dad that the Protestants had planned to burn down all the Schartz farms that night. I still find it impossible why my father didn't try to verify this crazy idea that Lawrence had. That night my father and I stayed up all night with firearms at the ready to protect our farm. It must have been that the phase of the moon was not right because the Protestants never showed up. I think that this incident ended Lawrence's self-proclaimed role as spokesman for the Schartz families.

ELEMENTARY SCHOOL

The elementary school curriculum at that time consisted of reading, writing, arithmetic, science, and music if it didn't interfere with scheduled classes. Most textbooks were purchased from kids who had moved up to the next grade. Subjects and textbooks rarely changed so textbook costs were not very high. Clothing worn by the students at Zook School was plain and consisted mostly of hand me downs from older brothers or sisters. Teachers, once established, spent the rest of their career in the rural school systems.

Discipline was never a problem while I was in school. Just the threat of being sent to the principal's office quickly restored control. I never saw a kid sent to the "office" in the 12 years I attended Zook School. I remember very vividly an incident that happened to me in the second grade when we had just come in from recess and were lined up at the drinking fountain to get a drink before going into the classroom. Our teacher, Mrs. Collins, grabbed me by the arm and shook me and said, "Don't you ever push anyone in line again." Even today I swear I never pushed anyone. That experience left an indelible mark on my personality. Pushing someone in a line would cause Mrs. Collins to suddenly appear and could lead me to the office where the fabled paddle would be applied to my behind.

For the first several years Mom packed our lunches for us until the community decided to offer a hot lunch program. The kitchen was located in a frame building that had previously been used as an industrial arts classroom. The interior was framed up but there was no finishing work on the inside so it was dirty and dark. A local lady was hired as the head cook and another was hired as her assistant. They cooked and served our lunches in this outbuilding until an unused classroom could be remodeled into a kitchen. I never realized that I owed her a hearty thank you for what she did for the few Catholic kids whom she cooked dinner for. Every Friday she served fish sticks to all the kids. Everybody loathed the fish sticks. It was when my classmates called me a mackerel snapper and blamed me for having to eat fish sticks on Friday that I became aware of any verbal evidence of discrimination.

The first few years in school an all school function or production was prepared. These events always were evidence of how talented and ambitious the teachers were. There were never any tryouts, but the students were assigned to certain parts in these productions. When I was in the fourth grade I was informed that I was going to be Pinocchio in a musical play of the same name. Our music teacher that year was a recent college graduate and saw this as an opportunity to show the world what she could do with a group of farm kids. When we were given our playbooks I took it home to show my folks. Mom sat down at the old piano and we started learning the songs I would have to sing. My sisters, mother, and I sang quite a lot but they were mostly Lutheran hymns since she had grown up singing them in their Lutheran household.

As soon as I learned the songs we started in on the spoken parts. At rehearsals I was the only one who knew the songs because everyone else had to learn their songs at school. Pinocchio's mother was played by an upper classman in high school. Her name was Phyllis Barstow. She graduated the following year, I believe. After her graduation and until the last time I saw her, my name was still Pinocchio to her. On the cover of the playbook was a sketch of Pinocchio; my Mom made a cap and curled up shoes that the picture illustrated. The teacher told me that I should make the three noses that were required when Pinocchio told a lie. I made them out of construction paper and taped them beside my nose. If I was careful they stayed on fairly well, except the third one. The picture in the book showed a very long nose with small twigs and leaves at the very end. By the time I got it constructed it was so heavy that the tape couldn't hold it up. When I pointed this out to the teacher she said, "Well, I guess you'll just have to hold it on your nose." I think it was about the time she was wondering how she got herself in this predicament. We finally reached that point where, the old saying goes…"Ready or not, here I come." None of the students knew or cared about the outcome. Everyone was just glad it was over with.

Another play that complex was never attempted again. Generally a grade school musical recital would be given once a year. A Christmas recital was presented at Christmas and the high school music students would present the pieces they performed at the league music festivals.

HIGH SCHOOL

Dating among our high school students was not prevalent, however a few of the students did have steady partners. Dating students from other area towns was limited by the fact that boys didn't have cars or their parents wouldn't allow it. In the forties and fifties the kids south of the river began to make a few friends with the kids in Larned and farm kids from north of the river when farm families began to go to town on Saturday nights to market their produce, go to the movies, get haircuts, pick up parts, and visit with friends and neighbors. Larned was our nearest town and just eight miles north of our farm. Saturday night in town was something everyone in the family looked forward to all week. The kids would maybe go to the movies or meet friends or classmates forming groups at the soda fountains in the numerous drugstores. The local bakery also had a soda fountain and a large area filled with wrought iron tables and chairs.

The streets would be crowded with cars double parked on both sides of the streets with a lot of honking and good natured yelling and gawking adding to the excitement of Saturday nights in their town. Friends and relatives from other small towns relate that Saturday nights in their towns also experienced this unique social phenomenon. This social event lasted until TV was introduced in the mid-fifties and died nearly as fast as it started. Us kids from south of the river were called "sand rats" by the kids from the north side of the river. The soils north of the river tended to be heavier and very flat. As we grew older the term sand rats nearly disappeared except among us who had become farmers in the area where we were born. The only time I hear the term is when two farmers meet who developed a friendship many years ago on our visits to town on a Saturday night. Of all my youthful memories the fun and excitement of a Saturday night in town ranks at the top. I wish my children and grandchildren could have had this experience as well.

In the early fifties a businessman in Larned started a youth oriented hang out for young people. He had a jukebox, a small dance floor, a couple of pool and ping pong tables, and had pop, and sandwiches. Early on it appeared that Sandy's was going to be a good place to hang out. As Sandy's place became more popular in the area the customers started to get older and were being frequented by older single men that had been drinking beer before they arrived. Fights broke out when they got too friendly with someone's date. On Monday mornings there were always stories of a fight that was seen in the alley behind Sandy's. It was usually between a local boy and someone from a neighboring town. The business only lasted a few years before Sandy closed it down because of the trouble.

The one thing that happened about once a month on Saturday nights was when my mother decided that I needed a haircut. In the forties there were four barbershops on Larned's Main Street, all having four barbers. Barber customers had their favorite barbers and By God no one else would dare cut their hair, so Saturday night was always a busy night for the barbers. When you walked into the shop you were at the end of a line of six to eight men waiting for their turn at their favorite barber. It never seemed to fail that one or two of the customers ahead of you would want a shampoo as well as a shave along with a haircut. This would easily double the wait time. It was not unusual to leave the barber shop at 11:00 p.m. or later. By this time most of my friends who were in town for the same reason had gone home. One barber in particular had cut my hair as long as I could remember. His name was Bliss Frankinburger. Bliss was a jovial man with a moustache and a big cigar in his mouth at all times. I considered Bliss a relative just like another uncle. Bliss always kept a conversation going while cutting my hair. Mostly he teased me about girls. No subject was out of bounds with Bliss. It must have made my hair easier to cut if I was blushing.

The boys' hairstyles were all the same, rather long in front and tapered in the back. The long hair in front was always hanging down in our eyes especially during basketball games. One of my teammates had a sister who was two years older. She suggested that she give him one of the new permanents that had just been put on the market so that women could give themselves curly hair. When Herb showed up at school with curly hair we boys razzed him unmercifully while the girls all thought the curly hair was neat, encouraging the rest of the boys to get their hair curled as well.

We all noticed that when Herb started sweating during sports, his hair curled tighter, which kept it out of his eyes. Once the boys realized that curly hair didn't get in your eyes, we started acknowledging that maybe there was something to this curly hair idea. I have always thought that the pressure from the girls had absolutely nothing to do with the decision by myself and the rest of my teammates to go the curly hair route. We were teased unmercifully by all of the teams we played. We got even by badly trouncing them in every game but two our senior year in high school.

After sixty years of reflection on the curly hair incident I must admit that the girls had perhaps played a minor role in my decision. It was shortly after I agreed to let my mother and sister curl my hair that I would be forced to face Bliss for a haircut. As I took my seat at the end of the line I saw Bliss look at me every once in a while. Every time he looked at me I would scoot down on my chair an inch or two. By the time it was my turn in Bliss's chair, I was nearly lying on the floor. I got in the chair and he put the cloth apron on me. He stepped back and slowly walked around me and the chair all the while looking at my hair. After he had circled me he whispered in my ear just loud enough so everyone could hear, "Tell me, do you squat to pee?" Many times in my life I have been embarrassed, but never as bad as that moment. This incident is deeply burned into my memory and every time I think of Bliss, which is quite often, I have to smile.

Shortly after this incident, Bliss retired from barbering. He bought a pool hall located beneath Vin's Pharmacy which was the largest pharmacy in town. I, along with my friends and acquaintances, had been introduced to playing pool as a substitute for walking the streets on Saturday nights and Bliss's pool hall became our fun center on Saturday nights or any other time we were in town.

The boys' athletic events were the highlight events of the school year. While I was in high school all of the boys went out for sports. Boys were never too light or small as no excuse was tolerated. If you were a boy you went out, period. The gyms in all of the schools were nearly identical in size since most of the schools were built in the twenties and it seemed they were all built from the same plans. Most of the gyms were about 50' long and 30' wide. Some gyms had the stage sticking out about four feet onto the floor. In my four years in high school we got one set of new basketball uniforms. Our football uniforms were from the twenties. Our helmets were of soft leather and were so soft you could fold them double and carry them in your rear pocket. Our shoulder pads were patched up. They were taken to a canvas repair shop every fall so they could be sewn back together, otherwise we couldn't keep them on. When we played a game where all the other kids' uniforms matched we could only look and be envious.

Six local teams made up the South 50-6 league. Those teams were Zook, Belpre, Pawnee Rock, Radium, and Garfield. When I reached my sophomore year in high school our football and basketball teams started being recognized as having the potential of developing into a better than average high school team. There were four boys in my class all over 6' in height. In such a small rural area it was unusual to have even one boy on a team as tall as 6'.

MODEL AIRPLANES

One day when I was in the third or fourth grade, as I walked into school, I saw some of the high school boys flying small model airplanes in the gym. At that time airplanes were a novelty seldom seen in central Kansas. When an airplane was heard overhead everyone would rush outside to watch it fly away. Today it seems ridiculous that such a common sight could cause such a commotion. I had always had a fascination with insects and birds' ability to fly. The building of airbases in central Kansas early in WWII only fueled my desire to learn all I could about flight. My education consisted of flying magazines that I bought with the change I received when purchasing dad's cigars at Lynch Drug Store after church. Dad would give me a dollar with instructions to buy two Swisher Sweet cigars he could smoke when we got home. Miss Lynch, who owned the drug store, and in no small way was instrumental in shaping what I became, would look over her glasses and ask me if I was old enough to smoke cigars. She noticed that I always bought airplane magazines. As the years passed her magazine racks always had new and different airplane magazines.

The airplanes that the high school boys were flying were give-aways with a tank full of gas that their parents received when they gassed up their cars. The boys allowed me to hold and inspect these marvelous flying things. They appeared to be constructed of small wooden sticks covered with light paper. That day in school all I could think about was how I could build one of my own. That became the starting moment that I began to realize if you wanted something bad enough you could build it yourself. It took me a couple of weeks to glue enough flat toothpicks together that sort of resembled the wood sticks in the models. I had no idea what a blue print was or that it had to be the first step in any construction.

My mother finally got tired of having glue all over the table, myself and anything else that was close by, but I kept trying and finally had glued enough toothpicks together to build a structure sort of resembling an airplane. After the framework was done it was time to cover it. I searched the house and the only thing that resembled the covering on the models was the toilet paper in the bathroom. The mess with toothpicks and glue was bad enough but when I added toilet paper to the mix my mother really became agitated.

When my mother went shopping, my sisters and I went along. It was on one of these shopping sprees when we found ourselves in Duckwalls. As we browsed around, way in the back, I found a few model airplane kits. What a wonderful find for me! My sisters and I had learned it did no good to ask for anything while shopping because it just wasn't going to happen. I asked my mother for a dime to buy the model but mom said no. I was very excited to know that one of those models could be mine for 10¢. I resumed trying to make toothpicks look like airplanes.

Model airplane magazines kept showing up in Miss Lynch's magazine racks and I would buy them with the change I got back from the cigars for dad. On my ninth birthday, my parents gave me one of the models from Duckwalls. That became one of the defining moments of my life.

One of the lessons I learned from my toothpick and glue episodes was that when you tried to glue something together be sure you have the correct glue for the job. One of the magazines had an ad for glue specially formulated for model airplanes. On our next trip to town I convinced my mother that I had to check at Duckwalls to see if they had the glue for model airplanes. I ran to the back of the store and sure enough, there was a whole box of tubes of glue, but it was 10¢ a tube. I could only hope I wouldn't have to wait until my next birthday to get the tube of glue. My mother relented and gave me the dime. I don't remember if it was the box with the model inside or the glue that thrilled me the most. From that day till I met Jewel every spare minute of my time was spent modeling. It was through modeling that I learned to read blueprints, how to spot weaknesses in structures, how to reinforce those weak spots without adding any more weight than absolutely necessary, and a host of other construction details.

It also made me realize how important mathematics was in design and construction. I wonder how much curiosity of mine might have been satisfied if my high school math teacher hadn't been more interested in talking about basketball, seldom asking us to open our textbooks. I decided if I ever had children I was going to insist that they get a good education. Many years later one of our daughters asked me, "How come there was never any discussion as to whether we would go to college? It seemed that we always knew we would go." That question proved that at least in one small way we did a good job of parenting.

BOYS' ATHLETICS; GOAT'S HEADS; DISKING THE GRIDIRON; COACH HOROSKO

The boys' school athletic events were always well attended by parents and friends. At the football games parents' cars were parked all around the field. The actual playing fields after the season ended were forgotten until about two weeks before the first game the following fall when the men of the community realized that a game was coming up and it was time to spiffy up the gridiron. In the meantime the most dreaded and nasty weed in western Kansas had formed a carpet on the field. That weed was the dreaded Mexican sandbur, "the goat head," as it was commonly known. It was a low growing vine that had millions of seeds that had two ugly and very sharp spines that protruded from each side of each seed pod. The spines were long and sharp enough that they could easily puncture the tires of the day. The favorite tool used to destroy them was a tandem disc. A tandem disc is a farm tool that chops up the residue on the soil surface and mixes the residue with dirt.

A football field readied for playing with a disc looks very nice from a distance, but upon closer inspection almost all the stickers made their appearance. They seem and actually are waiting for some fool to get knocked down and rolled onto their waiting spines. The spines are about a quarter of an inch long. If one was to enter the bottom of your foot they are so sharp that they would continue until they would be stopped by your knee bone. It was such a field that all of our football games were played on.

The football shoes we wore were the fourth thing that God created after the earth, the sun, and the sky. When the cleats were worn out they could be unscrewed and replaced with new ones. When it rained on the field after it was prepared the cleats on our shoes would pack the dirt and sandburs down until it was as hard as concrete. When a player made a cut or sharp turn his cleats screeched in protest. Since the shoes were passed down from one grade to the next invariably the last couple of boys would have to wear their basketball shoes from the previous season since the football shoes were so worn out. In my four years I never saw a new pair of football shoes on any player in our league.

Six man football was the game our league played. The team was comprised of a center, two ends, a quarterback, and two halfbacks. Eleven man football teams scoffed at six man football as not being football at all. However on a percentage basis, our small league had more players who played Division 1 and professional ball than any league in the state. The most famous was probably Oliver Spencer who started all four seasons at KU and was drafted by the Detroit Lions. After he retired he joined John Madden of the Oakland Raiders as a defensive line coach. I remember when I was a senior playing Trousdale where Ollie went to school. We dreaded when Trousdale had the ball because we knew that Ollie would be coming right over the center and all of our team would be on the ground in his wake. But he was a true gentleman because after he made his touchdown he would come and help anyone who was unable to get up.

Our basketball games were all played in the school gyms except when we played Lewis. Ball games at Lewis were played in their city hall which had a concrete floor. The ceiling was thirteen feet high and after they placed a couple rows of chairs against one wall the floor was only about 25' wide and maybe 40' long. The rules in those days, compared to today, make it nearly impossible to compare the two games. However, the basketball shoe problems couldn't compare with the football shoe problem either. Bill Wiggins' drug store was the only place in town that sold basketball shoes. He always got his first shipment in the late fall. Within 20 minutes of his getting his latest stock of shoes in, all the boys knew it. If Bill had your size you bought them because you never knew when his next shipment would come in.

In my senior year we all knew who would be on the first team because we had all played together since seventh grade. We knew that the team would be made up of the senior boys: Herb Bowman and John Kirchgassner at 6', Jim Pfister at 6'4", and myself at 6'2". The fifth spot would probably be Charlie Clowers who was a 5'10" junior. This lineup would average a tad over 6". Our team since the seventh grade had been taller by quite a bit than any other area teams and had seldom lost a basketball game to any team in our league.

In my senior year, our coach, Steve Horosko would become a controversial figure in the community. He was married and had a three year old daughter. 1949 was the beginning of the McCarthy era, which was the leading headlines in all the papers. Everyone was looking for any communist in our midst. Mr. Horosko was a strange man who taught civics and coached. His classroom was on the top floor of Zook High School facing the east windows. We would go to his class and might discuss some headlines in a recent newspaper, but generally his assignment would be a written comment that had been discussed in an earlier class. These comments were to be completed and handed in at the end of the period. While we were writing he would sit on the edge of his desk and gaze mournfully out the windows of the classroom.

Generally he would start the class with a short lecture which always had a political theme. These lectures should not have seemed unusual since his class was civics, but as the year progressed the lectures began to take on a strange overtone and very seldom did the students discuss this with their teachers or parents. Mr. Horosko was beginning to talk about Joe McCarthy more and more. Senator McCarthy's rants about the communist's takeover of America inflamed the country and nearly incited riots in the streets. The country hadn't been in such a panic since Pearl Harbor.

One day near the end of the school year Mr. Horosko was lecturing our civics class while he was perched on his desk. He seemed in a daze as he looked out the window and said, "You know, it is not fair that some people have so much money while some do not. The government should see that everyone is treated the same." He continued rambling and closed the lecture with the statement that declared that he could make his three year old daughter into any kind of person he wanted her to be. Even to a bunch of farm kids his lecture sounded radical.

When we went to the locker room to get ready for baseball practice a sign had been taped to the door that said, "Does Horosko know what a communist is?" As I came down the stairs I saw Mr. Reed, our principal, looking at the sign on the door. He removed the sign and passed me on his way to the office. When we came in from practice the school board was assembled in the office. Since the school term only had a week or so until summer break, I guess the board had decided to wait until after school was out before doing anything. Horosko had been offered his job back for the following year at a previous board meeting. Rumor said that the board had withdrawn the offer of a new contract for the following year.

About a month after graduation I was at the Collins Service Station which was situated about a quarter mile from the schoolhouse. In any other community it would have been known as the local watering hole. But because of local religious beliefs, liquor and beer just evaporated the minute it got near the Zook community. I was drinking a Coke when Tom Horton, whose home was about two blocks from the school, came in. After we exchanged our thoughts about the weather, Tom asked me if I had been interviewed yet. I told him I didn't know what he was talking about. He said that the previous week an FBI agent came to his house and interviewed him about what he knew about Steve Horosko. Tom proudly showed me the card that the agent had given him. The card identified the card holder as an FBI agent on assignment for the House Un-American Activities Committee under the direction of J. Edgar Hoover. Later that summer Tom told me that he had heard that the Horosko family had been relocated to some detention facility that housed suspected communist sympathizers. That was the last thing I heard about the man who coached my teammates and I in my last year at Zook High.

RECREATIONAL ACTIVITIES; SPORTS

As I look back on growing up on a farm I tend to feel sorry for today's boys growing up in cities without the wonderful things that I took for granted while I grew up. I have always wondered at my father growing up in a motherless family of five brothers and five sisters and how that affected him and eventually me. I'm sure it had to affect him and his siblings as to the role as parents. My father loved baseball and he was always sure that I had a baseball, glove, and bat and until I was in high school we always played catch or he would pitch to me while I learned how to use a bat properly. The first football or basketball games that my parents ever saw were when I participated in those games at Zook. They never missed a single game while I was in school and although they didn't really understand what the rules were they knew that if my team had the highest score we won. While I was in high school Dad found out that Larned had a summer baseball program and made sure that I would participate in the program. .

As a sophomore I started in the American Legion program in Larned. Players were eligible until they graduated from high school. After graduating, the Ban Johnson program was available. The B.J. program was very popular in the forties and fifties because few of the rural kids went to college, but they still liked competing at some level. Larned became the hotbed of baseball in the forties and fifties because of a fry cook who had a small restaurant just one half block off of main street. His name was Bert Wells. Bert was the lead scout for the Brooklyn Dodgers. The American Legion baseball program is for boys of high school age which is when a boy begins to show promise of becoming a potential major league prospect. Bert quietly became the architect of the Legion programs in Larned. He brought Lou Drazic to Larned to coach the Legion team. Lou had been a catcher in the Dodger's organization but had torn up his knee just after he was called up to join the Dodgers. Bert got Lou a job with Duckwalls and he quickly rose to manager of the store. Lou was six years older than I, and a Catholic, and since the Catholic Church in Larned was rather small at the time he and I became friends. Lou found a Catholic girl in our church and married her. I was thrilled to serve as his best man at his wedding.

The Legion program was a national program and had strict rules about how many players on a team could come from outside of a town's area. Bert overcame this obstacle by bringing a prospect to Larned and placing him in a local fan's home as the fan's close relative. It wasn't long until our team had four or five players who were from all over the country. Bert and Lou could watch how the transplanted player progressed, and if he showed promise, Burt would sign him. If not, the kid was sent home.

In high school and my early years in the legion program I was a pitcher. In my senior year of high school I was throwing the javelin and tore up my shoulder. After my shoulder healed as much as it ever would, I could only pitch three innings before it gave out again. It was during the years of sheer joy playing ball and dreaming of one day signing a contract to play with a major league team came to a screeching halt. My shoulder problem plus the fact that I never learned to run well became obvious when a player from a neighboring town joined our team; Harold Patterson was only about 5 ½ feet tall as a freshman but was already showing the skills of a great athlete. I pitched batting practice to Harold on his first day of practice. Normally, pitching batting practice required simply getting the ball over the plate. On my first pitch Harold ripped a line drive to left field. He did the same on my next two pitches. Lou, who was watching from the dugout, came to the mound and told me to start throwing him some curves. I soon found myself pitching as if I was in a game. This kid was unbelievable. He hit one over the left field wall in Moffet Stadium. Lou sent him to the outfield to catch fly balls and he covered the entire outfield and caught everything Lou hit him. Normally an outfielder would throw the ball to a cutoff player who would then relay it to the catcher. Harold would rear back and throw it to the catcher with unbelievable accuracy. This freshman had won a starting spot as an outfielder at his first practice.

We all knew we had witnessed something very special that day. After only one practice Harold caused me to reconsider my dream of playing in the big leagues. If, as a freshman, he could dominate so completely all of the skills of a ballplayer, my lack of skills would doom me to never be more than just an average player. I was lucky to play two seasons as a teammate with Harold Patterson. It seemed in every game he would do something that seemed impossible.

In my last year in the Legion program our team was scheduled to play in a tournament in Wichita. Our players and coaches were excited about the tourney because we had been hearing of a phenomenal player from Commerce, Oklahoma who would be playing in the tournament. By this time Harold was well known throughout central Kansas and everyone wanted to see if the Oklahoma kid was as good as Harold. Burt Wells had tried to sign the kid from Oklahoma all summer but hadn't been successful. The week before the tournament we heard that Mick Mantle, the kid from Commerce, had signed with and reported to the Yankees.

At the time the rules of the Kansas High School Activities Association forbid a high school athlete from signing a professional contract. Bert Wells would have to wait two more years before he could try to sign Harold to a Dodger contract. Meanwhile, as Harold got older he also got better. When Harold graduated from high school he and his family had decided that Harold would go to college first before he signed a professional contract. Harold had chosen KU as the college to attend. He went on to be a four year letterman in football, basketball, baseball, and track. Upon graduating from KU he was drafted by the Detroit Lions football team who traded him to Montreal in the Canadian Football League. He went on to set most of the records still standing as a receiver for Montreal. When he retired from professional football he returned to Rozel where he joined his family in the dirt construction business.

When I got too old for the Legion program I was asked to join the Ban Johnson program that was starting up in Macksville. I played three years for Macksville until I was 21 when I was too old for the Ban Johnson program.

Competitive sports existed in the rural areas for the athletes who still wanted to compete in the form of town teams. Baseball town teams existed in the towns across the Midwest while basketball town teams were mostly in the rural areas. The introduction of television in the mid- fifties ended both baseball and basketball town teams. Unfortunately, the girls had no organized athletic events as the Title 9 ruling was still a number of years down the road. Becoming a cheerleader was the only thing that a girl could hope to achieve athletic-wise in high school. Tryouts for a cheerleader was always a big deal for the girls.

DRIVING THE BUS; SERVING ON THE SCHOOL BOARD

We were hauled to and from school by a Model A Ford school bus. The bus had bench seats along both sides. Generally the bus would be nearly full by the time it picked us up because we lived close to the school. We were the last on and the first off. The busses were driven by boys in the upper classes from our high school. All the boys dreamed of the day when we might drive a bus. As I got older the $30 a month for driving seemed a princely sum indeed. I don't remember that discipline was ever a problem on the bus.

One incident does come to mind. There was a family who lived about three miles away from the school. The whole family was so shy that they appeared to be possibly slightly mentally challenged and were seldom seen out in the community. The family had two sons who were a couple of years apart. Their bus driver was one of the orneriest kids in school but his father was on the school board so his antics were pretty much ignored. He convinced the brothers that he could only stop to pick them up. When they were delivered to their home they must jump off the bus while it was still moving. The boys never doubted anything they were told.

On the day that the driver tried out the new procedure he called the boys to the front of the bus and told the boys to hold hands and when he said jump they would leave the bus together. Thirty years later the driver was telling a group of us about it. He still thought it was hilarious. He told us he had nearly stopped when he yelled jump as he watched in his rear view mirror as the two boys rolled down the side of the road. The following day the boys's parents called on the principal and asked that if the bus couldn't stop, could it at least slow down a bit more so the boys wouldn't get so scratched up. If this were to happen today, no one could even imagine the consequences. I saw one of the brothers at his uncle's funeral several years ago and he showed me a watch that his employer had given him for his 55 years he had completed at his firm.

In the mid fifties, the president of the Zook School board was suffering from cancer. When he died the board asked me to fill his unfinished term. When I accepted the position the teacher contracts for the following year had already been signed by the board. As the summer wore on we began to hear from parents of the high school students. They were taking their kids out of Zook High and enrolling them in attendance centers that were nearer where they lived. By mid-summer it became quite clear that what the board thought was an issue we would eventually have to face was suddenly a reality.

The Larned district which was only eight miles away was the first to contact us. Alva Turner, the superintendent, met with our board and assured us that they would welcome all of Zook's students. Although the defection of our high school students had been painful, we still had a viable grade school enrollment. But the board knew that once a family's high school student had changed attendance center it was just a matter of time before the younger members of the family would choose to change schools as well. As the summer drew to a close we started to hold open meetings with the patrons of our district to try to explain what the district was faced with. These meetings were a disaster. Parents blamed everyone from Stalin to me for trying to close the Zook School. Facts were not allowed in the debates that followed. Generational friendships evaporated. Those who knew what was inevitable stayed quiet while the radicals railed about the loss of community. The board finally gave permission to Larned and Macksville to send busses into our district to pick up any high school students wishing to go to Larned or Macksville. The Zook school board retreated and licked the wounds which were inflicted during the debate concerning the closing of Zook High. Although the enrollment in our grade school indicated that before long we would be faced with the closing of our grade school as well, the attitude among our patrons had calmed down somewhat. But it still remained uneasy and distrustful.

Because of the turmoil of the late summer we had forgotten that we had signed contracts with the high school teachers for the upcoming academic year. We had a meeting with an attorney and found out that since we had signed the contracts in good faith we must pay the teachers whether they taught at Zook or not. When the patrons found out about this we found out the problems of the late summer was a picnic compared to what we faced from the local taxpayers. There is no way you can win an argument with a uninformed person and since the public was convinced that all this pain was caused by the board, we would just ignore it. We soon discovered that it takes two to have an argument. If one doesn't participate the argument soon ends but the hate lasts a long time. Zook remained an attendance center for grade school for several more years. Our grade school enrollment began looking like what had happened to our high school. Every year enrollment dropped by 10% or more. Finally the board decided in fairness to our students and since the federal government was calling all the shots on how a school should be run and was threatening to cut funding, we should just bite the bullet and close the grade school. Today nearly 45 years later Larned and Macksville find their enrollments dwindling just like Zook did.

Consolidation was a very stressful time for the small rural schools. It was the consolidation issue that spelled the death knell for many communities. Neighbors blamed neighbors for their kids having to go to different attendance centers. Some of the animosity remains today, 50 years after the decision to close the schools.

A.A. DOERR; GRASSHOPPERS; HAYING; HOPPER DOZER; DDT

In the late twenties, a young man by the name of A.A. Doerr rode the train to Larned and decided to make it his home. He was a blacksmith and opened a shop south of the railroad tracks where the Pawnee County Co-op office now stands. The machinery of the day was very basic and simple and prone to break down frequently. Since most equipment was manufactured in the eastern industrial cities, parts were not readily available, and shipping parts by rail was slow and unreliable so a blacksmith was a town's valuable asset. Years later Doerr would be recognized as a classic entrepreneur. He quickly recognized the needs of the area residents, built a hardware store and obtained the first International Harvester dealership in Kansas. His firm quickly added a car dealership, a furniture store, and a mortuary. He built a fine mortuary, one of the first in central Kansas. Up until that time mortuary services were provided by the local furniture stores.

His blacksmith shop was always crowded with the local farmers' equipment waiting to be repaired. Double A, as he became known by the local people, also saw the need for water tanks to provide an easy way to furnish water to the area livestock producers. So he designed, built, and sold sheet metal water tanks. His tanks were light enough so two men could easily load them on a truck or trailer and haul them to another site. His tanks became so popular that he built a new factory to produce them. The new factory was called, Doerr Metal Products. In the forties, he started building steel grain bins. Until the introduction of the Doerr bins most farms had wooden frame granaries to store grain. Most granaries were too small and expensive so the steel bin was quickly embraced by the farmers. He laid a train track that ran directly into his factory. In doing so, the metal needed for his stock tanks and steel bins could be unloaded onto the floor of his factory. As more of the native grass was broken out for wheat production, the machinery got bigger and more complex. Because of this, repairing farm equipment required a steady supply of steel. Normally, iron salvaged from old or worn out farm equipment was used. So, to those of us who needed a piece of steel, Doerr Metal quickly became our go-to place.

Walking our alfalfa field in the spring of '39 with my father reminded me of walking through a mud hole. Each step produced a wave in front of each leg, the difference being that the waves were young grasshoppers instead of water. Dad slowly shook his head and said, "It looks like we'll have to plant more Atlas this spring." Atlas was the name of Dads favorite forage sorghum he used to supplement his alfalfa.

Surprisingly, rainfall was not the usual limiting factor in alfalfa production at this time. Grasshoppers were another matter altogether. If you were an alfalfa grower, the spring brought a preview of what you could expect the yields of your alfalfa crop to be. As plants began to green up in the spring, the young grasshoppers would start to emerge and if the numbers were high you knew you would probably have to plant more forage crops to supplement your alfalfa in order to produce enough feed for your livestock through the winter months.

I'm sure that 80 years tends to color your memories a bit, but recalling some of the grasshopper hatches of those years makes me shudder. That spring, as in the previous five or six years, the weather remained hot, dry, and windy... and the hoppers thrived. Normally alfalfa was harvested about every month usually starting at the end of May and then monthly through the summer. Grasshoppers hatch without wings, which develop about month after hatching. Once they are able to fly, they can move great distances to find new fields to feed. About a month after hatching, they have pretty much destroyed everything in their vicinity that is growing. Our mother always took lunch to the field when the men were working. When we drove into the field she pointed out the clouds that were visible around the tractors, which were pulling the mowers that cut the alfalfa off at the ground. She said that the clouds that were normally dust were actually grasshoppers being chased up by the machinery.

Alfalfa production was very labor and equipment intensive. My father and his four brothers (Lawrence, Julius, Eddie and Albert) each had a piece or two of hay machinery thus reducing the overall cost. They helped each other with harvest when haying season arrived. Any extra labor was made up by neighbors who traded labor for the use of our family hay equipment.

Most of the larger farms had huge barns. The upper parts were used to store feed for the farm's livestock, which were confined to the lower floor during blizzards in the winter. The bigger the barn the more livestock the farm could handle.

The barns had a track system built into the peak of the roof. High up on the roof a trolley ran on the track which carried a long rope that pulled the hay off of the barges, which brought the hay from the fields to the barn. The trolley carried grappling hooks which were hooked into the hay on the barge. A team of horses or a tractor was hooked onto the end of the rope. As the horses or tractor backed away it pulled the grappling hooks loaded with hay up to the peak of the barn through the huge door and into the hay mow. As the trolley moved into the barn on the track the hay could be dropped anywhere the man in charge wanted, by simply pulling a rope which unlatched the grappling hooks. Then, the stacking crew would spread the hay and pack it in the upper floor of the barn. When filling a barn with alfalfa hay, a crew of at least 15 men and 10 kids were required. The men did the work and the kids just got in the way. A boy quickly learned which of the men on the crew you stayed away from. Although I never actually heard of any boys losing their lives at the hands of the stacking crews during haying, we kids were aware of the probability!

Generally, when the boys began to annoy the men, they were merely handed a pitchfork and put to work helping distribute and pack the hay. When you were handed that fork, you were no longer a boy, but a part of the haying crew. When you were made a member of the stacking crew there were a few rules you quickly learned. The first rule was you never left your pitchfork lying around or propped against the stack. Fork handles were quickly found by the grasshoppers who quickly made a meal of it. An hour of their dining would leave the handle so rough it was unusable. When quitting for dinner or at night all pitchforks were shoved handle first into the stack so that the hoppers couldn't get to them. Anyone who forgot to put the handle into the stack would spend the afternoon with blistered hands from the rough handles. The veteran stackers would never tell a new member how to store their forks and would tease them unmercifully for rest of the day.

The second rule was when the pitchfork was left on the ground or shoved into the stack the teeth of the fork should always be left pointed toward the ground. Anyone impaled by a fork left the wrong way might justifiably break the handle over the guilty one's head.

The third rule was you never interfered with the stack bosses' decision as to where the next load of hay was to be placed on the stack. The title of stack boss was never handed out, but rather earned by the most intimidating or experienced member of the stacking crew. Before the end of the day everyone was so tired there wasn't any need for rules or thoughts of challenging the stack boss. Putting hay in the barn soon began losing favor, and farmers began stacking their hay in the fields and hauling it to the cattle as they needed it.

By the early 1940's front end loaders began showing up in the hayfields. They were quickly modified with large baskets that held the hay and could put the hay on a stack just where the stack boss wanted it. Hay that was correctly packed and stacked was amazingly weather resistant and quickly became the choice of most farmers.

In the early forties, Doerr Metal introduced a new product for the Ag market, which they called, "The Hopper Dozer." Visualize a bathtub 10 feet long. One side of the tub was approximately 1' high while the other side was about 5' high. Both of the ends were square. The 5' back side was slightly curved toward the front side. The bottom of the tub held from five to ten gallons of kerosene. This whole thing was bolted to the front of a truck or tractor. After the hay crop was stacked or hauled to the barn, the truck or tractor to which the Hopper Dozer was attached would go to the hay field and the operator would drive back and forth through the field. As the Dozer went through the field the hoppers would jump or fly ahead of the Dozer, hit the back side of the tub, and fall into the bottom, which was filled with kerosene, killing them immediately. However, those that jumped around the end or over the back side of the dozer were able to lay eggs for following generations. It was necessary that the operator stop when he reached the end of the field and scoop out the dead hoppers and replenish the kerosene.

Today this practice seems amusing, but it seemed to the farmers at that time to be worth the investment and time. At least they could brag about how many hoppers they had killed. Walking through the field the day after the hay had been removed, and the Dozer had been used, would convince any skeptic that the Dozer had indeed reduced the number of hoppers significantly. But I think because the food supply had been removed the hoppers had simply moved on to greener pastures. The advent of aerial spraying of pesticides quickly doomed the Hopper Dozer and very few can be found today.

In the mid forties, our crew was just finishing a hay field when an airplane landed in the field. As the pilot stepped out of his plane and started walking toward us, the grasshoppers made their little waves in front of his feet as he walked over to where the crew was standing. Most of the crew appeared to be in shock as few had ever been that close to an airplane before. When the shock began to wear off, I heard the pilot tell my father, "I won't charge you a penny to treat this field, but I'll come back tomorrow and if all these hoppers aren't dead, you don't owe me anything, but if they're dead, then you can pay me." I remember well how the crew laughed at him for making such a claim that he could kill all those hoppers. This guy was not only a pilot, but crazy as well. Quickly the deal was closed and the pilot got back in the plane and took off. He flew to the end of the field and started the turns that would become the classic aerial turns that in the years ahead from miles away would identify an aerial sprayer.

The following morning when we went to the field to finish the stacking, we witnessed the first of what would become the miracle of agricultural chemicals. Every one of the hoppers was dead! Unbelievably, there was not a single live hopper in the entire hayfield. While some of us were trying to find a live grasshopper the plane returned. The pilot was grinning as he climbed out of his plane and walked toward my dad. As we walked to the plane it felt and sounded like we were walking on Rice Krispies as the dead hoppers crunched beneath our feet. Dad's first words to the pilot were, "I'll write the check if you'll tell me just what in the hell it was that you sprayed on this field." The pilot answered, "It was DDT. We have used it on places where mosquitoes were a problem for our troops on the ground." Another new word was about to be added to my vocabulary, "environment." Despite its unbelievable ability to kill insects, its residue was soon found in the blood and tissues of birds and mammals all over the world. The shells on the eggs of birds were becoming so thin that they didn't survive until hatching. This nearly wiped out the bald eagle as well as many other bird species. After being banned it took nearly 60 years before the bald eagle population had finally recovered.

The experience with DDT in many ways was a blessing because chemists had to look at persistence as the first thing when they started formulating a new pesticide to be marketed for agriculture. DDT is still used today in some third world countries where insects are a threat to the human population. The use of it is strictly monitored and controlled by the World Health Organization and the EPA. I think that the return to normal rainfall and the widespread use of DDT so weakened the hopper population that they never were able to mount a threat to growing crops again.

Visiting the Blacksmith and Becoming an Engineer

My father was a good customer of Hank, the local blacksmith, who kept Dad's plow and lister shears sharp, but also repaired or modified his tillage equipment. Dad would stack in the corner anything that needed a blacksmith's expertise so that on the next rainy day we would head for a visit with Hank at the Smithy Shop. I always looked forward to riding along on these exciting trips. As long as I remember it became wonderful to be included. I always thought if I was ever adopted by anyone, I sure hoped it would be a blacksmith who would choose me.

Walking into a dark smithy shop, darkened by the smoke from the forge used to heat the metal, was to me a wonderful experience. If the smithy was sharpening plow shares I would always try to guess if he would use his big hammer or if he would go to his trip hammer to start sharpening it. A trip hammer was machine driven by a belt that ran up to a line shaft in the ceiling. The hammer was driven by a cam controlled by a foot switch. The further down he pressed on the switch the faster the hammer rose and fell. He would place the part he was working on in the coal fired forge and turn on the blower which would bring the coals in the forge to a white hot heat. It was so hot it hurt my eyes just to look at the coals. A few minutes were all it took to get the metal hot enough to work. When the part was red hot he would remove it with a huge set of tongs and go to the trip hammer to draw the metal out to its original shape. The first blow or two would send sparks all over the shop, but as soon as the part started cooling down the sparks would diminish as he continued working the piece. I was in complete awe at how he could manipulate anything made of iron so easily. His carbide torch used to cut iron was always a delight when he needed to cut through steel. When he welded something with his electric welder it was always a marvel as well. He soon recognized that I was interested in what he was doing and when he had something to weld he would give me his spare welders' helmet so I could get up close and watch him magically join two pieces of iron.

I have always wondered if my interest in blacksmithing was a genetic thing as my maternal grandfather, among other skills, was a blacksmith, or if it was because the kind blacksmith let me watch him do his magic with his welder.

One day when I was in the seventh grade, I came home from school and my dad said, "Let's go to the shed so you can see what I bought today." He opened the door and there sat a new electric welder. The welder the blacksmith had was a huge machine on wheels so it could be moved around the shop. This was about the time vendors began to realize that the farms that dotted the landscape were in fact a source of potential sales. It was such a salesman that sold my dad the welder. Dad said, "Now we won't have to go to the blacksmith when something breaks." The welder was about 30" high and 18" wide and came with an assortment of welding rods. By supper time, I had managed to use all of the sample rods. The next day we went to Larned to get more rods, but no one in town had any. Dad knew a guy who ran a hardware store in Great Bend and was sure he would know where we could get more rods.

On the way to Great Bend my dad said the first thing we were going to build was a cab for the tractor. He said he would check the junk yards for an old truck cab and we would make it fit on the tractor. This would be the first of many things that we made through the following half-century. The tractor cab was the most daunting project anyone could imagine. The first challenge neither of us had considered was how we would cut all the metal off the cab that we didn't need. I soon found if I increased the heat of the welder, I could burn right through the unwanted tin of the cab. This used a lot of rods and left a very rough edge on the tin. The easiest way to describe it would be like chopping a tree down with a hammer. Dad and I soon found out that to get the most out of the welder, we were going to need several other expensive tools as well. It was several years before my dad got tired of all the rough and ugly cuts I made with the electric welder and bought me an acetylene torch. I was sure my dad lay in bed at night thinking of things we were going to build. I never saw my dad even try to weld with our welder, but he sure kept me busy with our projects. I'm sure if every father bought his twelve year old son a welder and a pile of iron, the world would soon be flooded with blacksmiths.

When I got all the extra iron hacked off of the old truck cab and finally got the mounts made, we were ready to mount it on the tractor. Dad had forgotten that the doors on the cab wouldn't work because the rear tractor wheels were in the way. We finally decided to get on the tractor the same way as before----get on the rear of the tractor. That meant that the rear of the truck cab would have to be removed also. When the doors were removed we were left with just the windshield and a piece of tin over our head. I don't think this was exactly what dad had in mind when he dreamed of a tractor cab. Anyone who has ever done welding will agree that the hardest thing to weld is thin iron, like the metal on the body of a car. It's like trying to weld ice. When you strike the arc, it immediately melts a hole through both pieces. Move ahead a bit, strike the arc again, and another hole appears. This was the first lesson I learned on the tractor cab project. Dad seemed to be pleased with the way we were progressing on the build however, and could hardly wait to try it out. It was anything but beautiful to look at. If you looked closely it appeared that a truck had run into the back end of a tractor at a speed of just under 600 miles per hour. It looked as if everything behind the doors had been blown off by the impact. When it appeared that nothing else could be added or removed, we declared the project completed.

When I came home from school the following day, Dad had tried to cover up my welding with a couple coats of paint. The sun shining through the holes in my welds were evidence that the fabricator was less than an expert at welding sheet metal. If I thought that welding the whole thing together was hard, Dad's admitting that the thing was a complete failure was much harder for him. After half a day in the field, he would appear to look as if he was made completely of soil. The wind swirling around the tractor would deposit dust on the inside and right on top of him. The only things recognizable were the whites of his eyes and his teeth. Being a farmer, he sure wasn't going to complain about a little dust. Unbelievably, he never complained that removing the back of the cab so he could get on and off was a terrible idea. Enclosing the rear of the tractor in sheet metal and a glass enclosure however, brought problems we had not even considered. The gear noise from the transmission and differential was so loud it was like being trapped in a huge drum. A day inside the cab would leave you with ringing in your ears. Only after a night's sleep would your hearing slowly return to normal, only to be faced by another day of noise torture. Dad's determination and resolve lasted about a week until he couldn't stand it any longer.

My father later surprised me when he decided that we needed an oxy-acetylene torch so I would no longer have to cut iron with the welder. The oxy-acetylene torch made working with iron much faster and easier and speeded up our projects immensely.

In the late thirties Ford Motor company released their new tractor, the 9N. It proved to be a radical departure from previous tractor designs. It was smaller by half than most of the tractors popular with the farmers up to that time. The engine was the same engine that had powered the popular Ford Model A cars. It also introduced hydraulic power to the ag industry. The tillage tools to be used behind the tractor were built by Ford also. The tools were hooked to a pair of lift arms on the rear of the tractors. These arms were raised and lowered by a hydraulic pump that was inside the tractor. The raising and lowering of the implement was controlled by a lever near the right side of the operator. The novel hydraulic and mounting on the tillage tools were so efficient that the small tractor could do nearly as much work as the much larger tractors of the day.

When they were first introduced most farmers bought them as utility or chore tractors, but when they were hooked to the Ford machinery they quickly became farm tractors. Most operators didn't appreciate how much power the Model A engine had as a tractor. Since the hydraulic system was all inside of the tractor few realized that mating the tillage tool to the tractor and being controlled by hydraulics was the reason for the tractors' amazing efficiency. All four wheels were easily changed to different widths so it could be used for row crops. My dad bought his Ford tractor in 1940 and it quickly became Corrine's tractor when we plowed. When Dad realized that was mostly because of the hydraulics he began to dream of putting hydraulics on his larger tractors.

So as it happened, the winter issue of the 1946 Sears and Roebuck catalog offered a new product that caught dad's eye. It was a hydraulic kit that could be mounted on farm tractors. Dad immediately ordered one because he realized that hydraulics were going to start a transformative era in agriculture. When we unpacked it, Dad remarked that we would probably have to go to Hank's blacksmith shop to get it installed as some machine work would be needed to install it correctly. Thus began the second chapter of working with metal for me.

Back against the far wall of Hank's shop were several pieces of equipment that I had never paid much attention to, as I never saw Hank at work there. When Dad inquired about the installation, Hank quickly assured Dad that he could do it. Dad looked forward to driving his tractor to Belpre, where Hank's blacksmith shop was located, because he had just had rubber tires installed on his tractor which had been converted from the steel wheels that had been on the tractor originally. During the school year I only got to go along after school and on Saturday when Dad went to the shop, but during the summer, anytime Dad went, I got to go along. When Dad had a big project like the installation of the hydraulic pump, we would spend the entire day at Hank's shop watching. Dad always warned me to be sure and stay out of Hank's way when he was working. Hank must have been awfully hungry to put up with us every day while he worked. I have always wished I could thank him for answering all the questions that he answered for me. His patience forever impacted my life and what I was to become.

The installation of the pump required that he remove the tarps from the three machines at the back of his shop. The machines were a lathe, a mill, and an industrial drill press, plus a couple of electric grinders. When I watched Hank chuck a square piece of steel into the lathe and slowly turn the square piece of steel into a perfect shaft, it took me several days to recognize what I had witnessed. I guess I had just thought they were hatched from some kind of eggs along with other things that I didn't know or ask questions about.

After Hank had successfully installed the pump we figured out that the installation of the pump was just the tip of a very large iceberg. We had the means to remotely control our equipment, but anything we wanted to control would have to be remodeled to respond to our needs. Most of the equipment in use at that time was horse drawn equipment. All that was required to convert it consisted of removing the horse drawn tongue and replace it with a tongue so that it could be hooked to a tractor. Hank and Dad discussed this problem at length and decided that perhaps a plow would be the first piece of machinery that was to be remodeled. Dad's four bottom plow was the first piece of equipment that received the makeover. The original lift mechanism consisted of a mechanical lift of the left front wheel of the plow controlled by a rope running up to the tractor. When the rope was pulled, the lift would engage and either go up or down depending on which position the lift was in when the rope was pulled. Any adjustment after that had to be made by two handles on the plow. They decided that the hydraulic cylinder in the kit could perform all these functions if it was installed properly. The installation took place while I was in school, so I didn't get to witness all of the installation process, but from my conversations with Dad, I began to wonder if the dream of hydraulic controlled equipment might be destined to the ever growing pile of failed projects at the rear of our shop.

One day I came home from school and Dad informed me that they finally achieved success with the plow. When I finally saw the plow, with all of the weld scars, I knew that it had been a real challenge even for Hank. With the plow success, Dad was having a hard time deciding which piece of his equipment would be the next to be converted to hydraulic control, so the four row lister became the next piece to be converted. Since its conversion took place during the winter I wasn't able to observe its conversion, but after it was pulled home my respect for Hank and his ability to solve mechanical problems reached new heights. Even nearly seventy years later, I don't think I have ever seen a more remarkable bit of agricultural engineering. For me I wouldn't even try to describe it because of its complexity while being absolutely reliable. Never in the 25 years that we used it, did it break down or malfunction. In my opinion very few Ag products can make such a claim. Hank refitted all of our tillage tools to hydraulic control and they all performed spectacularly.

It was a couple of years before tractor manufacturers offered hydraulic as optional equipment and tillage tools were all still offered only with manually operated control systems. When manufacturers finally began offering hydraulic controls on everything did the hydraulic era suddenly begin to impact the way farm tillage was to be practiced.

As I experimented with my building and design projects, I began copying Hank's designs for the hydraulic conversion for a few neighbors who wanted their equipment converted. One of my uncles had purchased a riding lawn mower designed and built by a farmer blacksmith in western Kansas. It was the first riding lawnmower that most had ever seen. It had a 9 hp Wisconsin engine, a Model A Ford transmission, and a 24" cut. When my dad first saw it, he wanted one just like it. So it became our next project. The mower turned out very well and was used on our farms for 25 years. When my dad showed someone the mower he always said, "Omar built it." One of the viewers commented that I should patent it. I knew that a patent would only be issued on original designs and since it was a copy there was no way I could get it patented.

Our original tractor cab project was the first of many failures that we would eventually doom to the discard pile behind our shop. Though our failed projects were many, we slowly became more intelligent as to what we could make work. All through this learning process Dad never lost his enthusiasm for trying something new. I couldn't help but share in his enthusiasm when his next idea entered his head during my days in school. He continued going to junk yards to pick up iron or anything else we needed to finish one project or start another.

LEWIS CATTLE; LARNED AS PREMIERE ALFALFA PRODUCER

No one has ever given enough credit to a legendary Hereford cattle breeding family just outside of Larned, John M. Lewis, who named his farm Alfalfa Lawn Farms. He and his two sons Walter and Joe became known around the world as the leading breeders of polled Hereford cattle. Joe and Walter both attended K State and belonged to every club and organization that had anything to do with cattle and agriculture. They both were in K State's cattle judging teams and competed in the world's most prestigious livestock shows. All three served as president of the Hereford Cattle Association. Their calves would win both live and carcass shows anywhere in the world. John had used the abbreviation ALF as the first letters in his pedigree lines identifying that this animal had originated at the Alfalfa Lawn Farms of Larned, Kansas. I don't know of a logo in the cattle industry that is known any better than ALF.

In the forties dwarfism began showing up in some of their calves. K State thought that the small blocky animals that the livestock judges preferred in the shows were to blame. But Joe and Walter didn't believe that was the cause. They began searching through their extensive pedigree files and finally settled on a bull that their father had bought many years before in England and had carried the gene for dwarfism. They immediately contacted the association and K State with their findings and began culling anything that was related to that bull. The culling decimated their herd and their cattle were never able to achieve the dominance that they had enjoyed for so many years.

After many years of dominance by the Alfalfa Lawn Cattle of Larned and by way of association, Larned, in later years, would become known as the premier alfalfa production region of Kansas and truckers looking for hay for dairies and feed yards came to Larned first. Alfalfa plantings exploded in our part of the state in the seventies. Everyone wanted to get into it as it was unheard of that we could grow something that could be sold so easily.

We became educated in the ways of unscrupulous business practices as truckers would stop in the fields while you were putting up hay and would bid on the hay in the stack and want to buy all the hay you would raise that year. It turned out to be a real learning experience for us producers as no one knew these truckers. When it came time for them to pick up their load they might pick up several loads and pay cash for them, and then tell the producer that the yard they were supplying had built a large hay storage shed and wanted it filled right away so they would bring several trucks to fill the shed. They would arrive several days later with enough trucks and load all the hay and as soon as the farmers went to do chores or eat supper they would all leave and the farmer didn't know who they were or where they were from because they had paid cash on the first loads. This scheme worked several times before word got out what was happening.

Most truckers, though not all, were down and outers who could barely scratch together enough money to buy an old worn out truck and get into the hay business. Many times getting paid was like pulling chicken's teeth. It took us producers only a couple of years before we had developed a relationship with a reputable trucker who was honest and became their primary buyer. New business firms, whose only business was custom harvesting and marketing of their customers' hay crops, began to show up. These custom operators enjoyed a booming business. Most of these custom operators included marketing of the hay as well. This service helped weed out the unscrupulous truckers and fewer and fewer reports of hay thievery were heard. All of the hay that the truckers brought was baled, and semis loaded with hay heading west became common place. All of the hay was baled in what became known as small bales, which measured 16"x18"x48". The balers were manufactured by most of the major machinery manufacturers.

LIVESTOCK AUCTIONS

One activity my Dad always enjoyed was attending the local livestock sale. Fred Doll had a sale facility next to the creek south of Larned and on Thursdays he held a livestock sale. Since nearly all of the farms grew livestock of one kind or another most farmers attended his auctions. If a farmer wasn't in the sale barn watching the livestock being auctioned he would be outside visiting with neighbors and friends. Only harvest or illness seemed to limit the crowd of farmers at the auction. As I write this I am amazed at how rapidly sustenance farming was replaced by grain productions. As I grew up there were farm families on nearly every quarter section. Every family had a few cows and hogs, a flock of chickens or turkeys, and a houseful of kids and they survived on 160 acres. When these homesteads were settled most left a small acreage in native grass for their small herds of cows and horses to graze and all had barbed wire fences to contain their livestock.

When these subsistence farms gave way to grain production the buildings were razed, the remaining grass was broken out, and the fences were taken down. These changes seemed to happen overnight. All of these changes were driven by the Second World War which enabled farm families to head to the cities and higher wages. As grain production increased livestock production nearly disappeared especially on the high plains of Kansas. Livestock only thrived on lands not suitable for grain production. Cattle ranchers were now found in these hills and breaks not suitable for grain production.

Most of the large scale cattle production was in the mountains and arid areas of the mountain states. As size and efficiency of farm equipment increased so did the price of good farm land. Farm land value quickly reached $100 an acre, a price only dreamed of a generation before. About the only land sold at auction was to settle an estate so as to quell a family who preferred money over land ownership. Most land sales were by private treaty and neighbors only became aware of them when the change of ownership was published in the local newspaper.

GROWING UP WITH GUNS; HUNTING PHEASANT/QUAIL; PARSONS GROUP

After World War II a new business sprang up. It was the merchandizing of surplus goods that was used to fight the war. Surplus stores opened in nearly every town in the country. It was unbelievable the goods that these stores offered to the people who had to do without during the war. Kansas City had a surplus store made up mostly of wheeled vehicles from Jeeps to 4x4 trucks. It was from this dealer that my Uncle Lawrence acquired a Jeep. Vernon, his son, was a sophomore and I was a freshman when he bought the Jeep.

Vernon and I had both had grown up with guns in our hands. I am not sure if this practice was the way all boys from farm families were raised or if it was just the way our fathers decided to raise their sons. We both had started with BB guns before we started school and we were accomplished marksmen by the time we were ten years old. We both got 22 rifles for Christmas in1942. Both of our fathers were very good shots with Uncle Lawrence being the best shot of the two. I once saw Lawrcnce bet a neighbor that he could hit a penny thrown in the air with a 22 rifle. The neighbor bet him and he hit eight out of ten that the neighbor threw in the air. Sundays always found

Vernon and me driving the jeep through the fields hunting jack rabbits with our 22's. The late forties and early fifties were extremely wet and the fall always brought many ducks and geese to the many potholes in our area. The pheasant numbers were exploding and the state had instituted a three day season on them. The season on pheasants always brought many hunters from all over to hunt them.

A couple of car loads of hunters from Parsons, Kansas stopped in one early morning when our dads and us boys were getting ready to go pheasant hunting and we invited them to hunt with us. This started a 20 year friendship with the group from Parsons. They never missed an opening day of pheasant season in all those years. They all lived on farms and tried to get us to come to Parsons to hunt quail with them but the quail season always fell during the busiest time of the year for us as we were always planting wheat or filling silos when quail season opened. In 1952 the state fish and game commission instituted a split quail season with the second half opening the first of December. Vernon and I decided to go to Parsons and hunt with our friends on the opening day of the December season.

We were not prepared for the difference of lifestyles we encountered at Parsons. It appeared that many of the customs of the Ozark people had spilled over into southeastern Kansas. We found it strange that marriage among the farm kids were arranged by the parents of the girls and boys. Most of the kids were married by their sixteenth birthday. Another thing we found was that hunting was a way of putting food on the table for these people. The men knew exactly where every covey of quail was located within three miles of their homes. On our first morning of hunting as we walked along the timber that grew along a small stream one of the men yelled "squirrel" and everyone converged around the guy who had yelled. They all began searching for the squirrel. With eight or nine people looking it wasn't long before they had the squirrel in their game bag. The following morning at breakfast Vernon and I were served the squirrel while everyone else ate quail. The men were all great shots and could have easily killed all of the quail in a covey. But they always made sure that a few birds were left to rebuild the covey.

All of the men lived on farms while most of the farms were too small to support a family. Many of them worked at the Sunflower Ordinance Factory that made artillery shells for the government. In the eighties, the last of the original group passed away and their sons either moved away or no longer hunted. Our thread to Parsons was finally broken.

MILK SEPARATION

A bucket calf is what they called the calves that were taken from their mother when the mothers were milked for home use. Our calves were kept in the barn and fed the milk after the cream had been removed by a separator. The separator was an ingenious machine that you poured the fresh milk into, whereupon it separated the cream from the milk. After the milk and cream had been separated the skimmed milk was fed to other farm animals, including hogs and chickens. Hogs in particular were fond of the skimmed milk. When we went to the barn to milk, the hogs would recognize that in a short while they would be fed the skim milk and would fight for a place at the trough where it would be fed.

Our milk cows were not dairy breeds, but were mostly beef breeds and were not high milk producers. The cream produced from the six to eight cows generally amounted to about one to one and one half quarts per milking. The cream was taken to the house and placed in the refrigerator. When a couple of gallons had accumulated Mom would then churn it into butter. Any cream left over went into a 10 gallon cream can. When full the cream was taken to town and sold at the produce store. The sale of cream generally provided enough cash to buy sugar, salt, flour, and most other kitchen necessities plus a small amount of cash.

The bucket calves were kept in the barn until they were big enough so they could survive on their own with the rest of the herd. Bucket calves required a lot of care as the loss of their mother's milk was very stressful and, being confined in the barn, any disease was always a threat. In spite of all of these hardships most survived and were later added to the herd.

Doing chores required two to three hours twice a day so it seemed that a very short day was left for field work. This had been the regimen for generations so each new generation accepted it as a way of life. This way of life slowly changed in the forties and fifties as farmers began to phase out their livestock herds, primarily milk cows. This was caused by farms increasing in size, better grain yield, higher prices for their grains and smaller families. The loss of grazing acres as the remaining grass was broken out was also a significant factor in the demise of livestock production. About the only native grass that remained was on land thought to be unfit for cropping.

MEETING JEWEL ; MARRIAGE; HONEYMOON

It was shortly before my senior year in high school that I met Jewel. It was love at first sight for me. Not so for Jewel. She and her family had moved to Zook during the summer from Belpre, a small town eight miles south of Zook. Since she had three older sisters the boys from Belpre kept the road hot between the two towns. She didn't have a steady boyfriend in Belpre, but she had a hard time convincing me that all the boys from Belpre were only coming to Zook to see her sisters. When she was a junior and I a senior, we started dating and continued until after she graduated. Jewel's mother was against our dating, as her grandfather was a Methodist circuit rider and disliked Catholics. My being Catholic was a sure sign that I was up to no good in her eyes. It took nearly thirty years for her to accept me and my motives. It took our four girls and two sons to finally bring her around and accept me and our family.

It was around this time that Uncle Julius had bought a 640 acre farm five miles southeast of my parents' farm. Sadly, Uncle Julius died suddenly of a heart attack at the age of 39. His widow, Aunt Hazel, asked me if I would like to farm her farm. My first answer was no, because I didn't have any money to buy equipment or to fund an operation of that size until I could grow a crop. When I told my folks of my decision Dad said, "We need to talk about it." He said that an opportunity like this will probably never happen again in your lifetime. "When Hazel has her equipment sale, I will buy just the essential equipment to put in your first crop and anything else you need you can use mine. We will farm together and it will work out fine." Our combined livestock herd consisted of dad's 25 head of cattle and my four head that dad had given me as bucket calves while I was in high school. Since combining dad's and my two farms didn't leave enough time for me to work at blacksmithing for family and neighbors, I would concentrate on keeping our combined farm equipment repaired.

Jewel and I had talked of getting married, but since I didn't have a job or any income other than the cream I got from milking my parents' cows, we planned to wait until I could afford to marry. Suddenly I was a farmer and we decided to get married.

We married on January 29, 1951. When a classmate, Jim Pfister, heard we were going to get married he wrote me and invited us to visit him and his new bride in Harlegen, Texas. Neither Jewel nor I had been out of Kansas before so we decided to head to south Texas and visit Jim and Madalyn on our honeymoon.

January 28th brought a severe blizzard to Kansas. It was still going on the morning of our wedding day and by 2:00, when we were to be married, the thermometer showed -20°. Our flowers all froze when we left the car for the rectory where we were to be married. We had decided to spend our wedding night in Pratt where the new nine story Roberts Hotel had recently opened. We spent the first night in the tallest building between Topeka and Denver. When we were ready to leave Pratt the following morning the temperature was -22°.

Our car was typical of most cars of the time. It would not start. I walked to the corner where there was a filling station to try to get them to jump start the car. All the service people were gone out to help everyone get their cars started and I had to wait an hour before someone got back to the shop to jump start our car. They charged us $5.00 and since between us we only had $96.50 a fairly large hole had been blown on our honeymoon budget. Had we realized what lay ahead of us we would have pointed the car north and gone back home. We left Pratt and headed south to Oklahoma City. The roads were snow packed with huge drifts on either side. Being the head of the house now I kept telling Jewel that we would surely run out of the storm soon. We probably averaged 30 mph on our leg to Oklahoma City with snow packed roads and blowing snow all the way. It was about this time when Jewel got sick with

128

one of her migraine headaches. She would tell me to stop so she could throw up, and I would have to be sure we could get moving after we stopped. We spent our second night at the south side of Oklahoma City in a cold, drafty motel with Jewel throwing up all night long. Luckily our car started in the morning and we headed for Dallas.

Soon the snow started slacking up only to be replaced by rain. Suddenly, we realized that the rain was freezing. The freezing rain on top of the snow packed roads was making driving hazardous to say the least. It seemed there were more cars in the ditches than on the road.

Fortunately, we went through Dallas at about 2:00 PM missing the rush hour traffic. When we left home we had planned on two days down, three days with Jim, and two days back. In two days we were only half way to Harlengen with no idea of what lay ahead on our way to south Texas. We headed for Houston which lay on the coast of the Gulf of Mexico where we knew we would encounter more tropical weather. Jim and Madalyn had written to tell us to be sure and bring our swimsuits so we could spend at least one day playing in the gulf. We knew we were about to get out of the ice which was now beginning to accumulate on the power lines and trees. The ice on the roads looked like it was 4" thick and since the roads were all two lanes. The only way you knew if you were on the road was if you had your wheels in the ruts made by the traffic ahead of you. There were many more cars in the ditches than we had seen previously. On one stretch of new highway where the ditches were deeper we came upon a stretch where a car going into the ditch would wind up in water as deep as the top of the hood. The people sitting on top of their cars looked lonely and wet. We waved as we went by on our way to a warmer climate. The rains intensified while the temperature dropped.

When we got to Corpus Christi we thought we had seen all that a winter storm could do. We were unprepared for what lay ahead. We began seeing power lines snapping under the weight of ice, and cars came fishtailing towards us hopefully getting to a ditch before we hit them. When we finally got to Corpus it was like driving into an abandoned city. There wasn't a light to be seen in the whole city. Not a stoplight or another light to be seen. Car wrecks were everywhere as people drove into intersections and were not able to stop or avoid a car coming from the side streets. A few hardy souls had figured out if they placed a candle on the dash it would melt the ice on their windshields. Many of the drivers appeared to have a candle flame on the end of their noses as they went merrily on their way. We would drive cautiously up to an intersection and check every direction to make sure no one would hit us while we were crossing. It was rather amusing watching the wreck scenes at the intersections as a car would come sliding into the intersection only to be faced by several cars sitting at odd angles with fenders and bumper s hanging at odd angles and drivers and passengers standing around yelling and waving at each other. People would fall down when they tried to get out of their cars. No one had warned us that this was the way our marriage would begin.

Our gas gauge had slowly been moving toward the E on the dial. But, because of the terrible driving conditions I didn't pay much attention to it. I suddenly noticed that we had to have gas. I told Jewel to watch for a gas station so we could fill up. She finally saw a station with some guys standing outside and told me to pull in. As I pulled up to the pump one of the guys started towards our car. When I told him to fill it up he just laughed and said, "Sorry, but we haven't had power since yesterday morning and without power our pumps don't work." We visited for a bit and when we told him of the terrible driving conditions and all the accidents he said, "You are now in south Texas where no one has ever seen ice on the roads or tried to drive on it." When Jewel asked about the candles on the dashes of the cars, he explained that most cars that were sold that far south didn't have heaters or defrosters installed at the factory so the candles would melt a small area of ice on the windshield. When asked about a motel close by he just laughed and wished us luck. He said he had a friend who had just bought a motel two blocks south and we might try it but we probably wouldn't have any luck there because all of Corpus Christi had been without electricity or phones for the last 24 hours. We had been driving the last two days with the radio on trying to get the latest weather reports but the reports were sketchy because of loss of power. The service man said that they were warning anyone who needed a warm place to spend the night to go to any public building like schools, libraries, or hospitals where blankets and warm food would be available. The temperature was in the lower 20's but would drop to the lower teens by morning. It became clear to me if we were going to drive out of this predicament our only hope was to head for Mexico City. By now I was concerned about our gas because the hand on the gauge was well past the E and I knew there couldn't be much left in the tank.

We decided to check the motel we had learned about at the gas station. As we pulled into the motel the only sign of life was three candles in one of the windows. I stepped into the lobby and the owner appeared from a back room. He was dressed in a huge coat like a shepherd in Montana wears with a big furry hat and a scarf that if stretched out, would have nearly reached back to Houston. His first words were, "I'm sorry but we are closed because of the cold weather. All of our plumbing is frozen up and a lot of it has burst. If it thaws out we are going to have a big mess." I began explaining that my wife and I had just been married three days before in central Kansas. We had been driving on snow and ice ever since and that my new wife had been ill nearly all the way and that we were out of gas with no gas available because of the power outage and that all we really needed was just a place to get out of the rain. He stood there and just looked at me with a sympathetic look on his face. He finally said that he had one room that the pipes had not yet frozen solid, but that there was no heat in the room. If we wanted he could give us some extra blankets but he didn't know when or if the pipes might start leaking and if they started leaking we would have to leave. I told him we would take a chance on the pipes not leaking and really appreciated the offer. When I offered to pay him, he just smiled and said, "I would never charge anyone who obviously has more problems than I do." The next morning before we left we went to thank him again. He explained that nearly all of the plumbing was placed on the outside of the buildings in the city because it was cheaper than enclosing it in the walls. Since it rarely froze, this type of construction worked fine. He and his wife had lived their whole lives in the area and had never experienced any weather even remotely like the past two days. We left the motel thankful for the owners who allowed us to stay in their one unit that had escaped damage.

The morning came with the sun out and the glistening of the ice which covered everything. The trees were nearly stripped clean of branches. The power and phone lines lay across the streets and hung from the few poles left standing. Fenders, bumpers, and pieces of glass littered the intersections where the night before all of the accidents had occurred. Wrecked cars that wouldn't run were double parked on all sides of the intersections. The ice was starting to melt when we remembered that we were nearly out of gas. We passed several service stations obviously closed. We began discussing what we would do once the car quit. There aren't a lot of options that will work under those conditions. We decided to continue on and when the car quit we would try to figure out what to do then. Three or four miles later the engine sputtered and then died. I steered it as near as I dared to the ditch filled with water.

We had just stopped when an old pickup stopped behind us. An old Mexican man got out and asked if I was out of gas and I said yes. He said he had some gas but it was $5.00 a gallon. While I was trying to figure out if I would pay the highjacking fee he was asking, a carload of soldiers pulled up behind the old pickup and several soldiers got out. Our car was still painted with "Just Married" graffiti applied by friends. The soldiers walked up to the Mexican man and me and wanted to know what our problem was. When I explained that I was out of gas, but that this gentleman had gas so everything was under

134

control. One of the soldiers asked what the old guy was charging for the gas and I said $5.00 a gallon. He liked to have had a fit. The soldier started yelling in Spanish at the old guy. I don't speak Spanish so I don't know what he said to the old Mexican, but it really got his attention. He nearly jerked the door off his pickup in his haste to get going. I stood there with my mouth hanging open as the old Mexican roared away. Here I am out of gas and the only gas within 200 miles is speeding away. The soldiers were gathered around cussing about highway robbery before I was able to remind them that I was out of gas. The one who chased the Mexican off said, "We will push you out to the base where you can get your car filled up." He said that he would drive our car while his buddies pushed it with the car they were driving. He slid behind the wheel and with a few bumps from their car we were on our way. We found out that the soldiers were all from Nebraska, and that we were only a couple of miles from the base where they were stationed.

When we entered the gate to the base our driver had his window down and yelled at the guard at the gate. The guard waved us on through. A couple of blocks later we rolled into the service station where our gas tank was filled. I went inside to pay for the gas followed by the soldiers who had started teasing me about being just married. They then said that as a wedding gift they were going to pay for the gas. Then two of them grabbed both of my arms and led me back to the car where they threatened to kiss Jewel if I didn't leave. We left the base bewildered by the happenings of the past 18 hours.

The weather was rapidly improving and the ice on the roads was turning to slush. We were coming into the area where the citrus trees were grown. The orange, grape fruit, and lemon trees resembled squat Christmas trees as the branches had all been broken off and made piles around the bases of the trees. The ice and the bright colored fruit added to the look of brightly decorated Christmas trees. Some groves still had the sprinkler systems operating which added to the surreal devastation. Grazing lands divided the orchards. Dead cattle dotted the landscape. At that time the cattle were mostly of Brahman breeds to handle the hot humid weather and insects. The shock of the cold wet weather was devastating to the cattle industry of south Texas. The radio was still issuing warnings to the locals as where to go for food and shelter. Another 25 miles put us on rapidly drying roads and warmer weather. We continued on to Harlengen and found Jim and Madalyn home. They were very worried as we were a day late. We had tried calling when it became obvious that we weren't going to be there when we told them, but with the phone lines down we were not able to contact them. It was obvious that the three days with Jim was going to have to be shortened to a day and a half if we were to be home in time for the reception my parents had planned to celebrate our wedding.

Jim and Madalyn were disappointed that we wouldn't be able to do all the things that they had planned. After our experience on the drive down, we decided not to go back the way we came down. We had had all of the gulf coast we could stand.

Jim suggested we head northwest to Uvalde. Uvalde was the home of "Texas" Jack Garner who served as Franklin Roosevelt's first Vice President. As we drove northwest from Harlengen we saw field after field of vegetables, compared to the wheat fields of Kansas. We began to appreciate what it took to feed our country. The fields were dotted with migrant workers planting, weeding, and harvesting vegetables. It was very different from the mechanized farms in Kansas. We had stopped to eat and check the map when we realized if we continued west on the road that Jim had suggested we would have to back track to the east to be south of home. Jewel said she would find a road leading north that might eliminate some of the backtracking. After a bit she said she had found a short cut of about 25 miles in length. The map showed the short cut to be a secondary road. She figured it would shorten the trip home by at least 75 miles. We were both pleased of her find. When we reached the intersection of the short cut we turned north. We had no idea that three hours later we would again be at the same intersection.

The secondary road started out as a paved road for about five miles and then it turned into a gravel road. After another couple of miles it turned into just two ruts quickly getting rougher and narrower. I began to get a bit apprehensive and told Jewel if we passed or saw anyone we would stop and ask about the road ahead. Just over the next hill was a farm; as we pulled into the yard we were met by a scruffy looking individual surrounded by a bunch of scruffy looking kids and dogs. I told him we needed to get to the highway about 25 miles north and wondered if we could get there from here. He got down on his knees and surveyed the underside of our car, got up and said, "I think you can make it alright." We pulled out and headed north once again.

The ground was rapidly getting more hilly. We topped a hill and at the bottom was a river. On the other side was the road going up the hill. We pulled up to the river and talked about our options. The landscape had changed from soil to flat rocks. We got out with the scruffy farmers words ringing in our ears. The water was as clear as drinking water and the rocky bottom was easily seen. The water wasn't deep enough that it could get in the car and we figured that by then we didn't have but a few more miles to go to reach the highway. We carefully eased into the river and started for the road on the other side. The river was about 40 yards wide at this point. The cars at this time were prone to drowning out, even if very little water was thrown by the fan back over the engine, so I was aware of this as the water was a couple of inches from the bottom of the doors. I drove slowly to the other side of the river and we breathed a sigh of relief as we started up the hill. We topped the hill only to be greeted by another hill. As we topped the second hill there was the river again, only instead of the road on the other side, there was a huge rock bluff with a large painted arrow pointing to the left. As we sat there pondering our circumstances a Dodge Power Wagon came into view around the bluff in the river. It was loaded with fence materials and two Mexicans. As they continued down the river in front of us the Mexicans gave us a friendly wave. I watched closely to see if they hit any holes but it appeared to me that the rock bottom was as flat and smooth as a concrete highway. The loss of time dictated that we proceed because we had already invested a couple of hours on this shortcut. We pulled into the river and started the left turn that the arrow indicated. As we passed the bluff the car missed out a couple of times and died. I had experienced a drowned engine a few times, and knew all you had to do was remove the distributor cap and wipe the inside and outside and wipe the spark plugs and their wiring dry, and then start it up. There were chunks of ice about a foot in diameter and a couple of inches thick floating down the river. I removed my shoes and socks, rolled up my pant legs and got out of the car. I opened the hood and began wiping the water from the plugs and distributor cap, closed the hood and got back in the car. It started right up, and we were underway. We had to go about 150 yards before the road again came into view. The road out of the river was very steep but after holding our breath we finally reached the top.

We were greeted by several more hills with the path clearly visible ahead. As we topped the second hill there was a large sign on the side of the road that stated: Prade Ranch, Do Not Enter. We sat there stunned. It seemed the only option was to turn around and go back. If we ignored the sign and continued ahead the possibility of the Prade Ranch having a gun tower on the next hill was very real. Having our car shot out from beneath us didn't seem like something to look forward to.

The car drowned out twice on the way back stretching our lost time close to four hours. As we went past the farm where we had stopped for advice, the farmer was standing in nearly the same spot where we had left him 4 hours earlier, however the kids and dogs were gone.

We drove until nearly midnight that day trying to make up the time that the Prade Ranch had cost us. The next morning found us roaring north and into the aftermath of the blizzard of a few days ago. The roads were dry and clear of snow so we were making good time in our haste to be home the following day for the reception, plus I had a small herd of hogs that I had started in high school hoping to generate some cash until I had a wheat crop to harvest. Dad and Corrine promised to look after them for me while I was gone, but the sows would be ready to farrow by the time we were to return, so there was no time to waste in our adventure homeward.

As the years passed and our fiftieth wedding anniversary approached, we began to discuss where we wanted to go. We had no trouble deciding we must return to the place of our exciting river crossing on our way home from our honeymoon. As we started west out of Harlengen, Texas, nothing looked familiar. As we approached the turn off that would take us to the river, the area had taken on a more urban look. If Jewel hadn't kept the maps of our honeymoon travels it would not have been possible to find the place. A convenience store stood at the intersection where we turned at the shortcut fifty years before. We stopped and went in hoping that someone could help us find what we were looking for.

Fortunately, we found the store proprietor on duty and after we explained what we wanted she immediately perked up and her south Texas heritage took over. A smile came over her face as she told us she had been born and lived her whole life in the area. When we explained that we had crossed the river twice before we turned around at the Prade ranch sign, she laughed and said that most people had turned around and went back when they first saw the river. She explained that when we saw the ranch sign we were less than two miles from the road we had been seeking. When I mentioned that we had seen an article titled "The River That is a Highway" in some magazine in the fifties, she laughed and said that the article had been an embarrassment to Texas because it had relocated the road a couple of miles to the east where they only had to build one bridge to cross the river. She went on to explain that it was no longer possible to drive the old road as the right-of-way had been crossed with barbed wire fences by local ranchers.

Jewel and I decided to cross the river on the new road but for some reason crossing the river on a modern bridge just wasn't as thrilling and romantic as we remembered it from 50 years earlier.

MORRILL ACT AND OTHER GOVERNMENT PROGRAMS

As a boy growing up in the 30's and 40's I was not aware of a bill called The Morrill Act of 1862 and how it would impact the rest of my life. It was introduced by a Vermont congressman, and signed by Abraham Lincoln in 1862. The legislation would allow each state to establish a Land-grant college, funded by a 30,000 acre grant to focus on military tactics, agricultural, and mechanical research. The bill would also allow each county in the state to establish an extension office where its residents could access any of the research conducted by the state Land-grant colleges. Each county would elect a board whose job was to set the focus on the needs of its residents. The board would then hire a county agent whose job was to help the residents' access any of the research done that would apply to their particular needs. It was in the early 50's before I became aware of our local extension office.

Until that time if you asked a farmer how or why he did something, his answer was always, "Because that's how dad or grandpa did it." It was not very scientific, but it worked for the farmer. This was the philosophy my father also lived by. It would take a generation before that answer was put to rest and farmers in our part of Kansas began to embrace technology.

Crops remained pretty much the same throughout the mid-century. Forage crops were used for livestock feed, wheat, (which was introduced by European immigrants), and of course vegetables. Alfalfa was grown to a lesser degree, because it was so labor intensive. The amount of acres a farmer grew was dictated by the number of cattle and horses he had to feed. Generally, if you had three cows and a couple of horses, ten acres of alfalfa would yield enough forage to get through the winter.

In the thirties, the government passed a law that allowed local Ag communities to form local Farm Cooperative Associations governed by local grain producers and any profits were to be distributed back to the members who bought stock in the Co-ops. The Co-ops themselves were not taxed. The only taxes collected came from taxes paid on the distributions of profits made to the stockholders. The formation of Co-ops and especially the tax structure was not well received by other businesses up and down Main Street. Early in the formation of Co-op their focus was only on the handling of grains, but it wasn't long before the Co-op Board of Directors began to realize that the taxation laws allowed them to expand into many sidelines other than grain storage alone. Co-op hardware, fuel, tire stores, and even farm machinery bearing Co-op logos became common fixtures in the small towns in the high plains. Co-op aggression was only limited by how aggressive the local Co-op boards of directors were. The animosity between the Co-ops and the businesses up and down Main Street still simmered when we retired 60 years later.

BANK LINES

A couple of my cousins and a few of our friends had enjoyed fishing for catfish in the Arkansas River just five miles north of our farm. About once a month during the summer the men would go to the river and set bank lines. In the evening our wives and kids would show up with picnic supplies and set up on a sandbar in the river. All of our kids were toddlers with the older ones just passed the walking age. Seldom was the water around the sandbars over ankle deep so it was easy to keep an eye on the kids. While our wives laid out a picnic lunch the men would run the lines the first time. We would set 25 or 30 lines and catch five to ten fish each time we ran the lines. The size of the fish would vary from two pounds with an occasional four pounder. After we ran the lines the first time our wives would have the picnic set up. We would eat and play with the kids until nearly dark when we would pack up the kids and our wives would head home. The men would then run the lines again and if the catch was good the men would go home. We needed enough fish to have a fish fry at one of our homes the following Sunday. If we didn't catch enough fish the men stayed on the river and ran the lines again at midnight. A few times we would run the lines again at two o'clock. The final run was made at sunrise the following morning. After the last run the catch was cleaned and we went home. We always caught more fish than we could eat and we looked forward to our next trip.

Around this same time the young farmers had heard rumors that several flood control dams were being studied on the Smokey Hill River about 70 miles north of Larned. The unseasonal rainfall in the mid 40's had caused a lot of flooding in central Kansas so it wasn't long before the US Army Corps of Engineers had started construction on a dam called Cedar Bluff west of Hays and a second one known as Kanopolis sixty miles east of Cedar Bluff. At last we would have access to fishing, camping, and water sports. It took a couple of years before construction was complete and the lakes began to fill.

FLOODING; COTTONWOODS; JACKRABBITS; BLOWING FIELDS

The late 40's and first two years in the 50's were extremely wet. Heavy rains and snows saturated the soil and filled the low places in the fields with excess water. It soon became obvious that a new stream was about to dump all of the excess water into the Arkansas River near Pawnee Rock. The headwater appeared to start near Trousdale, 18 miles south of our farm, and would cross the west side of our section. The county commissioners of Edwards and Pawnee Counties were discussing the dirt work that would be necessary to open a channel to the Arkansas River. It wasn't long until bullfrogs became common in the mud holes and ditches. In some areas the ponds covered 160 acres. Hunting bullfrogs became a favorable sport among many people during this wet cycle. Bullfrog hunting was done at night using flashlights and it was easy to catch enough for several meals in a couple of hours.

Cottonwood trees started germinating along the edges of the mud holes and quickly got too big for them to be killed by normal farming practices. In the sandy areas where these ponds formed, Cottonwood forests were soon established and their remnants can be found today 65 years later. At the height of the wet cycle it was not unusual to have ¼ to ½ of the tillable acres in a field under water. We always had two tractors in the fields during this time because it seemed one was stuck in the mud at all times. A heavy log chain became a necessity when going to the field so equipment could be retrieved from the mud. The parts of a field not under water would be farmed normally and as the mud holes dried between rains the dried out perimeters would be farmed. Some small mud holes would remain late into the fall and could not be planted to wheat.

As this wet cycle finally played itself out and our weather became more normal, a new menace reared its head. Suddenly jackrabbit numbers began to explode. As I write this I feel as if the jackrabbit incident must be fiction, but too many facts remain that prove the tale to be true. It started in the summer of 1952 as we plowed the wheat stubble. It became apparent that the rabbits had had a very good spring as their numbers were much higher than normal. Rabbit habitats are pretty much destroyed by plowing wheat stubble. The rabbits just moved over into the row crops or wheat stubble left standing for summer fallow. In the previous year you might see two rabbits per mile while driving down a road. But now there were rabbits on the roads as far as you could see. The Extension Office began offering free Strychnine poison to farmers along with instructions on how to build bait stations to kill rabbits.

As the season slipped into winter and the only green thing available for the rabbits to eat was the new wheat seedlings their numbers increased as they moved out of the grasslands. If I was to guess the number of rabbits on my section of wheat, the number would have been in the tens of thousands. The Extension Service said that ten rabbits would eat as much as one cow. A cow will only consume the leafy portion of a wheat plant but a rabbit will eat a plant off at the ground thus killing it. My brother in law Bob Brack and I spent a couple of nights a week driving around my section shining spotlights and shooting the rabbits with 22 rifles. We probably could have killed more if we would have raced around the section and simply ran over those that didn't get out of the way. I am sure if as many rabbits were ran over by vehicles today as were ran over in the fifties, we would see several conservation groups lobbying to protect the poor rabbits from cars.

With the rabbit numbers that high they tended to tamp the soil down until it was as smooth as a cement floor. Since they had killed the wheat plants there was nothing to hold the soil in place and when the winds came up the soil began to blow. To me the most discouraging thing about farming was when my fields started blowing. This was always a possibility on our sandy soils south of the Arkansas River. Those soils were prone to blow for seemingly no reason at all. Few things can seem as futile as pulling into a 640 acre field with a tractor and a 16' tillage tool and hope to stop a dirt storm that limits your vision to perhaps 100'. This happened to me many times in the fifties.

I often wished I had been born with the outlook of a neighbor of mine who was our township Assessor. Once a year he came around and made a list of everything we owned so the County could determine how much taxes we owed. One day he arrived to assess us just as the wind was coming up and the dirt in my field was starting to blow. I asked him if we could make the assessment later because I needed to stop my ground from blowing. Melvin always smoked a pipe and was as laid back more than any human had a right to be. He slowly said to me, "Let me tell you how I handle ground that is blowing. I will go home and tell my wife to get ready to go to Great Bend. We would go to the Elks Lodge and have a nice dinner then play cards with some of the other members until about 9:00. When we came home the wind would have gone down and I'd have saved all that time and money trying to stop my blowing ground." I was never able to embrace his solution of my blowing soil. It would be 50 years before technology would bring the solutions that nearly eliminated the wind damage to crop production.

Meanwhile the rabbit problem intensified. Farmers began talking of organizing rabbit drives like they had in the thirties. When it seemed that the rabbits were going to drive the farmers from the land their numbers began falling and a year later they were seldom seen. By the time I retired you might spend a week on the tractor and not see a single rabbit.

STARTING A FAMILY; SINGING SCHARTZ SISTERS

The 50's remain a blur in my memory punctuated by the birth of our first five children within the space of seven years. Our sixth and final child, Jim, was born in 1963 and was a welcome addition to our brood.

When the anesthesia wore off after child number five and Jewel was told that her new baby was a girl, her response was, "Good now we can have our quartet!" She hadn't told me she had a quartet in mind, so this was news to me. Music was always a very important part of Jewel's life. When I first met her she played the piano and saxophone. Our first home had a piano left by previous owners. It was old and had seen a hard life; some of the keys no longer worked. Jewel could change her piano arrangements so the non-working keys never were missed by anyone listening to her play. She had learned to play as a youngster and had never really learned to read music.

Once on a trip to the east coast to a niece's wedding reception, one of the guests was an opera singer. There was a piano in a corner of the reception hall and Jewel naturally was drawn to it. Before long a group of the guests including the opera singer, had formed around the piano and were singing as Jewel played. After one of the songs, the opera singer asked if she knew a particular song and she asked him to sing it for her. She immediately began chording and before he finished the first verse she was playing along perfectly. After the sing-along broke up the opera singer came to our table and told me, "Do you know what an exceptional piano player your wife is? I have been involved in music all my life, and I have never seen anyone who can play any piece of music after just briefly hearing it!"

By the time our youngest daughter Carolyn was two years old, Jewel had her singing with her three older sisters. Cindy was four, Susan was five and Sharon was seven. The Singing Schartz Sisters took to singing like ducks to water. In the fifties, barber shop quartets became one of the favorites of the listening public. One group was the Lennon Sisters who were highlighted on many of the variety shows popular at the time and another was the McGuire Sisters on the Lawrence Welk Variety Show. Jewel began working out the arrangements of their songs and teaching them to our girls.

I think Carolyn might have been three when the girls began singing in front of the public. One of the things that always made it so enjoyable watching them perform was the fact that Carolyn was so conscious of how they looked. When they took the stage, she would always check out their costumes and if a collar or sleeve didn't look right to her she would just go and make the adjustment she thought was needed. It didn't bother her if they were in the middle of a piece or the last event on the stage, they had to look good to her.

One of the challenges of quartet singing is finding songs with the voice range to make it sound right. I don't know if it was because they had started singing so young and had developed their voice ranges or if two of them just naturally had voices in the lower range while the other two were proficient in the higher ranges, but they harmonized perfectly. As I stated earlier, Jewel did all of their arrangements and made all of their costumes. As they got older she began doing some choreography to get some movement along with their harmonizing. From the very beginning, Jewel had to turn down engagements as she felt the girls performances should not impact their schooling or family life. Our kids were active in 4-H so the 4-H activities were always a venue where they performed. Soon they were performing in surrounding counties and at any gatherings that required entertainment. They performed several times at the State Fair. It became obvious that Jewel and I would have to make some hard choices about what we wanted for our girls. If we really wanted them to succeed, then they were going to need a professional manager, formal voice coaching, a choreographer, a costume maker, a money manager plus a host of the other professionals that we knew nothing about. It was about this time that many of the youth that we had admired watching in the movies were reaching young adulthood, and were wailing about their unhappy childhood. They felt they were exploited by the professional that had managed them in their youth. We didn't want our kids saddled by these kinds of memories. We decided that when our oldest, Sharon, entered junior high school, the girls would stop performing. I'm sure it was hard for Jewel to turn down all the requests for them to perform, but we had reached the decision that it was best for them. As Jewel and I talked about it in the following years, we felt we had made the right decision.

BUILDING A FUTURE

Our first wheat crop was a very good one and it looked like farming was a good choice as a profession. Our second and third crops proved how rapidly things could change. The second crop was hit by hail and only produced half as much as the first one. Dry weather decimated our third crop and we began to talk about leaving the farm for a job that would produce a paycheck. The economy had tanked and jobs were scarce. We increased our hog herd hoping to increase our income. Our cow herd numbers remained low because it takes a year for a cow to produce a calf and at least three years for that calf to reach maturity and be added to the herd as a producer. I spent all my time making all the adjustments that were required as my shop work consisted mostly of trying to keep our aging equipment repaired and operational.

Brother Greg was born in 1946 when I was fifteen, and Gordon was born in 1952. Greg was only two years older than our oldest child Tony, and Gordon was a year younger than Tony and the same age as our first daughter Sharon. It seems Jewel and my early married life seemed to be molded from our parent's lives, our kids' early lives and our constant concern over childhood diseases. However, by the early fifties vaccines had been developed for most childhood diseases except polio. Since my sister, Carol Jean, had died in 1948 at the age of 12 from Bulbar Polio, we always wondered if polio might strike our kids as well. Few people had any idea that the release of the polio vaccine in 1955 would eradicate this terrible disease.

After all of our family had received the new polio vaccines and after the harrowing experience with Carol Jean, we had relaxed many of the self imposed restrictions on our summer activities. Most notable was our kids enjoying the local swimming pool. If the weather permitted Jewel would load up our kids along with my two younger brothers and head to the pool. Neither Jewel nor I ever learned to swim, and we wanted our kids to learn. They all took swimming lessons. It was always very satisfying when one or the other of the kids would proudly tell me that they had swam across the pool that day.

The Zook Rural high school closed after Greg's sophomore year and both brothers finished high school in Larned. Both boys lived at home but when Jewel planned any activities for our kids they were always included. It always felt that they were our kids as well. Our oldest five children attended Zook School through sixth grade until the school was closed at the end of Carolyn's sixth grade year. Our youngest son Jim, born in 1963, was educated in Larned.

Greg and Gordon learned to drive tractors at about the age that I did. Jewel and our oldest son Tony started doing field work as well, and suddenly we had more tractor drivers than we had tractors. In another year they were operating combines as well. Our acreage continued to grow and more of our time was required in the field. My two brothers helped during the summers but when they had to go back to school in the fall, dad and I could barely keep up.

Both Gordon and Greg had more than their share of mechanical aptitude. Greg decided he wanted to become a diesel mechanic and enrolled in a trade school and studied diesel mechanics. Gordon went to Hutch Junior College. When Greg completed his schooling he was drafted into the army as a tank mechanic. Gordon joined me on the farm. Greg was deployed to Viet Nam where he repaired tanks for the army. When he was discharged he joined Gordon and me on the farm. Their joining me was to be nearly 20 years of good fortune for our farm as it freed me of much of the day to day duties so I could concentrate on other pursuits. I was able to work on projects that I had thought about during many hours on the tractor.

EARLY ALFALFA PRODUCTION

In the forties and early fifties hay production was a slow and laborious process. Producers first mowed their hay with sickle mowers pulled by horses and later converted to tractor pulled. After it was mowed and dried out it was raked into windrows by rakes also from the horse drawn days, then it was baled. A field just baled with the bales all in rows across the field was always a pleasing sight to me. The next haying development was one that held back the development of large hay operations in the forties and early fifties. The hold up was due to the large labor force required after the hay left the baler. After baler design moved from the stationary design to tractor drawn, the capacity of balers was dramatically increased. The most popular way of handling the bales was trailers pulled behind the balers with a man on the trailer stacking the bales after being ejected onto the trailer by the baler. When the trailer was full it was replaced by an empty trailer. The full trailer was then pulled to the stack site where several men would unload the trailer and stack the hay into larger haystacks. This method of stacking the hay was very labor intensive and attributed to the relative lack of interest in alfalfa production in the forties and fifties.

In the mid fifties New Holland introduced a new machine that would revolutionize and bring hay production to prominence as a major crop in the Midwest. The machine was a self propelled stacker which would pick up and stack bales dropped on the ground by balers. The machine practically eliminated the manual labor required to produce hay. Balers and stacker capacity began to improve by leaps and bounds through the rest of the twentieth century bringing alfalfa acreage to nearly match wheat and corn. Suddenly the capacity and reliability of farm equipment was replacing the labor intensive ways of farming. Most of the grasslands of central and western Kansas that had escaped the plow in the early part of the twentieth century was converted to grain production. Labor had been replaced by mechanization. Only small pockets of farmers who farmed the way dad did it remained.

ASCS LOAN PROGRAM

Early in my farming when I participated in the loan program my delivery point at the end of the contract was the local Co-op. But by the third year the government decided to erect steel bin sites in the county seats. Most of these bins held 5000 bushels of wheat and used farm augers to fill the bins. When they started this program it was a headache and since it slowed the process down so much the famers were hard to handle. It was not unusual to wait in line for an hour or more to unload and another half hour unloading. Until the change to the binsite storage system, the grain went to the Co-op and in ten minutes you were on your way to get the next load. So by the time you got your load unloaded at the binsite you were already mad at how inefficient this system was.

I had used the loan program for four years. In 1953 we got a good rain just as we finished harvesting wheat and if we hurried we might get the plowing done before the ground got too dry to plow. Because Jewel and I had purchased what we called the half section of farm land, that meant we were in a hurry to get our plowing done before it got too dry. If you were able to plow right after harvest you had more time to get the soil ready for planting in the fall. Because I had received government loans in the past, I thought I had my stored wheat ready to apply for the loans. I got up at 5:00 in the morning and went to the ASCS office. I got there before 6:00 because I knew if I got there at 9:00 when the office opened there would be a line of farmers waiting to apply. By arriving at six I would be close to the front of the line. I waited until the office help arrived at 9:00 and followed them in. By the time they were able to start processing it was 9:30. When we started working on the loan the loan officer wanted the paper that was required. I replied that the paper she was asking for had never been required before, and she said that the law had been changed and I must present the paper before she could authorize the loan. Steam was coming out of my ears as I left the damn office.

When I got back to the field and started plowing I had wasted nearly six and a half hours and had accomplished nothing. When we stopped at noon dad asked me if I had gotten my loan, and I replied no, that I had made my last trip to that office and would never participate in another government program as long as I farmed. Dad shook his head and said "You better think about it or you and your family may starve." I had made up my mind that I would rather quit than let Washington tell me what I had to do! 40 years later as my friend and accountant John Jansen was doing the last tax work for our farm, John said to me, "Do you realize how much money you left on the

163

table by not taking advantage of the farm programs all the years you farmed?" I replied "John do you know how much satisfaction I got from not being under the thumb of Washington bureaucrats?" John smiled, and said, "None of my farm customers could have done it." As I look back over my life as a farmer I made many mistakes but that decision as far as I am concerned was definitely the right one.

HERBICIDES; CORN

I always subscribed to agricultural magazines. In the early fifties a new word I didn't recognize was becoming more prevalent. That word was herbicide. I became interested, and began researching the topic. While the word was becoming more common in the magazines, I found out there were companies who were about to market these products. I went to Cliff Manry, our County Agent, and asked if any information was available on these new weed killers. He was aware of herbicides, because K-State had been involved in some of the early research on the herbicides. He promised me he would get any information available from K-State. A few days later he called and wanted me to stop by. He told me he had contacted the head of the agronomy department at K-State and they were excited about this new product, but it would not work on sandy soils or soils low on organic material of which made up all of my farm soils. Herbicides exploded in farm publications. Every new issue seemed to introduce new herbicides. All of the first herbicides were designed for corn. And since I wasn't growing corn I could only hope that before long a milo herbicide would be available. The following year a milo herbicide was put on the market, but it wasn't to be used on sandy soils or soils low on organic content. I was determined to see if I could use it and got ready to try. There weren't any spray rigs on the market except very primitive ones used to apply 2,4-D to pasture lands. I bought one of these rigs to start trying to see if I could make herbicides work for me.

I went to my local Co-op to buy my first herbicide, but they didn't have any so a call was made to Geigy, the chemical company, and they sent me ten pounds. When it arrived I read the label which was actually a small booklet. I nearly backed out of trying it. It was mostly a list of 'Don't use this product if...' The name of the product was Maloran and it controlled or suppressed nearly all of the weeds that were present in my milo fields. After reading the claims I was more determined than ever to learn how to use it. I had just finished planting my milo when I received the Maloran. Fortunately, it was to be applied pre-emerge which meant after planting, but before the milo emerged. The label said to apply two pounds per acre of the material, but under no circumstances was it to be used on sandy or low organic content soil as it would severely injure or even kill the milo. If used on these soils there was also the danger of carry over which might kill anything planted the following year.

This could be a problem I hadn't even considered in my haste to embrace this new miracle. My test plots consisted of starting using the material at 1/8 pound per acre and increasing the rate by 1/8 pound until I reached the two pound recommended rate. My spray boom was 20 feet or eight rows. It took me almost a week to get all the rates applied. But I had started to try to achieve what I had dreamed of in the beginning and that was to be able to do away with cultivating. Every farmer knew that the earlier you cultivated the better it worked, but the timing was critical because it always seemed it needed to be done just when you were in the middle of wheat harvest. If you got rain at this time it not only slowed harvesting, but the weeds in the milo would get ahead of you. I knew it was important to control weeds in the milo early on or they would be a problem for the rest of the season. Any competition with weeds would reduce the milo yield. The ideal thing was to be able to suppress the weeds until the milo formed a canopy and shaded the soil. Weeds don't grow well in shade, so it was imperative to help the milo form a canopy.

Cliff happened to come by while I was putting my test plot in, and stopped because he had never seen anyone spraying a freshly planted milo field before. After I explained what I was doing, he just shook his head and left. I caught him several times during the summer checking the plots. In August, Cliff introduced me to Tom Threewitt who had just been promoted by Geigy to head the herbicide research in Kansas. At the time none of us realized that our introduction would turn into a 35 year association. Tom's job was to find where he could put out test plots and monitor the effects of herbicides on crops to see if there was any carry over effect on crops following herbicide applications. A few days later, Tom stopped and asked if I would be interested in providing the land for his test plots. Since he would be testing any new herbicide being formulated in Geigy labs in Bern, Switzerland, I immediately accepted. It seemed to me to be a win-win situation. I would be able to see the results they made in the earlier formulations, but I could also see any new products they wanted tested in the field. What I learned from Tom in the ensuing years, in my opinion, was equal to a doctorate in agronomy.

As the years passed we began to see indications of herbicide resistance in some of the weed species. Not to an alarming degree, but this was not what the chemists had even considered. Tom's test plot indicated that after six or seven years of continued use, Maloran was no longer effective because of weed resistance. When Tom pointed out this disturbing news to the Swiss chemists who visited the test plots, they weren't too concerned because they had new formulations ready for field testing that would obviously not have this problem. Sixty years later, resistance is still the number one herbicide problem especially when a mono culture is practiced such as corn grown on the same fields year after year.

The introduction of new herbicides year after year has masked the problem of resistance. It took the researchers fifty years to realize that they were attacking the weed problem in the wrong way. Instead of trying to develop an herbicide that would kill all weeds and not harm crops, they needed to breed crops that weren't harmed by the chemicals. It wasn't until Craig Venter discovered the genome in all living things that technology finally gave scientists the tools to genetically modify any living thing including crops for feed and foods. Giant strides were soon made in crop breeding when herbicide resistant genes were inserted into the normal crop plants. Today, 2012, genetic manipulation of host plants seems to be the acceptable direction that herbicide research is going. It's easier to make a herbicide that is deadlier to all weed species and then insert a gene of resistance in the chosen plant species.

GRAIN DRYER ENTREPRENEUR

The summer of '58 was nearly normal except that we had a bit more rain than in the early fifties, which was dry. We had a decent wheat crop, and the milo looked promising. Most of the milo was a hybrid milo introduced two years previously by DeKalb Seed Company. Their new hybrids had performed well in the state yield plots and farmers had enthusiastically responded by replacing the old standby varieties of milo with the new hybrids. It had rained in early September which was perfect timing to get the new wheat crop planted and established before winter set in.

The weather remained cloudy with fog and light drizzle throughout the time of wheat planting, which lasted till around the tenth of October, however we never got the killing frost that usually occurred around the middle of October. One fact that went unnoticed was that the new hybrid milos had a ten day longer time to reach maturity than the old varieties had. If the weather had been normal during September and October this would have probably gone unnoticed. But the cool weather and no killing frost in mid October allowed the milo to continue growing. When it finally frosted the tenth of November it was too late for the warm windy weather that milo requires to finish maturing.

With the old standard varieties, the later plantings were harvested around the first of November. Normally a couple of weeks of Indian summer followed a killing frost around the middle of October. But the cloudy damp weather continued through October and into November. Any hope of a dry down of the still growing milo during an Indian summer after a frost was not going to happen this year. Farmers who had planted early had done some sample cutting nearly a month earlier, but because the new hybrid required an extra ten days to reach maturity the moisture content was around 20%, a full 5% above the benchmark of 15%.

The local elevators would normally take early wet milo and as the milo dried down would blend it with the earlier wet milo. If the sun came out for a few days, farmers would do some more test cutting and find the moisture as high or higher than it had been a month earlier. The constant test cutting soon filled the elevators with wet milo and no dry milo to blend with it. Soon the elevators started piling the new milo on the ground. I had seen in the farm publications a new machine that allowed farmers to harvest early and at higher moisture content and then drying it down to a safe storage moisture level. I wrote to Bchlen Manufacturing to see if there was a dealer in our area who carried their new dryer and they pointed me to Doonan Truck in Great Bend. I had increased my milo acreage considerably the previous spring and I was getting nervous about the prospect of having to let my milo freeze dry before harvesting.

It was becoming apparent that the hybrid varieties were prone to lodging (falling over) if they were not harvested early but it had never been a problem with the old familiar varieties. I had bought a tractor from Wendel Doonan a few years previously so when Jewel and I walked in Wendel waved us into his office. When I expressed my interest in the Behlen dryer he expressed his disappointment that more local farmers had not shown more interest in drying their grain. He had ordered several dryers for his inventory and since no one had shown any interest in it, he had set up one of the dryers at Hudson Flour Mill and was using it as a display model. He took Jewel and I to Hudson to watch it working. At first I was only interested in drying my own grain, but as I watched the local elevators pile more and more grain outside their facilities I thought that maybe I might be able to get a contract at our local Co-op and dry some of their growing inventory of wet milo.

The local papers were starting to run feature articles about the looming problems elevator operators were going to be facing if drying weather was not forthcoming. I explained to Wendel that I was very interested in buying a dryer, but I needed to talk with my banker first as I thought

172

I might want to try to get a contract with the local Co-op for custom drying as well. Wendel told me not to take too much time as farmers from Nebraska had been calling, asking if he had dryers for sale because their dealers had sold out. I decided pursuing a contract with an elevator would help me secure a loan with my banker. When I approached the Co-op manager, he brushed me off. The president of the board of directors of the Co-op was in the office when I made my pitch to the manager. He followed me out and asked me several questions. The last question was, "If we agree on terms, how soon could you start drying?" I replied, that after looking at the setup in Hudson I thought it would take a full day to get set up and I could be drying the following day. The president's parting words were, "I'm going to call a special meeting of the board tonight. Come back tomorrow for our decision."

When I walked into the office the following day my heart sank as the manager was more confrontational than he had been the previous day. He told me to wait in the meeting room until the board arrived. I didn't know what to expect from the board, but I felt that his attitude didn't look promising. When the board had assembled the board president cut right to the chase. His first statement to me was, "If we can come to an agreement on how to work out the bookkeeping on the operation you can start drying as soon as you can get set up." Jewel and I had discussed that the bookkeeping was going to be a headache, so I had the answer for the board. I told them the dryer was designed to hold 400 bushels of grain. Any less grain than that and the dryer would not work. And as far as the moisture to be removed, that would be calculated when the grain was delivered by the farmer. The office would merely figure what the average moisture was when it was delivered.

I had questioned the operator of the dryer at Hudson about the timing of the drying cycle. He told me that since they had started drying, the time necessary to dry 400 bushels had been a constant two hours per 400 bushel batch irrespective of the moisture content and it had remained that for three weeks. To verify the 400 bushel batch we would load the dryer three times and then average the loads and the average would be the batch size. I would then keep a daily log of the number of batches which I would turn into the office every morning.

Wendel was charging nine cents a wet bushel, so I decided that would be my charge as well. The elevator had about 50,000 bushels of wet milo in the elevator and 75,000 bushel was piled outside at $.09 per bushel. I would gross $11,250 on the milo that was already on hand. We had agreed if either party had a complaint we would immediately have a meeting and a solution would be worked out or the contract would be terminated. I took my figure to the bank and showed them to Stan Moffet who loaned me the $5,000 to purchase the dryer. I called Wendel Doonan and asked how soon he could deliver the dryer. He said it would be delivered that afternoon.

The Co-op board had told me that I could set up anywhere I chose. I had picked a spot just outside the main elevator on the east side about 50' from the pits where the grain was dumped. There was a manhole inspection port about 5' above the ground that, when slightly modified, would be perfect for filling the dryer. A door to the left of the filling port led to a rubber conveyer belt that would carry the dried grain to the main leg which would then take the grain to where they wanted it in the elevator. I would use a joint of irrigation pipe running from the dryer to the conveyor belt.

The dryer was about 14' long, 10' high, and 8' wide and had six bladed propellers in the front and a large propane burner just behind the propeller. My tractor sat in front to furnish the power to load and unload and to power the propeller. An open space about 4' in diameter ran from just behind the propeller to the back end of the dryer. This was called the plenem chamber. When drying, the plenum chamber was pressurized and heated by the propeller and burner. The heated and pressurized air was then forced out of the plenem chamber and out through small louvers in the chamber into an 18" blanket of grain surrounding the plenum chamber. The blanket of grain was contained by the outer skin of the dryer which was perforated by small louvers. The rear end of the dryer had a hopper which fed into a vertical tube which had an auger inside.

When filling the dryer the grain would go into the hopper and then up the vertical auger. The vertical auger had paddles on its upper end which would then throw the grain toward the front of the dryer. It took about ten minutes to fill the dryer with 400 bushels of grain. The paddles on the top of the vertical auger were covered by a cap that could be rotated by a crank on the back of the dryer. The cap had a discharge port built into it so when unloading the cup with the port it was turned away from the dryer and into any direction the operator wanted. An auger ran from the front to the rear on the inside of the drier.

To unload, the operator engaged a clutch to power the auger that was in the bottom of the dryer, which carried the grain to the vertical auger, which carried the grain up to the paddles, and out of the port. Unloading also took about ten minutes. When unloading the port on the cap it discharged the grain into the irrigation pipe previously mentioned. There was one potential problem involved in the unloading cycle and that was the operator forgetting to check that the belt that took the grain to the leg which was about fifty feet away either stopped or was failed to be started at the beginning of the unloading cycle. If the belt was not running, the 400 bushels of grain would wind up on the floor. The basement that housed the belt was dark and had a lot of hardware in the floor which made shoveling the grain back onto the belt a bitch.

I would be remiss if I failed to introduce you to an employee of the Co-op at this point. Jack "Dempsy" Artz was a bear of a man standing 6'7" or an inch or two taller, and I believe I first met him when I was in the first grade. I remember wondering where in the world he could buy bib overalls that large. His arms were larger than Dad's legs. His shoes, like his overalls, made me wonder where he purchased them. My first memories of Jack were of him shoveling coal out of the open topped coal cars that were parked on the railroad tracks next to the coal bins. I wish I knew how many coal cars he shoveled out in his career. Jack was the only employee I ever saw unloading coal cars at the Co-op. As I remember it, the coal came in several sizes from about the size of your head down to about walnut size. The different sizes were separated in the coal bins where the customer chose the size he wanted. When we pulled up to the bin Jack would jump out of the coal car and help fill our gunny sacks. When filled, he would grab the sack and place it on the floor of the back seat as the '32 Chevy Dad drove didn't have a trunk. It was always a chore for the folks to remove the sack of coal from the car because it was so heavy and was difficult to maneuver past the front seat and the door frame. When Jack put it in the car he did it as easily as if it were a sack of bread. Jack was still employed by the Co-op when I started drying milo for them. He was always the first to work in the morning and never left at night with a job unfinished.

Jack always started his day asking how I'd got along during the night. I had an extra cup in the pickup so Jack and I could have a cup of coffee to start the day. I doubt that any two men in Larned could have done the work that Jack did in his job with the Co-op. During the day he would stop by to make sure I didn't need anything. We became good friends and when he died I could only hope that he considered me a friend as well.

Getting set up required that the dryer was more or less level and a propane tank was needed to furnish fuel for the large burner on the dryer. Since the Co-op had a propane business, they got me hooked up to the dryer. All the other modifications I did myself. Our first load went into the dryer on the day I had told them I would start. The Co-op customers soon found out that the Co-op would be able to dry their milo and the rush was on. Because of the large pile in the parking lot, it was hard to maneuver farm trucks around the facility. There were a few shouting matches every day. I had hired Benny Bowman and Les Davis to operate the dryer while I cut my milo. As the fall days grew shorter and the cloudy damp days persisted it became obvious that the thirty days that I had hoped for were going to stretch out long into the winter. My original plan was to dry 24 hours a day until I got the outdoor pile all picked up and dried. Benny and Les got along well drying until I finished my harvest. Les, who was having back problems, decided if he was going to recover from the surgery that his doctor recommended he would have to have it done before Christmas. Benny had a new job waiting for him after the first of the year. I began running ads for help in the Tiller and Toiler, but the only applicants I got were quickly passed by because most were looking for indoor jobs or weren't mechanically inclined. Benny and Les were getting close to our goal of eight loads or nearly 3,500 bushels per day. The wet grain on hand would last well into January.

Since we were the only dryer in the area, milo was being shipped in from outside of the Co-op's trade area. About 10 days before Christmas we finally got the pile in the parking lot finished. Les had quit on the 15th of December. Benny was working days and I ran nights. Jewel was taking phone calls from the few applicants for Les's shift.

I had been milking cows for cream money that fall before milo harvest but it looked like Jewel would be stuck with the milking on the antique milking machine while I ran the dryer. She reluctantly came to the barn while I taught her how to become a dairy maid. Jewel grew up on a farm but had never been near cows before. She was scared to death of them and nothing I said or did convinced her that they weren't dangerous. When milk cows go into the barn to eat their grain and the farmer walks between them to close the stanchions, which hold them during milking, they will always swing their butts together, trapping you in between them. I thought I had warned Jewel that we had a couple of cows that were experts at this tactic. Generally, a good slap on the rump of one or the other was all it took to get them to move apart. On the morning of her solo milking, sure enough they trapped her and she couldn't get them to move apart. I have no idea how long she remained trapped. I'm sure it was sometime before she planned her exit strategy. She knew that the rear end of a cow was dangerous because she had heard the horror stories of people being kicked by horses and cows, but she didn't recall any stories about people being bitten by a cow.

She climbed up on the top of the stanchions and released them one by one. I guess it was fortunate that I wasn't home or our marriage and my life would have ended on that fateful morning. When she related the story to me there was little doubt that she would never become a milk maid. This episode marked the end of ever having homemade butter on our table again.

The wet milo continued to dribble in as the harvest began to wind down. Some farmers had put wet milo into bins on their farms hoping a market would develop before warm spring weather would cause the milo to start to spoil. The government had a loan program available for milo producers, but the milo had to test # 1 to qualify. Until the moisture was down to 15% it was not eligible for the loan program. I asked Mr. Brown if he had any objection if I ran an ad in the paper that pointed out that the Co-op had a dryer and could make the wet milo eligible for the loan program. Mr. Brown said the Co-op would see if the ad could be run as a public notice. The notice ran the week before Christmas and farmers started hauling in wet milo. The elevator quickly filled and piling in the parking area began again. I had originally planned on going to one 12 hour shift after the first of the year because it was looking like the milo run was starting to come to an end. When the piling in the parking area started again it became obvious that we were going to have to stay on the 24 hour program for at least through January.

I had been unable to hire anyone to take Benny's place and I wanted my dryer available to dry as much as possible. The elevator industry took notice of how important it was to offer drying to producers. Several firms announced that full automated continuous flow dryers were being readied for installation before the next fall harvesting season. The alarmed Co-op began preparations to install a new dryer in their elevator in January. Since I wasn't getting any new applicants for the day shift and Benny's departure was drawing near I was getting nervous. The pile of milo in the parking area wasn't getting much bigger, but the milo kept coming in. We shut the dryer down on Christmas morning, but I started it back up that afternoon.

I decided if I couldn't get a new employee I would just run the project 24 hours a day by myself. Each batch took about two hours to run, ninety minutes to dry, and thirty minutes to empty and refill. I could sleep between batches. Jewel didn't particularly like the idea, but I felt that we could make it work if she would bring me a dinner with enough leftovers for supper. I would shut the dryer down on Saturday evening to go home, shower, and have a meal with the family. That is how we started 1959.

Nearly two weeks into the schedule a young man who had graduated from high school the previous spring woke me up by tapping on the pickup window. His name was Vince Simmons. He said he heard I was looking for help and he was looking for a job. His family and I went to the same church and we watched Vince and his brothers and sisters grow up. Vince had worked during summers for a farmer north of town. He caught on quickly and after a few days I felt he could handle the job well. As the delivery of wet milo slowed we went back to 12 hour days. I would usually be at the dryer by six in the morning to service the equipment for the day's run. Vince would start loading at

182

8:00 and his last load would be done at around 4:00 P.M. We continued this pace through January and early February. The later part of February we only started the dryer if we had three batches to dry.

I had decided that I would stop drying the first of March so I could start my field work to get the milo ground ready for the spring planting. The last week of February, Vince and I started tearing down. The Co-op's own continuous flow dryer was nearing completion but would not be operational until wheat harvest in June. It was not until then that I began to realize how fortunate we had been to have participated in a once in a lifetime event. The extremely wet fall, the development of grain drying, and the association of the Co-op had allowed us to repay all of the money we had borrowed to survive during the tough days of the early fifties. None of this would have happened except for some unique and wonderful people I met along the way.

CATTLE OPERATION

My experience with cattle had been traditional. I learned to do it just as Dad did it. But here again, modernization was starting to make itself known. Our operation consisted of around 25 cows. My folks had purchased a quarter of sand hill pasture southwest of Larned. This grass was used for grazing during the summer. Aunt Hazel had 320 acres of sand hill pasture which I rented. A neighbor had a herd of Angus cows and had been trying to convince me to get into the Angus breed. He came by one day and said he was going to an Angus production sale in Illinois and he wanted me to go along. I only owned about five cows and since I had 320 acres of pasture I needed more cows to utilize the grass that I had rented. We got on the train in St. John and headed for Peoria where the sale was to be held. We were met at the train station by Forest Lemons who was the Illinois Secretary of the Angus Association and a farmer in the Peoria area. In reading my farm magazines I had read a lot about the Corn Belt, and now I was able to see it firsthand.

We stayed in the Lemons' farm home. Mrs. Lemons gave us a tour of the old farm house and told us a bit of its history. Apparently Abraham Lincoln had either lived or spent a lot of time in the area. She said that when he was in the area he always stayed at this house. When she showed me to my bedroom she proudly said that my bedroom was the one that Lincoln slept in while he was a guest in the house. She was so sincere that I never questioned her statement. The house was a two story rectangular brick building with solid brick walls at least two feet thick; even the interior walls were as thick as well. The house had indoor plumbing which had obviously recently been installed as the plumbing ran through the floors and on the outside of the thick inside walls.

After supper, Forest gave us a tour of his farm. I was fascinated by the corncribs which were all empty. When I asked him about them he said that it was the second year that they were empty because he had bought a new combine with a two row corn head and no longer harvested his corn with a corn picker. As we toured the local farms I saw how the farms had kept their livestock out of the mud in the winter months: their mechanical shellers had two conveyers; one carried the shelled corn and the other carried the cobs from the sheller. One wagon received the grain while the second carried the cobs. The cobs were hauled to the corrals and dumped on the ground that held the cows and hogs. The hogs would quickly root through the cobs searching for any grain that remained on the cobs. The cobs would then form a base for the next layer of cobs. It was not unusual to see a layer of cobs two feet thick in some of the corrals. The use of combines would eventually ruin the Corn Belt as a cattle area because corncobs were left in the fields instead of being used to keep the livestock out of the mud. It became evident that there were always consequences when a change was made in agriculture practice.

I relate this next incident only to point out that very often you must pay tuition to learn the lessons of your chosen profession. Mr. Lemons had an elderly neighbor who had recently been diagnosed with a terminal illness. He and his wife were trying to sell everything and move into Peoria to be near the doctor and hospital. He had 20 head of nice Angus cows for sale. The cows were bred and would start calving in about four months. I am not sure if I decided to buy the cows or if Forest decided that I needed them. Forest knew a trucker who would take them back to Kansas for me. I now owned 20 registered Angus cows. I anxiously waited for them to start calving. The first indication that something was wrong was when one of the cows aborted her calf about a month early. I immediately took the dead calf to our veterinarian, Dr. Coddington, to see if he could figure out what had happened. He autopsied the calf and found nothing wrong and suggested that it might have been caused from the stress of moving. Ten days later I found another aborted calf. Dr. Coddington said that he would take the calf to K-State and let them figure it out. A week later two more cows aborted. After all the cows finished calving I had six live calves. Dr. Coddington and I waited for nearly two months before we heard back from K- State. I was amazed at the number of diseases they had tested for. The only disease that they got a positive response on was a new sexually transmitted disease called Vibrio. Since the cows had aborted at the right time they said they could positively diagnosis that my herd had Vibrio. There was nothing that could be done to cure the infected cows but to sell them for slaughter. I had purchased the cows at a slight discount when I bought them but I still lost around $100 a head.

With the booming feed yard industry the cattle industry was changing in a dramatic way. Previously, fat cattle for the restaurant and hotel market were produced in the Corn Belt by corn farmers who purchased calves from the mountain states and finished them on corn on their farms. But because of the cold wet weather the cattle used so much energy to stay warm and dry their performance was poor. Suddenly feed yards started springing up all over the high plains. Some of these yards were started by cattle feeders from the Corn Belt who were trying to get a warmer, dryer climate.

Manufacturers in these areas were quick to design, manufacture, and sell specialized equipment that was required by the growing feeding industry. Livestock trucking firms were springing up everywhere. Alfalfa acreage doubled, then tripled to supply the feed yards with alfalfa. Specialty feed mills with nutritionists on staff opened and became a booming business. Fat cattle buyers who bought cattle for the packing plants were seen throughout the area. Huge trucks were hauling fat cattle to the Kansas City packing plants and bringing feeder cattle to the feed yards soon were as common to see as a farmer's pickup.

A new cattle industry was being instituted in our area. That industry was to become known as a wintering program. Freshly weaned calves were bought in the areas of Colorado, New Mexico and Montana where large herds of cows and calves were traditionally grown. The calves were then shipped to Kansas where they were grazed on wheat pastures and milo stalks. The ideal weight of these calves when purchased was 400 to 450 pounds. The goal was to sell them the following spring at 700 lbs.

The weaning process is the most stressful time in the life of a cow. Usually it takes about ten days after a calf is taken from their mothers before they quit bawling and searching for their mothers and start to eat. Their guts have to get used to feed without the milk from their mothers. Any change in the weather further stresses them and being in a weakened condition they can quickly succumb to any disease that comes along. Calves that were weaned and started on feed at their home place always demanded a higher price by the producer, but since the mortality rate can run as high as 10% most producers choose to get rid of them as soon as they were taken from their mothers. When the calves were loaded on trucks and spend two or three days on the road enroute to the buyer they usually arrived in a sorry state. They were still bawling for their mothers. They were hungry, dehydrated, and had been exposed to who knows what on a dirty truck. Usually the first thirty days after receiving the calves dictated whether you made a profit or just gave away your feed and labor.

The prices remained stable for nearly ten years. You pretty well knew about what the calves were going to cost and what they would bring the following spring. The lack of wheat pasture was always a factor in how profitable the program was. When I sold my cows I decided to try the calf wintering program. I started with 100 head and had a respectable gain in my first year in the wintering program. Through the following years the only sure thing was that the first month was always exciting. You almost had to live with them because they would die if not treated promptly. The grazing of newly emerged wheat had been studied extensively at K-State and at the Hays experiment station. Their research had shown no adverse yield reduction from grazing of the young wheat.

One seldom recognized technological advancement that also spurred cattle production was the electric fence charger. Until its invention, if a field was to be grazed, a barbed wire fence had to be built surrounding the field. Most of the fields had been fenced when they were first farmed, but by the early forties those original fences had fallen into disrepair from neglect. Two men can build two miles of electric fence in about 6 hours. Instead of barbed wire, smooth galvanized wire is used for electric fences. Steel rods with insulators serve as posts and after cattle get used to an electric fence it does a great job of containing livestock.

The one downside of an electric fence is high winds. When wind speeds increase, tumbleweeds break loose and are driven by the wind and when the weeds hit an electric fence they will tear it down. If the wind is accompanied by snow the snow can cover a fence. During snow storms cattle will always drift with the storm and if the fence is down from the wind the cattle will go right over the fence and keep right on going until either they find shelter or it quits snowing. It was not unusual for cattle to drift 25 miles during a blizzard, but usually the drifting cattle would stop at a shelter belt or one of the creeks that run through the area.

One of the dreaded possibilities was that the drifting cattle would get mixed up with someone else's cattle and then had to be separated before they were returned to their home field. These instances of drifting cattle didn't occur very often but was always in the back of your mind when you had cattle on wheat pasture. Water was mostly hauled to the wheat pasture for the cattle. Breaking the ice in the tanks was a job that had to be performed every day throughout the coldest part of the winter along with checking on the health of the herd. Cattle needing treatment were roped and treated in the field.

Generally the health of wheat pasture cattle remained good during this grazing part of the program so the time required for treating sick cattle was at a minimum. The weight gain on wheat pasture was always good and the cost minimal. So wheat pasture became one of the driving factors that moved the industry to the Great Plains. The 400 lb. calves that had been purchased the previous fall would weigh 600 to 650 lbs. the following spring after the winter on wheat pasture. These cattle were then sold to the feed yards where they were fattened for market.

GREYHOUNDS; COYOTE HUNTING

I doubt that with today's definition of recreation, the following story would fit into that category. I vaguely remember my father coming home with four greyhound pups. Even today I don't think there is a more attractive breed of dog than a greyhound, especially when they are just pups. I wish I knew the reason why he got four instead of just one. He had a neighbor who hunted coyotes from horseback and perhaps Dad liked the idea. Anyway, I quickly picked the largest dog as my dog. Ring was brindle in color with a white stripe around his neck. My sister, Corrine, picked a small blue female as her dog. The dogs were kept in the barn and always got a large pan of milk when we milked. Dad shot jackrabbits to feed the dogs as well as the milk that he fed them.

Dad had recently purchased a Model A pickup and built a dog box that fit in the bed of the pickup. The box was about four feet long and three feet tall. A door on each side was hinged on the bottom and came up the side about two feet which left an opening of about one foot for the dogs to stick their heads out of the box. A latch at the top of the door was connected to a rope which could be pulled to open the door, allowing the dogs to jump out. We began training the dogs to load and jump out when the door was opened. We would go to the closest wheat stubble field and drive through it until we jumped a jackrabbit. When the dogs saw the rabbit they would start barking and we would pull the rope and the chase was on. We never let the dogs eat the rabbits they caught in the field. We always took them back to the barn where they were fed to the dogs.

On one memorable day we jumped a coyote and released the dogs. Coyotes are a bit faster than a jackrabbit. The dogs finally caught the coyote but didn't know what to do with it once they caught it. Jackrabbits don't fight back but a coyote surely will. For a while it was impossible to say who was fighting who. The coyote would get a hold of one of the dogs and they would be going round and round while the other three dogs simply watched in amazement. After all of the dogs had been bitten several times they had had enough and simply left the coyotes go.

Dad was pleased how the dogs did on their first coyote. Uncle Lawrence also had a pack of hounds and Sunday was the day when we went hunting. Dad and I were always at a disadvantage because we always went to church on Sunday while Uncle Lawrence did not. Lawrence always had a couple of neighbors who rode with him on hunts. Dad and Lawrence always planned where they would hunt on Sunday. We would rush home from church, load the dogs, and then take off in the direction they had chosen to hunt. Several times we never found them at all, but most times it would only take an hour to catch up with them.

Greyhounds that hunt in packs soon establish themselves as to what their function is within the pack. Generally the fastest dog becomes the catch dog. Their only job is to catch the coyote and hold him until the rest of the pack arrives. Then there are the throat and chest dogs whose function is to kill the catch. Occasionally we would jump a coyote that would whip the whole pack. We had several that we never got close enough to dump the dogs. These coyotes became legendary and stories soon became known among the local hunters. The season for coyotes generally started in October and finished in April. Our total catch for a season was generally about 100. The ears were removed from the coyotes and presented to the county treasurer who paid $2.50 bounty for them. In the early to mid 1900's coyotes and crows were considered vermin and counties paid bounties on them. I well remember the morning when we went to the barn to milk and found two of our greyhounds dead and the other two very ill. Dad said it was probably distemper that the dogs had picked up. The two sick dogs died that day. That was the end of our having a pack of greyhounds on our farm.

When I reached high school age I went coyote hunting with a couple of neighbors who had greyhound packs. I grew up with the idea that dogs and cats were just

194

farm animals like cows and hogs. Their role was to help control the vermin that was prevalent around the farmstead. My mother never allowed cats or dogs in the house, so the barn was always their home especially when the weather was bad. When the outbreak of distemper hit the farm it would kill the dogs and cats. Six months later, they would be replaced by strays who happened by our farm. Distemper is a disease that is carried by rodents, at least that was what I was taught. We were fortunate if we went a year without it striking our cats and dog. It wasn't until the early fifties that a vaccine was available to protect our pets from this deadly disease.

After WWII, the vehicle of choice for coyote hunting was the Ford model A. All of the body was removed and the dog box was built over the rear axle. The cowling which held the gas tank and windshield was retained. A pipe handhold behind the seat allowed a third rider to stand behind the seat. After the war, when vehicles started to become available, most car manufacturers began offering pickups with larger engines and more robust bodies. These newer pickups were quickly put to use by the hunters. The farmland south of the Arkansas River was ideal for hunting with a vehicle as there were no gulleys from running water that had to be avoided. Occasionally when the hunters strayed outside of their usual familiar areas hitting an unseen gully or hole would require the hunter to spend the following week repairing the vehicle so it would be ready the following Sunday.

Our group primarily hunted in a forty square mile area and most land owners allowed us to hunt on their land with few exceptions. Several times each winter, groups from the cities would come through our area. These groups might have ten dog wagons and ten chase vehicles. One or two of their vehicles would be equipped to run through barbed wire fences and on occasion we would hit a fence that had been built since the previous year. We would repair the fence before we left the area and try to contact the landowner whose fence we had damaged and repaired. The rogue hunters might run through a fence three times in a half mile and never repair a fence that they cut. A few landowners felt that all hunters knowingly destroyed fences and their perception made it hard to convince them otherwise.

As a young boy I remember an old farmer in our community named Claude Young who always went coyote hunting with my Uncle Lawrence and Dad. I don't know what role he played with my uncle and dad in getting started coyote hunting, but I do remember Claude reminiscing about how as a younger man he had hunted coyotes on horseback while his pack of dogs ran alongside his horse. We never went hunting without Claude as he always seemed to instinctively know where the best places to find our prey. As I remember, it was Claude's pack that was in Uncle Lawrence's dog box in the bed of his early thirties Plymouth pickup.

There was just enough room between the front of the dog box and the back of the cab for a hunter to stand. From his elevated position in the bed of the pickup he generally was the first to spot a coyote ahead of us in the wheat stubble and weeds. A flag consisting of an old rag nailed to a broom handle was always carried in the beds of the pickups. When a coyote was spotted the rider would raise the flag and everyone knew a coyote was spotted. The rider would then lean over the cab so the driver could see the flag and the rider would then point the flag in the direction the coyote was headed. Most of the time, it was only because of the rider in the rear that anyone was aware that a coyote had been jumped. Until Claude passed away he always rode as a spotter in the pickup with the dog box. The spotter position was then passed to Clarence Buhrer who was as avid a hunter as Claude had been.

I remember one hunt when I was about eight years old. It was a bitterly cold day with about 6"-8" of snow on the ground. It was a perfect day as the snow on the ground allowed us to see anything that was moving a half a mile away. We jumped a coyote and had dumped the dogs and they had caught and killed it just as dad and I drove upon the scene. As Dad and I walked up to the area, Clarence jumped out of the back of the pickup just as my cousin Vernon opened the door of the pickup. The top corner of the door caught Clarence right between his upper front teeth. Both teeth were knocked out and the corner of the door continued up to the bottom of his nose. An awfully lot had happened to Clarence in the short time it took him to reach the ground. We tried to talk Clarence into going to the doctor, but he wouldn't even consider it using the argument that the hunting conditions were perfect with the snow and that we might not see such good conditions the rest of the winter. We caught two more coyotes that afternoon. By the time we quit hunting Clarence had quit bleeding due to the cold wind and snow blowing into his face. The blood had caked his face from his eyes to his chin and around both sides of his face where his ears kept it from going to the back of his head. When dad and I arrived home late that afternoon and as I was telling my mother about Clarence's injury I passed out right in the middle of the kitchen. Mom and Dad thought it was because I was hungry and cold and had come into a warm kitchen that had caused me to pass out. But as I got older I realized that injuries and blood were apt to make me pass out or make it impossible to watch. Later in life I was able to perform most of the medical things that livestock required but I never learned to like it.

After Dad and Lawrence quit hunting I went with several neighborhood friends who ran dogs. Bill and Whitey Harris and Carl Bowman all had packs and hunted every weekend. Every county had bounties on coyotes and fur buyers would buy the skins. The bounties plus the skins would cover most of the costs minus repairs to the vehicles. Once a vehicle was used to hunt coyotes they were quickly modified so that they could stand the rigors required and even then, repairing them required a week of work so they would be ready the following weekend.

I purchased a 1951 two-door sedan from a local boy for $75. It quickly became my coyote hunting vehicle, which we referred to as our 'Hoopy.' I don't think I ever bought anything that sooner or later didn't succumb to my torch and welder in my quest to improve or make it better at what I wanted it to do. My '51 Chevy was no exception. When I finished it, the body from the back of the front seat to the rear bumper was gone, as well as the hood and front fenders. The front and rear axles were moved forward two feet. The back of the cab was covered with light sheet metal. Light sheet metal front fenders were added as was a roll bar and seat belts. An old Model T pickup bed was shortened to three and a half feet and welded behind the cab. The object of all of this butchering was to remove as much weight as possible and to distribute the weight as evenly as possible to all four wheels. The results were more than satisfactory to me. It drove very nice and because it was so light it was seldom in the shop being repaired.

In the early sixties new craze in communication was taking over the population; it was the Citizen Band radio. When we got our first CB's it was wonderful to be able to contact the house or any of my friends with this new miracle. However, in a few months time they became virtually useless. Reception would fade in and out. You might be talking to someone a hundred yards away and suddenly you were talking to some shrimp boat captain in the Gulf of Mexico. In a couple of years the FCC started licensing much narrower band widths that brought about Business Band radios. These radios were great and did what everyone needed.

These radios were quickly put in all coyote wagons. No longer did a rider in the back direct the driver with a flag but rather with a microphone. In February of 1972 we were hunting and just caught a coyote when someone called and said there was a coyote several miles away. We jumped in the Chevy and took off for where the coyote was sighted. Greg was riding in the right seat and Gordon was standing in the back. I figured it would take several minutes to get the dogs loaded and for the dog wagon to catch us. When we got to the area we saw the coyote out in the middle of a large alfalfa field. I started to slow down to jump the ditch and to try to hold the coyote in the alfalfa

200

field until the dog wagon arrived. The road was probably the least traveled road in the township and had never been graveled and on those roads the dust kicked up by a vehicle was unbelievable. It hadn't taken as long to load the dogs as I figured and the driver, Benny Bowman, had quickly caught up with us.

Benny suddenly roared upon on us as we were slowing down and hit us before he could even touch his brakes. I vaguely remember calling to my brothers to see if they were okay. When we jumped in both Greg and I were in such a hurry we forgot to put on our seatbelts. The sheriff who investigated the accident said we had flipped twice end over end and then rolled twice. All three of us had been ejected. The only injury to Greg was he lost his glasses. Gordon had a broken leg which had to be pinned and I apparently landed on my head. When I came to the following day, Dr. Brenner told me that I had missed having my neck broken by a mere hair's breadth. They kept me in the hospital nearly a month to be sure that after the swelling went down no damage had been done. It took until the following fall before I could work a full day. I remember a number of close calls in my lifetime but this was the nearest I came to becoming just another statistic.

BUILDING A BOAT

It was in the early fifties that we learned of a new water sport. It was water skiing. This news only inflamed our enthusiasm for Cedar Bluff reservoir to be opened to water enthusiasts. After we found out that it had reached its conservation pool size our group of friends and relatives would make several trips each summer to enjoy the lake. We quickly found a marina that rented boats by the day. The marina operator's boats were homemade and consisted of a boat made out of 10" aluminum irrigation pipe with a plywood floor. When the boat was stopped the water would come in the back of the boat and the floor would be covered by 4" of water. When the 25 hp. engine was started the nose of the boat would come up and all the water on the floor would run out the back and the whole thing would turn into a motor boat. To be a passenger on one of these boats was about as exciting as anything we had experienced. It was behind one of these boats that we learned to water-ski.

The only one of us who could swim was my brother-in-law, Bob Brack, who had worked every summer as a lifeguard at the Larned pool. Having him with us was always a confidence builder. We had a favorite beach where our kids could swim and play. Plenty of driftwood was always handy for campfires and our lunches always were built around tons of wieners cooked over the fire. We would all load up three or four times every summer and make the trek to Cedar Bluffs.

After several years we decided we would build a boat as the marina operator had gone out of business. A boat dealer in Hutch had an unfinished boat for sale plus a jeep inboard engine and transmission. We thought we had stolen it from him as we only paid $400 for an inboard boat. We turned my cousin Larry's garage into a boat factory and spent nearly every night for the next seven months finishing the boat. We always had plenty of help as everyone who enjoyed the weekends at the lake was always available and wanted to help.

The dealer who had sold us the boat had strongly suggested that we cover the boat with fiberglass as it would make the boat leak proof as well as adding to its strength. Because fiberglass was only recently invented no one knew anything about it and that included us. Our dealer friend also sold fiberglass and the resin to activate it.

Our boat costs began to escalate along with the amount of time that we were investing in it. We would put a layer of fiberglass on the hull and mix the resin to spread over the fiberglass to set it up, but the surface would end up as rough as a sidewalk. Our wives were recruited as sanders. As soon as we got another layer of glass applied our wives started sanding. The resin applied on the cloth consisted of two ingredients: five parts resin to one part activator. This ratio was very critical. Not enough activator and the resin refused to set up and too much and the resin would set up in the paper cups we used to hold the resin. When the resin started to harden it immediately got so hot that you could no longer hold the cup and instantly the brush being used to apply it to the glass cloth would be trapped in the cup. It soon became apparent that the air temperature was critical to the setup time of the resin as the ratio of activator to resin.

It took us a month to get the glass installed on the hull. We must have used a truck load of sandpaper. Once the hull had been glassed it was time to install the engine and finish the inside.

After we got the Jeep engine and transmission installed it was time to install the prop shaft. I had been elected to build the stuffing boxes for the rudder and prop shaft. The stuffing boxes were the waterproof holes in the bottom of the boat and allowed the shafts to go through the bottom of the boat and not let any water enter the boat. The angle that the engine and prop shaft sits in the boat is very critical. If the front of the engine is too high the propeller won't operate as efficiently as it is designed to. If the angle is too flat the propeller will hit the bottom of the boat. Once the angle of the engine is established the hole in the bottom of the boat can be cut for the propeller shaft.

When I climbed into the boat to mark where the propeller shaft would go through the keel of the hull I noticed that the keel didn't feel quite right under the pencil point. I pushed a little harder and the pencil slid into the keel at least two inches. The keel was little more than a shell. When a boat is being built the first piece that is put into place is the keel so the whole boat is built around the keel. The keel in our boat was ruined by dry rot. Dry rot can only occur when wood is unprotected and submerged under water for a long period of time and then allowed to slowly dry out. Some species of wood are more prone to dry rot than others. As my swear words resounded around the building everyone looked into the boat fearing that I was injured. When I explained what I had discovered everyone was stunned. We knew the original builder of the hull had never had the boat in the water and had either built the boat outside or stored it outside and rain had collected in the bottom of the boat. It appeared that the only solution was to carry it outside and have a good ole wiener roast. That night, for the first time in months, we were all home and in bed before midnight.

I didn't sleep all night as I tried to think of a solution to the problem. I called all of our group together at noon the next day and told them we would resume work that night. It was a very dejected group that showed up that night. I explained that since we had all the decking material on hand we wouldn't have to spend any more money to try to salvage the project. The first thing we did was to drill small holes as close to the keel as possible through the bottom of the boat. When we turned the boat over the small holes would show us exactly where the keel was on the inside. We would then screw the decking material to the top of the boat. The decking plywood would then hold the hull perfectly in shape while we removed the keel from the outside. I'm sure a marine engineer would have said it was impossible to remove a keel from a completed hull, but we didn't know that.

As we applied the fiberglass to the outside of the hull I was amazed at what a marvelous material it was. When the glass material was saturated with resin and allowed to cure it was as translucent as window glass. Every screw was easily seen through the fiberglass. We had to remove the installed Jeep engine before we closed the top of the hull with the decking material. Resting on its top on the floor, the holes were easily seen and would give us a perfect guide. We started removing the keel. I had decided that to preserve the integrity of the hull we would remove and replace the keel in three sections starting with the middle section first. I was the only one who thought that would work. A pencil line along the locating holes showed us exactly where the keel was located on the inside of the hull. When a Skill Saw followed the pencil lines we were rewarded with a thunk as the middle third of the keel fell out. The removed section was used as a pattern to make the replacement section. I had found when we glassed the outside of the hull that the resin used by itself was a perfect glue for gluing wood together. If there were any gaps in the glue joint, fiberglass was used as filler and saturated with resin which would create a joint stronger than the wood itself. The piece removed was used as a pattern for the replacement part. As the new section was lowered into the hull it was obvious that it was going to work just fine. We carefully glassed the replacement part just enough so it was perfectly placed and left it to cure overnight. Next we replaced the rear third followed by the forward third. It soon became obvious that the hull had not been compromised by our butchery.

After the keel was replaced we put several layers of fiberglass on the exterior of the keel and sanded it down. We turned the hull over and removed the decking from the top and fiber glassed the keel on the inside of the hull. The replacement had worked perfectly. We reinstalled the engine and installed the control cables that controlled the transmission and rudder. We had a local mechanic wire the gauges and ignition system and started the engine for the first time.

We cut and installed the formers for the decking. We thought we would try the boat on a local sand pit before we put on the final touches. It was now time to build the trailer for the boat. We finished the trailer in a few evenings and headed for the sandpit. Excitement was high as we unloaded our new inboard. Our wives and kids lined the banks as the two of us left the bank. Vernon was driving and as he headed out he shoved the throttle to full speed. The jeep engine exhaust rose to a mighty roar, but the speed only increased a little above a fast walk. We checked the engine installation and anything that might point to the anemic performance of the boat. Everything looked ok.

I left to find a phone to call an old friend who I had played baseball with and who had built his own inboard boat. His success had been our inspiration to build our boat. Jim Deighton worked as a road engineer for the county and said he would be out at noon to take a look. When he arrived and started looking our boat over the first thing he pointed out was that our propeller appeared to be too small and he doubted if the four cylinder Jeep engine would ever generate enough speed to pull even one water skier. The only good thing he liked about our boat was the transmission, which he thought was a good idea especially for maneuvering around docks. We pulled the boat home and began discussing what to do. Someone suggested we finish the boat as a fishing boat and sell it. Vernon, who was an avid fisherman, said he would never buy an inboard because it would not be maneuverable enough to fish off of. We finally decided to salvage the project and the only solution was to install a larger engine. I pointed out a different engine would require an awful lot of work. The first challenge was if we retained the transmission, an adaptor would have to be built that would mate the transmission to the engine, water cooled exhaust manifolds would have to be built, and a new water system built to cool the engine. Someone asked if I could build the adapter and manifolds while the rest would finish construction of the boat. It appeared that we had little choice at this point and I agreed to try.

We found a used 350 cubic inch V-8 Chevrolet engine to replace the Jeep engine. After I removed the transmission it became obvious that this project was going to require a lot of luck to make it work. If we had a lathe it would have been much easier, but we had no machine tools. All I had was a torch, welder, and hand grinder. It was obvious that if I couldn't build the adaptor there would be no need for the water cooled manifolds or the cooling system for the engine. Because we were having to do our farm work during the day and build a boat at night sleep was a precious commodity and most of the time we could have gone to sleep standing up. But we were young and didn't know any better. After three nights and way more luck than I deserved I finished the adaptor and the transmission was on the engine.

I started on the water cooled manifolds. On a normal engine the exhaust manifolds became red-hot if the engine is working hard. In a boat loaded with people and the exposed red hot manifolds, it is dangerous and uncomfortable for the passengers. If the manifolds are encased by a water jacket that has water circulating around the red hot manifolds nothing is ever hot enough to burn a person.

Home-made marine manifolds are tricky to build. I suppose that is one reason they are seldom seen on home-made boats. However, I don't remember seeing anyone ever looking for shop-made marine manifolds. I guess that might be why they are so rare. When I finished the manifolds and painted them they looked just like they were purchased from a marine specialty catalogue. The Jeep mounts were removed and we built mounts for the Chevy engine. As soon as the engine was installed we headed for the sandpit to see how it would perform.

Along with all of the normal gauges, we had bought a marine speedometer. Vernon and I backed the boat off the trailer and took off. Almost immediately the speedometer showed 35 miles per hour and settled on 40 mph. After everyone had a ride we loaded it up and took it back to the shop to finish it up. We had seen a boat at Cedar Bluff that had to be the most elegant boat on the lake. We met the owner at the marina and found out that it was a Chris-Craft. We decided we wanted our boat to be finished to look just like the $35,000 Chris-Craft. The boat had a teak wood deck. The only openings were the two cockpits with the decking covering the engine between the front and rear seats.

We called the dealer in Hutch and found the teak decking was available in a plastic covering that could be applied over a plywood deck. We ordered enough to cover our deck. We had been collecting pictures of boats so we could paint our boat just like our favorite picture. Johnny Berscheidt, who had painted machinery in the winter, was hired to paint our boat. When we asked him he got very excited because he had never painted a boat before. He began to check out the best paint to put on a boat, and had bought a new paint just released for marine use. When we read the instructions on the cans it sounded just like the resin used on fiberglass. It was a two-part paint. The primary paint was to be mixed with a catalyst. The paint had a pot life of one hour and then any paint left in the equipment had to be dumped out and the system cleaned before the next batch was mixed. Johnny insisted that the painting be done during daylight as it was easier for him to see. As he was just finishing the first coat the paint started to set up in his gun. He quickly headed for his bench to get the paint thinner and clean his equipment. The label on the paint said acetone was required to clean the paint equipment and of course we had none. By the time we got the acetone the paint in Johnny's paint equipment was as hard as a rock. We added the cost of replacing Johnny's paint equipment to the growing cost of our boat.

Painting and masking the hull had taken a lot longer than we had figured, but the finished boat was a joy to behold. Our boat had consumed nearly two years to complete and Jewel and I only ended up making three trips to Cedar Bluff to enjoy it. All of our kids had friends they wanted to take boating and unless we could stay a couple of days it wasn't worth the hassle.

I was getting a haircut when my barber asked if we had been to the lake recently. I explained how hard it was to find the time to get the boat, kids, food and everything ready and then come home with everything dirty and needing put away. It seemed a group of boating enthusiasts had leased an abandoned sand pit south of town and were recruiting new members. He asked if Jewel and I would be interested. Jewel and I talked it over and since it was only eight miles away we could go in the evenings without much planning and best of all we wouldn't have to drive four hours to get there and back. We used our inboard several times on the sand pit but since the sandpit was only about twelve acres in size the inboard was nearly too big, especially if any of the other members had their boats out at the same time.

One of the club's members whose kids had all left home approached me and offered to sell his aluminum outboard at a reasonable price and we bought it. Lil' Bo was a fourteen foot aluminum boat with a 25 hp. Evinrude outboard engine. The seller threw in a couple pairs of skis, ropes, and several life jackets and just like that our family had our own boat.

The CB radios we had installed in our home and in all our equipment proved very handy as Jewel and I could communicate instantly. CB radios were soon replaced with new FCC approved Business Band models, which offered a range of twenty-five miles and an operator's private channel. We replaced all of our CB's with the newer business band radios and though they were more expensive they proved to be just what we needed and we continued to use them until we retired.

If I was in the field and it appeared I could quit a half hour earlier than normal I would call Jewel and ask if she could get away to go boating. She and the girls would make sandwiches and when I came in the kids were in their swimsuits and ready to go. I would put on my swimsuit and a pair of pants and in thirty minutes we would have the boat in the water. We spent our next several years on this schedule. Our kids could have their friends join us and we generally had a couple of hours to enjoy the water.

We sold our share of the inboard to the original builders who continued to make trips to Cedar Bluff. Our own boat and the close proximity to the sandpit was just what we wanted. Gordon and Greg were always included and their friends joined us as well. All of our kids learned to ski behind Lil' Bo. We could ski until it was nearly dark, load up, drive home, back the boat into the barn, and be in bed at our usual time. That was how we enjoyed our summers until the kids had all left for college.

TANDEM TRACTOR; MECHANICAL END GATE

In one of my farm publication subscriptions, I saw a picture of a farmer in Western Kansas who had hitched two farm tractors together and had married two tillage tools together. He had eliminated one tractor operator. The idea intrigued me. But since our fields were much smaller in Central Kansas, I thought I could improve on his design considerably. The following winter I started building my own twin tractor project. The design of the Western Kansas farmer had the operator on the rear tractor with a long shaft running over the back tractor to the steering wheel on the front tractor by which he could steer the hitched together tractors. All four wheels remained on both tractors.

I wanted to remove the front wheels on both tractors, thus making the rear wheels on the front tractor into the front wheels of my twin tractor. This idea would require a unique hinge arrangement between the two tractors suspending the front ends of the tractors where the original front wheels had been. The front end of the front tractor stuck out the length of the original tractor minus its front wheels, which gave the tractor a very unique look. When steering, the front tractor swung side to side. We called it "The Snake." The steering was accomplished by placing a hydraulic cylinder between the two tractors which tried pushing or pulling the two tractors apart thus turning the rear tires of the front tractor into the steering wheels. The hinge and steering worked very well and the steering was accomplished with a tiller instead of a steering wheel on the back tractor operator's platform. The operation of the tiller arrangement was quickly adapted to by the operator. This feature was appreciated because power steering hadn't been used except in a few instances on regular tractors.

The clutching arrangement was also unique. The clutch pedal on the back tractor was linked to the clutch on the front tractor with a closed loop master to slave hydraulic system on the front tractor. This allowed the operator to disengage both clutches at the same time simply by depressing the clutch on the back tractor. A handle was installed on the back tractor which when pulled held the clutch disengaged on the front tractor. This feature allowed both tractors to operate independently of each other. This feature was used when hooking up to tillage tools or when maneuvering around the yard. The snake could easily maneuver in the smaller space allowed by a standard tractor. The turning radius was also normal.

An ignition switch for the front tractor was also close to the operator in the event he needed to stop the front tractor. The throttle was left full open on the front tractor and the gear selector was left on the proper field gear and through the following years was seldom changed. With the clutch disengaged and the front tractor not running the rear tractor could pull equipment down a road at normal speeds. Upon reaching the field, the operator simply engaged the clutch on the front tractor and the rear tractor simply pushed the front one and it would immediately start and was field ready. What the Snake taught us was invaluable as to what four wheel drive offered. We found out how important it was that when the entire weight of the tractor was placed on all four wheels the efficiency of a tractor more than doubled. A four wheel drive tractor that had its weight evenly distributed on all four wheels was almost impossible to get stuck. The snake lasted four seasons before the engines were worn out and was retired as our big tractor needs had changed when our cropping changed from wheat to more alfalfa.

Another of my early inventions was a self opening and closing endgate for trucks hauling silage. The conventional endgates of the time consisted of two doors that were connected by a latch in the center. When the driver arrived at the silo he had to get out of the truck, go to the back, unlatch the doors, swing them open, tie them open, get back in the truck, dump the load, then drive out of the way of other trucks, stop the truck, get out, untie the doors, swing them shut and latch them, get back in the truck and go back to the field. Most of these endgates were homemade and were constantly breaking or being torn off at the silo because when they were open the drivers would forget that the doors were open and would tear them off via the other trucks or equipment at the silo. I had noticed that a driver was spending an awful lot of time just getting in and out of the truck. I timed one of our drivers at the silo one day and knew if I could build an automatic endgate the driver could easily gain two more loads a day if he didn't have to spend all the time opening and closing his endgate. Since I had been thinking about it for several years it only took two days to build my automated endgate. My endgate swung up and over the rear of the truck bed. Once the driver started to raise the truck bed the endgate would automatically start rising. As the truck bed continued rising so did the endgate. After the load was dumped and the bed came down so did the endgate. The driver didn't have to get out of the truck any longer. We were harvesting silage using three trucks and by noon on the day I finished the endgate the crew agreed that the endgate had nearly eliminated the need of one of the three trucks. I was told by many people that I should patent it.

About a year later Tradewind Industries of Liberal who manufactured truck beds came out with an automatic endgate which resembled my endgate exactly. The design was so simple that they might have designed their endgate before they saw mine. It was when I saw their endgate

218

triggered a true interest in patenting any further ideas or inventions that I might construct.

IRRIGATION

One thing I quickly learned when I started farming was how important the timing of rainfall was to crop yields. The rainfall could be average or even above average, but if it was dry at the critical time, yields suffered. I watched the flood irrigators and it became obvious to me that irrigation was the way to increased yields. Our farmland was so rough it made machine leveling economically infeasible. There remained one alternative to machine leveling, however, and that was what was known as Side Roll Sprinkler systems. This system consisted of an aluminum pipe with a 6' wheel every 50' on the pipe. The pipe was hooked to the well by a long hose. There were sprinkler heads every 25' on the aluminum pipe. When the pump was started the sprinklers would water a swath about 100' wide the length of the pipe. When one or two inches of water had been applied the pump shut down and the pipe was rolled forward 100' and the pump was restarted. I visited with several owners of these systems and all had one complaint. They all complained about uneven water distribution caused by the wind. If the wind was from one direction when the system was started, and suddenly shifted to the opposite direction of the water pattern on the upwind side would be less than on the downwind side which affected yields and water patterns. I dropped the idea of this method of irrigation. However, these systems can still be found in areas that have low wind speeds or a constant direction of winds.

It became obvious that if I was to irrigate then we were going to have to move to a different area where machine leveled soils were available. A machine leveled farm west of Larned located near the Pawnee Creek came up for sale. This farm pumped its water from the creek. This was before the state banned pumping from streams. I talked to my banker about buying the farm and he suggested that I try to borrow money from The Federal Land Bank. When I approached them I was informed that I would need at least 30% equity before they would lend me the balance. Jack Hestor was the manager of the office and suggested that I try to borrow the 30% down payment from an individual and then they would lend me the balance. I had heard my Dad talk about several families in the Ellinwood area who had amassed huge fortunes from oil production. I decided that they would be the place to start trying to borrow the down payment. Today, 65 years later, it is hard to believe that I, only a few years out of my teens, had the nerve to approach those individuals with such a preposterous request. Needless to say they turned me down. Jack Hestor called me several times to see if I had any luck borrowing the down payment. I think he recognized how badly I wanted an irrigated farm. Jack became a friend who proved invaluable to me years later. The farm that we wanted had sold, but I continued looking. We continued growing wheat, milo, alfalfa, and cattle.

When we made the decision to irrigate one of the first steps we had to take is drill test a well to be sure water is available. I contracted Rosencrantz Drilling in Great Bend to do my testing. When the first test well was done I asked Rusty Rosencrantz what he thought of my water supply. He replied, "If you put an irrigation pump on this well and run it 24 hours a day until you die and you give it to your kids and they do the same, the well will be as good then as it is today." Unfortunately that attitude was what all consumers of natural resources believed at that time. The water in a well was not visible so there was no way to gauge how large it was or how long it would last. As irrigation development increased in the sixties it became apparent that a large part of the Midwest enjoyed a huge aquifer that started in the Dakotas and extended nearly to Mexico. It began at about the Western Kansas border and extended East to central Kansas. The thickness of the water bearing sands appeared to be around 100'. The thickness of the soil over the aquifer varied from 400' in the Western part of Kansas to around 10' in the East. Most of the water was deposited by runoff water from the eastern slopes of the Rockies, while the eastern reaches were deposited by excess rainfall that percolated down through the thin soils into the aquifer. Rusty's prediction would probably have been true if my well had remained the only well that tapped into the aquifer. Neither of us could foresee how quickly development would occur. Within five years over 100 irrigation systems would be installed in a five mile square around my test well. Soil scientist decades before had named this underground lake the Ogalala Aquifer and because it could easily be tapped for homes and livestock it was responsible in large part for the settlement of central Kansas.

When the laws governing the early settlers were written and adopted in the early part of the century, the water laws included a provision that if a county wanted to write and enforce how ground water in its boundaries were used, they could by petitioning the state. The state would then return the control to that county. In the late 60's Cliff Manry asked me to serve on a steering committee petitioning the state to give control of the county's ground water back to Pawnee County. Several counties in western Kansas had received control of their ground water from the state and were organizing ground water management districts to study the aquifer and how to best utilize their water. The County Agents from Pawnee, Barton, Rice, Edwards, Kiowa and Hodgeman counties had followed the western Kansas counties and felt that the governing of water usage could be better done on a local level.

They began the process by asking some of the irrigators to serve on steering committees that would inform landowners and municipalities of the county's intent. Serving on the steering committee proved to be very frustrating and rewarding at the same time. The committee was made up of one member from each of the counties. If the County Agents had not done such a great job of choosing their candidates for the committee the plan would have died before the first meeting.

I had been measuring the water level in my irrigation wells every year before I started running my systems in the spring. I had watched the water level decline by an average of 1' a year and by the time I retired in 1990 the level had fallen by 30' since the test wells were drilled in the 60's. Most of the steering committee had seen the same results on their wells and realized that some form of control was needed if irrigation was to be passed down to the next generation. The first task of the committee was to inform all of the large users of water that the use of water should rest in the hands of the local people. When we ran public announcement ads announcing meetings to implement local control of water we were lucky if 4 or 5 people would show up. Control could only be given back to the counties if a vote by the users requested it. We couldn't even get the city managers to attend. By our second meeting we were a very disappointed group.

One of our board members was a former member of the Kansas House Of Representatives who said the only way to get people interested in our meetings was to mention the tax issue in our public notices. Dick Wellman was a rancher whose ranch lay on the south side of the Arkansas River in Rice County. He was the only true cowboy that I knew in the central part of Kansas. His family had settled in the sand hills and became successful cattle ranchers. He irrigated grass for his cowherd and was the exact opposite of what I pictured a politician to be. He was quiet and unassuming but when he spoke it was obvious he knew what he was talking about. Years later he would drive into our yard to get repairs for his irrigation systems and we would spend the rest of the day visiting. I like to think of Dick as a good friend.

After moving to Olathe, I started going out for coffee once a week with a fine gentleman, Charlie Caylor, who was soon to become a great friend. After a couple of weeks one of us happened to mention Dick Wellman and we were amazed that we both knew Dick, who Charlie had known since both attended K-State. It was through Charlie that I learned what a unique individual Dick was.

Charlie told me Dick had published several books about cowboys, the old West, and was an accomplished singer and guitar player who had cut several records. Apparently Dick was close friends with most of the movie cowboys. Dick, John Wayne, Martha Rae and several other Hollywood cowboys had formed a group called "The Hole in the Wall Gang." They would load up their horses and meet in the Black Hills in South Dakota once a year for a week of riding and cooking over a campfire.

Dick, while serving in the Pacific during WWII, had been assigned to be the driver of Martha Rae while she performed with the USO entertaining the troops. When Dick was discharged he kept in touch with Martha and together they came up with "The Hole in the Wall Gang." Over coffee Charlie and I had talked of driving back for a visit with Dick, but it seemed there was always a conflict and we never made that trip. It was a sad day when we received news of Dick's death.

The press release that Dick had penned for our steering committee finally got the results that we needed to get the irrigators interested in the Ground Water Management concept. After several informational meetings the proposal was voted on by each of the counties. The proposal passed by a large margin and the Big Bend Water Management District # 5 became a reality. I was elected and served two terms as the director of Pawnee County. It was very satisfying to have helped organize and implement the district and watch its growth and the impact on the irrigation industry in Kansas.

JOHN JANTZEN; IRS; TAXES; FARM MANAGEMENT PROGRAM

On one of his visits to our farm when I told him that we were nearly at the end of our rope, Cliff Manry suggested that we join a new program that K-State was offering to farmers. The new program offered an accounting program which included four visits a year from a field man who would monitor our accounting records. At the end of the year a summary of all the farms that were similar in size and operation could be compared to our operation. Jewel, who did most of our farm bookkeeping, liked the idea because at the time she had been unable to find a bookkeeping format for farm use. During our first meeting with our field man we expressed the fact that if the opportunity presented itself we would leave the farm. He was an optimistic young farm boy who had just graduated from K-State with a degree in Ag accounting. He pulled his files from the previous year on the farms that were in our category and began comparing our books to them. It became obvious that as far as profitability we were in the upper 50th percentile of the farms of our size in Kansas. He pointed out that the thing that was causing our concern was the fact that we were just starting and hadn't started acquiring equity. He said that research had shown that by

1965 the world population would begin to exceed the ability to produce enough food for the world's growing population. When that point was reached we would see dramatic increases in the price of our commodities. His enthusiasm for a better tomorrow helped us lay aside our thoughts of leaving the farm.

As 1965 approached so did a nagging distrust in research. The researchers had forgotten to include the fact that fertilizer and improved plant breeding would allow production to outpace population growth. Through the years the Farm Management Program went through many changes especially among the field men who made the quarterly farm visits. The rural banks began to recognize that the field men offered an untapped source of potential farm loan officers which were in short supply. Seldom in those years would we have the same field man calling on us. The overall philosophy of the farm management concept remained unchanged but each new field man's ideas were different from the previous ones.

At our next quarterly visit we were introduced to a new field man named John Jantzen who was a farm boy from Iowa, and a Purdue graduate. John was an accountant who loved accounting and when glancing at a set of books was able to find an answer to any question that we might have. Jewel loved how he could interpret her accounting. John called on us twice before he told us that at our next meeting he would introduce us to yet another field man. After he left Jewel and I discussed how we hated to lose him and decided to call him. After we had made it clear how much we liked his accounting and visits we asked if it would be possible to retain him as our accountant. He told us he was thinking of starting his own accounting business in Greensburg and if his plans went through he would be delighted to have our account.

A few weeks later he called and said his new office was open and he would call on us just as he had when he was working for Farm Management. If we wanted he would retain the same bookkeeping method that we were familiar with. Jewel and I were very pleased at this turn of events. We had no idea how important our relation with John would be and how it would affect the rest of our lives. John's farm visits only lasted one year and were replaced by visits to his office instead.

On our first visit I was impressed by his huge library consisting of hundreds of volumes of Tax Law books on state and federal law. It soon became obvious that John's clients were made up of the most successful of the farmers who he had served as field man when he was working for Farm Management. Jewel had no training as an accountant but she soon had devised her own methods of accounting. Early on John tried to get her to adopt standard accounting procedures but she defended her method vigorously.

We seldom made a decision involving our operation without consulting John. Sometimes it was hard to catch John in his office because he was at a seminar involving farm tax law or new farming methods.

He was always very interested in the work I was doing on fertilizer placement versus the old broadcast method. I had been working on a new idea on changing the cultural method of seed bed preparation. John would stop by the farm occasionally to see what I was doing in the way of modifying my equipment to achieve what I wanted. One evening John called and suggested that we go to Boone, Iowa and attend a field day at a farm where the farmer was working on the same ideas of minimum seed bed tillage. At the demonstration of the farmers' method, John and I were amazed at the similarities of our methods to change the seed bed preparation. The farm was very similar to the experimental farms of Kansas. The farm's main goal was to test sustainable agriculture concept, which was very popular at the time.

John's method of handling tax payments drove Jewel up the wall. She was always very punctual about getting each year's accounting finished and given to John for making and payment of our taxes. When we delivered her finalized reports, she would begin to worry if John would get it done before the deadline. She called him constantly checking on how soon he wanted us to sign our returns and pay our taxes. John's mode of operation was always laid back and he never shared Jewel's sense of urgency. As the date drew close so did Jewel's frustration. John hadn't called and she couldn't get him on the phone. John had three secretaries in his office and they didn't know where he was either. Jewel started watching for agents from the IRS who she was sure would escort both of us to Leavenworth. He called two days later, and after Jewel had unloaded on him, he told her she needed to have more confidence in him. He told her he had filed for an extension a week before, and that the IRS agents were too busy to come and pick us up. I am convinced that Jewel's untimely death was attributive to her frustration with John. One of the services that were part of his package was, in the event of an audit by the IRS, he would represent his client at the audit and pay any fine levied by the auditor for accounting errors. This was small consolation to Jewel.

Auditing by the IRS was dreaded by every farmer. An audit of a neighbor's taxes was treated the same as a death in the family. Every farming community had horror stories about audits and auditors. When we were notified that our returns were to be audited Jewel immediately called John. He tried unsuccessfully to reassure her. We and John arrived at the courthouse on the appointed day.

Before our appointment John laid down the ground rules. We were allowed to give our names and say hello and then not to answer any questions that the auditor might direct to us. John said that all our returns showed him as the preparer. John said he would answer all questions from the agent. The audit was to cover our returns from the three previous years. The agent started out with procedural questions early in the audit and slowly got into specific deductions. He finally got to a claim of $9,000 that we had made on a credit card. The question went right over my head. John leaned back and said that was a new engine for one of my tractors. The agent said that no credit card company would accept that high of a charge on one of their cards. John pointed out that several card companies did in fact allow even larger charges on their cards if the card holder had good credit.

After two hours the agent announced that he had finished and thanked us. John reminded him that we wanted everything before and included in the audit to be declared as correct and signed by him. The agent gave us the document. Jewel and I were ecstatic. John merely reminded us that he had told us not to worry.

PAWNEE BEEFBUILDERS

A card club organized in the early fifties in our community was comprised of eight members of the local farm families and was very popular among our group of friends. We rotated the meeting among the members during the winter months. At one of the card club meetings after the card games were over and we were enjoying the dessert, Harold Koehn, Milford Zook and I were at one table visiting about our calf wintering programs. In the course of discussions we all agreed that if we were going to expand our feeding programs it was obvious that we would need to hire someone to manage those as we all had farming operations that required all of our time. We decided to build a commercial feed lot and begin selling our ag production to the feed lot and since we had all started irrigating at about the same time the plan was we would produce as much of the necessary feed as possible on our three farms. I had begun several years earlier expanding my alfalfa acreage to take advantage of the growing demand for hay in the western part of the state where several new feed yards had opened. The irrigators in Western Kansas decided that hay couldn't be grown in their part of the state so a great market for alfalfa developed in our area.

Since we were all customers of the First National Bank we went to see Stan Moffet, the bank President. After we explained what we had in mind Stan suggested we explore the idea further and he would check into how to finance the operation. We had already chosen the land we thought would work best for what we had in mind. A few days later we met with Stan again after he had arranged with Traveler's Insurance Company to finance the construction of the feed yard. Stan's bank would furnish the capital for the early costs until it became necessary for the large loan when actual construction began. Milford knew the family who owned the land we wanted. He contacted the family and they sold us the land. The three of us started visiting feed yards all over the high plains getting ideas that we could use in our yard. The one idea that every yard suggested was to plan and execute a drainage system before beginning construction because once built it was impossible to do the dirt work for a workable drainage system. We hired an engineering firm in Hutchinson to plan our pen layout so each pen would drain into a large ditch that would take any runoff to a large lagoon, where it could evaporate or, during extremely wet weather, could be pumped out on surrounding farm land. It was very expensive to do all the dirt work necessary for the drainage but in the following years it became obvious that it was money wisely spent. Our yard was the first yard built in

Kansas with the drainage work completed before a single post was set. The dirt contractor worked with a large fleet of construction equipment to get the dirt moved quickly.

We had decided that we wanted our manager to be on the job when construction began so he would be familiar with everything in the yard. Our search began at Kansas State. K-State was starting a program for feed yard management so we met with the professor and asked to interview any likely candidates. They had a young man who was just what we were looking for. Max Siegar was 28 years old and married, had a strong Ag background and was hungry. We hired him and he started work right away. Max's plan was to hire a construction crew and then choose his permanent crew from the construction crew. We had chosen the first of August as the day to open. We chose this day so we would be ready to receive new milo. It was late spring and it was going to rush Max to be ready in time. During our visits to other yards we found that they were started by farmers who had large acreages of feed grains, and had only planned to feed their own cattle, but suddenly found they had more customers than they had pen space.

With the research from K-State on grain comparison between milo and corn we decided to break from the traditional way of storing and preparing the grain that we would feed. We would take milo at harvest time and process it as we received it in huge trench silos.

Research at K- State showed that milo harvested at 32% moisture then processed and stored in trench silos was just as efficient as corn that was processed daily. A contractor had been building our two trench silos 200' wide by 400' by 10' high. These silos proved to be very versatile as the capacity was only limited by how high you wanted to pile the grain in them. The silos were constructed out of concrete and a large pad was poured at the end for storage of grain prior to processing. We purchased a large diesel powered roller mill that processed the grain. The processed grain fell onto a long conveyer belt which threw the grain into the silo. Farm tractors with bulldozer blades pushed and packed the grain into the silo. While the silos were being constructed a steady flow of local farmers were stopping and inquiring about how we were going to purchase grain and whether we would be buying local grain. It became obvious that procuring grain was not going to be a problem. We had formulated a purchasing plan for grain. A week after the grain was delivered we would pay the farmer 10% of the grain delivered to the yard. Then every 30 days another 10% could be sold. We would check what the local elevators were paying daily and we would pay 10 cents a bushel over the average price of the local elevator. The 10 cents a bushel above the local elevator price was very popular with the producers as prices rarely increased by 10 cents a bushel. On top of what the three of us produced we had contracted enough grain to get us through the first year. The silos were finished by mid July and Max had started pen construction.

In June after the dirt construction was completed and it was time to get the money promised by Travelers Insurance Stan called a meeting of the three of us. It seemed when Stan had asked Travelers to forward the money they had promised, that as of the previous Wednesday they had terminated all Ag loans. Since we had taken delivery of much of the needed supplies we needed cash badly. We spent most of the day with Stan trying to figure out what we were going to do. We needed $100,000 as soon as possible. The economy was showing signs of slowing down and talk of recession was making headlines in all the newspapers. This put pressure on borrowed money and land capital borrowing as well.

It appeared that we had chosen a bad time to take on such an aggressive project. We spent the whole afternoon with Stan trying to find a workable solution to the problem we faced. We finally decided to take the only solution that appeared feasible. We made a list of people that we would approach and offer to sell them a share of the yard for $10,000 in exchange for a seat on the board of directors. We pared the list to ten which would raise the $100,000 we so desperately needed. We approached the ten candidates and made the offer. We tried to include the people who we felt had the most to gain by having a feed yard in the area. We asked both presidents from local banks, the presidents of the largest implement dealerships, a driller who was drilling nearly all the irrigation wells in the area, the meat buyer for Dillon's grocery chain, a local attorney, a large farmer who had been feeding cattle in one of the yards in western Kansas, and a car and truck dealer who we felt would probably furnish our truck and pickup needs. Harold, Milford, and I were very upset to have to give up our ownership in the yard after all the work getting the yard that close to operational. We had reluctantly donated our labor and money we had spent to date to the corporation if we were allowed preference at the time the yard needed grain or hay. We decided to call our yard Pawnee Beefbuilders Inc., or PBI as it became known.

Thus began our education on the way a corporation functioned. We found the politics involved trying to get the votes needed to get a majority on an issue we felt very strongly about could take a long time and someone who we felt was a sure vote on an issue would change his mind at the last minute. Harold and I worked nearly every day to get the yard ready to open by the planned date.

We had noticed a large farmer in the area who I will call 'Bob'. He was showing up nearly every day and would always talk to Max although Harold and I knew him well. When we asked Max about Bob's interest in the yard Max said that Bob was pushing him to get a pen ready for some cattle he was about to receive. A few days later Bob again showed up and told Max that his cattle were being loaded at Eagle Pass, Texas and would be at PBI the following day. Eagle Pass was where cattle from Old Mexico were gathered and inspected by the Agriculture Department for shipment inside the U.S. Cattle from Old Mexico were called Corrientes, which to us meant you never knew what to expect until they walked or in most cases scattered off of the trucks. The Corrientes for the most part had never seen a man or horse in their lives. Because they have lived their whole lives in the brushy deserts in Old Mexico everything was a predator and was to be evaded at all costs. They had no idea what a fence, feed bunk, or waterer was, only that it was to be evaded by any means. When the Mexicans decided to round up their cattle they would go into the brush on horseback and start the cattle toward a gathering area. It is remarkable how quickly a domestic animal reverts to the wild.

The entire Mexican cow herd had no idea of what domestication meant. I would guess if they were able to round up 25% of their cattle they felt they had been successful. Since all of the Mexican's cattle were born in the wild and were so hard to catch, most arrived at Eagle Pass having none of the normal doctoring performed on them. They would arrive at the border with horns as big at

240

the base as a closed fist. Few if any of the bulls were castrated and had tails that drug on the ground. Most were infected with every parasite known to the bovine species. These cattle proved to challenge even the most dedicated cowboy. But because they were cheaper than U.S. calves, there was always a buyer for them. Feed yard managers hated to see them arrive. They were better than an open pen, but just barely.

Max had a temporary pen readied to receive Bob's cattle. When we opened the gate on the first truck the cattle looked as if they were being shot out of the truck with a slingshot. Fortunately, the first ones saw the fence on the far side and began to circle the pen. A few stopped at the waterer and began to drink. Occasionally one would stop at the bunks and would grab a mouthful of prairie hay that Max had put out for them. It soon was apparent that the cattle had been in another yard recently because their horns had been clipped, the bulls castrated, and all carried Bob's brand. Bob insisted the cattle had been loaded at Eagle Pass and came straight to Pawnee Beef Builders.

Everyone was so busy with construction that we forgot about the mystery of Bob's cattle. Posts were being driven and the lodge pole fencing was being installed. The veterinary barn and its pens were nearing completion. The waterers were being installed and the loading docks were finished. Max decided it was time to pressurize the water lines. The pump was turned on but the waterers remained dry. It appeared something was wrong with the pump. A quick call to our electrician, Warren Smith, and he showed up immediately. He quickly announced that the problem wasn't with the pump. One of the construction crew came up and said we had a bad leak in one of the pens. When we got to the pen the problem became obvious. We had decided to drive the fence posts instead of digging all of the fence post holes by hand. A fence post had been driven through the water line. As we began talking about it water began coming out around the next post. We decided that the best solution would be to repair each pen one at a time. We might be able to receive cattle as the leaks were repaired. Max took responsibility for the problem but we all should have noticed that the posts were being driven into the lines.

The only thing that could have been worse would have been if all of the lodge pole fencing had been installed. Upon closer inspection we found that the water line wasn't pierced by every post, but enough of them had hit the line. Because it was going to take a long time to do the repair, I think it was this catastrophe plus Bob's insistence that Max get a pen ready for his cattle, that began to push Max over the edge. Max's construction crew was working long hours getting the pens and facilities ready. Scales to weigh trucks and scales in the hospital area to weigh cattle were being installed. A 60' trailer house would serve as our office and bookkeeping center. A young secretary who worked for a local attorney was hired and was busy setting up the office.

A steady stream of potential feed grain customers kept Max occupied. We called a meeting of the farmers who wanted to contract their milo to the yard and explained that they would start harvesting their milo as soon as the grain moisture reached 32%. This was a novel idea to the grain producers because their harvesting experiences had always been to wait until their grain got dry enough to harvest and we were telling them that we wanted it wet. We had several professional feeders who toured our new yard and invariably they would ask where the mill that would process the rations would be located. When we explained that there would be no mill they would shake their heads and we never saw them again.

Max had enough customers lined up to fill the pens as fast as they were finished. Because Harold, Milford and I knew that we would probably have the yard in the fall we had planted every acre to milo that we could. Milo harvest started about a month earlier than normal because we wanted wet milo to process. Our pens were filling as quickly as they were finished and Max had pared his construction crew down to the number he wanted to help run the yard. This proved a great way to pick the working crew as they had all proven their worth with the construction crew and turnover of feedyard crew remained low for several years.

October 19th dawned cold and cloudy with a forecast of an early blizzard developing across the high plains. It started snowing around noon. I told Jewel that I thought I would go to the yard and help just in case it got as bad as the forecasters predicted. By 2:00 PM visibility was zero with hard winds out of the north. Two of us scooped the snow out of the feed bunks while the feed trucks filled the bunks with fresh feed. By dark, the feed trucks could no longer get through the feed roads in the yards and everything was snowed in. None of the crew could go home. The crew spent the night in a room in the vet barn huddled around a small stove. Someone had a bag of M&M's which we tried to melt in a pan of water on the stove. This makeshift coca was our supper.

Before sunrise we were busy digging out the machinery so we could begin feeding. When it became obvious that our equipment alone was not going to be able to clear the snow and feed the cattle, we started calling anyone we knew with large front end loaders to help dig out. The bunks were full of snow and frozen feed. The concrete pads that the cattle stood on while they fed at the bunks were piled with snow. The cattle could have walked right over the bunks. The cattle were hungry and bawling to be fed. The waterers were all covered with snow and had to be dug out. Snow had piled up in the silo and had to be dug out as well. It took a couple of cowboys and a tractor equipped with a front end loader to begin removing dead cattle from the pens.

We started on Bob's pen. They had reacted to the storm in a predictable pattern which was to bunch up tightly in a corner of the pen. When they do this they drop their heads until their nose is only inches from the ground. If it continues to snow they will suffocate and die. Prior to the snowstorm, Max's vet crew had done a good job pulling Bob's sick cattle out of his pen and getting them to the vet facility but they were still weak from the move. When we got the dead cattle out of Bob's pen the death toll was 8% of his cattle. While the loss was high it was less than we had expected. The death loss from the rest of the cattle was surprisingly low, due in large part to the warm ground temperature.

By late afternoon the alleys were clear and all of the cattle were fed. There was still a lot of snow to plow but the cattle were all taken care of. I talked to Jewel several times that day and she said that the roads hadn't been plowed yet so I couldn't go home. I spent the night with Harold and his wife at their home in Larned. The next morning dawned clear and warm and by nightfall most of the snow had melted and little remained to indicate the severity of the storm.

The monthly board meeting was held a few days later. Harold and I had noticed that something was bothering Max. He dropped a bombshell on the board when he informed us that Bob was demanding that the yard reimburse him for the cattle that had died. When Max informed him that was not the normal way that losses were handled in the industry, Bob replied that since we were new to the industry he would have us blackballed and we would never be able to fill the yard. That information raised the hackles on Harold, Milford, and me while it scared the snot out of the rest of the board members. The whole board had known Bob forever and no one could believe that he would ever make such a threat. The industry had always operated on a man's word or his handshake. That was the way cattle business was conducted. A written contract was unheard of.

After a long argument whether to pay Bob's blackmail demand, Harold, Milford, the other feeder, and I were out-voted and Bob was paid. Several years later Harold was at a conference in Denver when he was approached by a feeder from eastern Colorado. He inquired if Harold knew anything about Pawnee Beefbuilders. When Harold told him that he was the manager, he asked if he remembered Bob's Corrientes. The feeder went on to explain that Bob had put them in his yard originally but when they began to die faster than he could drag them out, he had called Bob and told him to come and get them. They continued to die and Bob continued ignoring him. His last call to Bob informed him that his cattle were being loaded and Bob should call the trucking company and give them destination instructions. The feeder thought he heard a truck driver mention Pawnee Beefbuilders and had wondered what the outcome was. He said that Bob would never feed cattle in Colorado again.

Shortly after, Bob started construction of his own yard. A few days after the board had voted to pay Bob's blackmail, Max submitted his resignation citing the job was too stressful. A special meeting of the board was called to discuss Max's replacement. Much to the board's relief Harold expressed interest in the management position. His offer was accepted by a unanimous vote by the board. Harold remained the manager until the yard was sold in the early 80's. He remained as manager of PBI until he retired in the early 2000's.

As I write this it became obvious that the yard was governed by the board but the major decisions were made by Harold, Milford, and I. One example occurred in the fall of 1973 when the industry was shaken by the news that corn blight was threatening the corn crop in the U.S. If the yield reduction was as great as was in the forecast we could be in trouble before the winter was over. We decided that we would buy corn as long as it was offered to us. We wound up with nearly twice as much corn as we had ever received before. The price of corn was slowly climbing as the industry was trying to figure out what the implication of the blight was going to be.

At the next meeting when Harold gave his 'corn received' report all hell broke loose. One of the board members had a business degree from KU and we felt that he was always trying to impress us with his business knowledge. He apparently had a professor who had warned him of the dangers of Contingent Liabilities. At every meeting he always wanted to know just what his contingent liabilities were. The two bankers on the board were also upset about the excess grain that we had on hand. The rest of the board remained silent. Harold had nearly ten years experience on how to manage grain inventory and his grain history indicated that at any one time he knew exactly how much we had fed and exactly how much remained in inventory. The beautiful thing about the feeding industry is that it can generate huge amounts of money. On the grain we bought we would shrink it back to the industry standard 15% but since the shrinkage was still in the grain when it was fed the shrinkage was sold at the price of the grain which could amount to as much as 15% profit on the wet grain. The industry standard shrink on stored grain didn't apply to grain that was processed and packed in a silo. Our records showed that we had no shrinkage on processed grain packed in a silo.

Customers paid 25¢ per head per day for yardage plus the price of feed plus the markup for processing and storage. When these costs are multiplied by the number of head in the yard it can easily be seen why the industry had grown by such leaps and bounds. The board member who was worried about his contingent liability began wanting protection on his share of the corn and several other stockholders fell into step with him. The bankers said they would check into it. A short time later they reported to the board. The government had a department that guaranteed stored grain but the cost made it nearly prohibitive. When the worrisome board member mentioned above heard that perhaps there was a program that would protect him from the dreaded contingent liability monster, he demanded that we buy the protection. The two bankers on the board were handling all our short term loans we needed for the purchase of cattle and equipment. They were concerned that perhaps our huge supply of grain might impact their ability to obtain the credit requirements of their loan offices.

Several special meeting were held to discuss the problem. When it became obvious that Harold, Milford, and I were going to be out voted we continued to voice our opposition to the idea. Harold had warned the board that not only was it terribly expensive, but to become involved with the government on a project of this size would become a management nightmare as well. His warnings fell on deaf ears. After all the office work was finished and the onsite inspections started we began to see that Harold's warnings were understated. The first problem was the storage facilities. The inspectors didn't know if the silos fit the criteria as approved storage facilities. They complained because there was no roof over the grain. They didn't like that we would be taking grain out of inventory to feed. We had no way to lock it up to prevent theft. What was our fire plan? Our bookkeeping files showed exactly how many bushels were in each silo. They complained about that as well and insisted on physical measurements to determine the amount of grain in the silos.

After nearly a month of BS from the government personnel, the contract was approved. During the life of the contract the monthly harassment continued. It was about this time when the government instituted another headache. It was the Environmental Protection Agency or EPA for short. The EPA inspectors descended on us like a locust plague. Most of the inspectors were recent college graduates who were determined to save the world from the likes of us. The inspectors examined every facet of the yard. The only citation that they issued was the dust that our hay grinder made while grinding hay. The feeding industry raised such a fuss over this ruling that they finally rescinded the dust clause for the preparation of feed for livestock. Nearly all of the feedyards had been cited for runoff problems by the EPA. Some were forced to close. It became apparent how fortunate Pawnee Beefbuilders was that we spent the money to shape our yard before construction began. Several of the large yards in the western part of the state are still trying to meet the EPA requirements today.

We had reached our maximum number which was 7,000 head. Over the next several years expansion would raise the capacity to 14,000 head. A new firm called Cattle Fax opened in Denver. They collected data on the cattle industry focusing primarily on the feeding industry. Their information was relayed to their subscribers by ticker tape. A subscriber could access any of the data in real time. The price of feeder and fat cattle, the number of cattle placed on feed the previous day, what the number of head slaughtered the previous day, and the tons of beef exported. Each subscriber called in information daily. This service proved invaluable to the feeding industry.

It wasn't long until Harold was elected to the board of directors of Cattle Fax. His contacts in the industry quickly became apparent. Shortly after, he was elected to the board of directors of the American Cattleman Association. He was making trips to Washington D.C. on behalf of the American Cattleman's Association. He was elected as president of the National Feeders Council and named The Manager of the Year of the Kansas Feeders Council. His exploits put Pawnee Beef builders on the map. In the early 70's, accountants and money managers became aware of the tax structure for agriculture and began moving client's monies into the feeding industry. Pawnee Beefbuilders found several movie stars among their list of customers, Steve McQueen probably the best known. The list also included many professional athletes, and big names from the business world.

When the feeding industry began its movement from the corn belt to the high plains the packing industry was forced to move as well. The old firms such as Swift, Hormel, and Armour were closing their plants in Chicago and Kansas City and being replaced by new and more modern plants closer to the supply of fat cattle in the high plains. Iowa Beef Producers built a slaughter plant in Emporia in the 50's. The cattle they slaughtered were all trucked from yards in the western part of the state. In the early 70's IBP relocated to Garden City into a new state-of-the-art cattle processing facility with a 5,000 head per hour capacity. Now production and processing were concentrated in a relatively small area. This concentration also meant that most of the allied manufacturers also moved to the western part of the state.

After the jittery start up, Pawnee Beefbuilders moved into a stable business in the seventies and early eighties. Deaths and retirement plans cut into the original board of directors. Their shares were quickly bought by the remaining stockholders while a few went to outsiders. Jewel and my plans to retire when we were 60 years old were nearly upon us. At a board meeting Harold informed the board that he had been approached by the Bass Brothers, an old oil rich firm from Dallas, Texas who were interested in purchasing the yard. Since a few yards were being sold to outside investors and their selling price was known throughout the industry the board agreed on a price and Harold was charged with trying to sell it. After several weeks of haggling, Bass Brothers owned Pawnee Beefbuilders. The era of my being a cowboy was over.

FISHING WITH HK

In the early eighties Harold Koehn and I started taking occasional weekend fishing trips in the winter. The trips usually began Friday afternoon when we would get in Harold's plane and head south for some destination Harold had heard about. We would be home before sunset on Sunday. Every year friends and business associates who owned planes would join us on those weekend jaunts. Most of these trips consisted of two, but as many as four planes. Since the planes were all four place planes there could be as many as sixteen fishermen involved. The first several trips were to Beaver Lake near Roger, Arkansas.

Sharon, our oldest daughter met her future husband Ron Garman while they were students at Dodge City Community College. After college Ron and his twin brother Don moved to Rogers and joined their dad in the family printing business. They were all avid outdoorsmen and each had a nice fishing boat and gear. Ron always wanted me to come to Rogers and go fishing with them on Beaver Lake. When Harold and I started talking about a weekend fishing trip, Rogers was the first place we decided to go. Harold had his own plane and it was only two hours to Rogers. In the early seventies Rogers was just beginning to boom. Sam Walton's Wal-Mart was fast becoming a real player in the retail business. J.B. Hunt was becoming a giant in the trucking industry. The Cooper family had just finished up Bella Vista retirement community. Don Tyson had finished a huge chicken processing plant, and Daisy BB guns had a manufacturing plant in Rogers. When Friday evening rolled around people from all these businesses would descend on Roark Printing to drink the free beer that Roark had on ice. We met most of the people from these firms and fished with a few of them. We watched Rogers grow from a small Ozark town to a bustling commercial center. When friends heard about our fishing trips it wasn't long till another plane-load of fishermen would join us on these trips to Rogers.

Our last trip to Arkansas was when we heard of a firm in Flippin, Arkansas that offered a guided two day float trip down the White River. Harold and I talked to our friends and wound up with ten friends and their wives on the White River. At first some of the wives didn't show much interest in floating down some river in Arkansas. But when we took off all the wives were on board. We landed in Flippin just at sunset on a Thursday evening. Charlie's guide service owned a bunch of cabins on the banks of the White River. They also had a nice convenience store right next to the cabins. We were to get in the boats at 6:00 A.M. the next day. At midnight it started raining. We were to meet at the store at 5:00 for breakfast. When Charlie counted heads, only about half of his customers were present. Someone said that those missing had assumed that since it was raining we probably wouldn't go. Charlie told us to go and get them up because the fish hadn't heard that it was raining. Charlie just happened to sell rain ponchos in his store, and when we got in the boats, nearly half of the fishermen were not happy campers. All of Charlie's customers had only to get in the boats at 6:00 and he and his guides did everything else for you. The tackle, bait, pop, and candy bars were all in the boats.

Charlie must have looked over the whole state of Arkansas to choose his guides. When you got in the boats everyone forgot that it was raining. The guides had all grown up on the rivers in Arkansas and kept everyone in stitches with their hillbilly stories. About mid morning a boat passed us that was loaded with something. When we asked our guide about the boat he informed us that it was the commissary boat. As we came around a bend, on a large sandbar, was a large tent with tables and benches all ready to serve us the trout that we had caught. The cooks had table cloths and flower arrangements on the tables and were cooking everything over an open fire. Even the most skeptical of the group agreed it was the finest fish meal they had ever eaten. By the middle of the afternoon the excitement of the morning and the delicious lunch had begun to wear off. The state kept this stretch of the river stocked with trout, about one pound in size. These fish were either dumb or awfully hungry because everyone was getting tired of catching fish. You would reel one into the boat and then 10 seconds later the guide would have your hook re-baited and back in the water. Around 4:00 we again came to the commissary boat on a sand bar. The kitchen tent was up and along the sandbar were five smaller two man tents. The small tents had 2 cots each complete with sheets, blankets, and pillows. Another tent had a complete bar and snack food. Before we left the boats, our guides took our orders on how we wanted our steaks cooked. The steaks and corn on the cob were cooked over an open fire.

We were awakened the following morning by the cooks fixing breakfast. We had pancakes and bacon, or if you wanted several different types of cereal were laid out. When we got up a heavy fog lay in a layer about head high on the river. For about half an hour you couldn't see any boats on the river, but standing in the boats you could see the top of the fog and the beautiful scenery of the river banks. We fished a little that morning but mostly we were entertained by our guides and enjoyed the beautiful river scenery. Late in the morning we came to the take out point. When we got on the bus that took us to the airport, the guides were busy cleaning the boats and loading them on a trailer. We all promised each other that we would make it a yearly event, but it never happened again. Now and again when it was cold or we had just made it through a bad stretch of weather three or four plane loads of our friends would pick a lake in the south and we managed to get in a couple days of fishing here and there.

CORN PRODUCTION AND CHEMICALS

Along with the occasional severe dry years, corn production in central Kansas was brought to a halt by the movement of the corn borer from the south. In the south, corn borers are known as the boll weevil. In the early part of the twentieth century when cotton production moved into western Texas, the corn borer followed the cotton. Strong southerly winds then carried the adult borers to Kansas where corn became the borer's favorite hosts. Unless a farmer knows how to identify the life cycle of the borer, he may not even know that his fields are infected until the field is just reaching maturity and suddenly, often in 24 hours, all the corn plants in the field fall over making harvest impossible. It's not a good day when a farmer finds his corn crop on the ground especially when the crop was intended to feed his livestock in the coming winter. In the seventies, with the adoption of irrigation, corn was again introduced to central Kansas. Most corn producers were soon reacquainted with the corn borer and it became evident why their fathers had quit growing corn. Just as in the fairy tale, the knight on the white horse gallops up and saves the maiden. Only this time, the white knight was the chemical companies trying to save the farmers from the corn borers. They brought with them their newest concoction -- an organic phosphate brew called Furadan. It took a season or two until the correct rate and timing were established. The protocol called for four aerial applications of Furadan, one every ten days. As with everything in agriculture these recommendations didn't take into account what the wind would be on the scheduled application day, or when a rain might appear, or perhaps the pilot who was supposed to apply the application might have partied the whole night before. We merely went ahead and hoped that the gods would smile on us.

The corn borer cycle starts with the adult female laying her eggs on the underside of the leaves. When they hatch, the tiny larva head for the stalk into which they bore. When they are in the stalk, they begin feeding on the inside of the stalk where the moisture and nutrients are carried to the ear of the corn plant. Once inside the stalk it is impossible to control them. As the inner part of the stalk is eaten away, only the outer part of the stalk holds up the plant. As maturity begins and the corn plant begins to dry down, the thin outer part of the corn plant can't support the ears and all the foliage. The first wind breaks the stalk off and it topples over. The corn borer has now reached maturity and leaves the corn plant and lays its eggs in the soil to await the next crop.

The four parts of the Furadan program are aimed at trying to intercept the adult borer while she is laying her eggs and when the young are making their way to the stalk. The timing depends entirely on past examples. You might miss the window of opportunity if the hatch is a few days earlier or later, or perhaps the variety of corn has a tougher or easier outer layer to bore through and many other variables that we don't recognize. Most farmers didn't know the definition of the word economics or the discipline involved. The $40 per acre cost was shocking compared with wheat because once wheat was planted there weren't any further costs involved. The cost of corn production is very high compared to wheat which previously was the principal crop grown in central Kansas.

With wheat production, seldom were herbicides or insecticides used. Fertilizer costs were generally about a third the cost compared to corn, and machinery costs were significantly less. Wheat yields generally were in the 25-30 bushel range giving a potential gross of $60 per acre, excluding land and labor costs. Irrigated corn meanwhile would yield 80-100 bushels per acre giving a gross of $160-200 per acre excluding labor and land costs. However, I only used corn borer costs in the above example. Other insecticides and herbicides plus special equipment also added to corn production costs. Economics was suddenly becoming very important in the choice of crops a farmer chose. Research showed that the better the farm management was the more apt the pressure from weed and insect pressure were higher than we had presumed. Higher rates of fertilizer not only increased yield, but also increased weed and insect pressure. However, stronger crop plants also allowed faster recovery when the insect and weed pressure were removed.

A new problem soon became apparent when the new herbicides were first used. The grassy weeds thrived because of the effectiveness of Maloran or Atrazine. Both are weed specific herbicides controlling only broad leaf weeds. With the broad leafed weeds suppressed, the grassy weeds thrived. It seemed when one of the problem weeds were controlled several new challenges would appear. One of the reasons a grassy weed herbicide was slow to be perfected was because both milo and corn were grassy plants closely related to the grassy weeds that grew in the soils of the Midwest. About 18 months after Geigy released Maloran and its sister herbicide, Atrazine, a grassy weed herbicide, Princep, hit the market. At last, a broad spectrum weed control was available. The only limiting factor was learning how to use them effectively while minimizing the damage to the crops. This meant years of test plot research which was slow to produce useful data because we still didn't know exactly what information we needed.

It was known that these products, while not perfect, showed great promise. Some of the questions that needed to be answered were: How does rainfall or irrigation timing affect the herbicide? What about cultural practices? Do fertilizer rates and timing make a difference? How about seed bed preparation and seed choice? What rates return the most control for the least amount of cost? Suddenly, being a milo or corn grower meant more than merely taking a few bags of seed to the field and planting it, just like dad did it, was no longer valid. Welcome to the world of technology. When the seed and chemical companies began expanding their research to the southern hemisphere, did we get the answers twice as fast, very little information that was needed could be gotten from a lab.

I have concentrated my remarks mainly on milo because corn wasn't grown as much in central Kansas because of the corn borer problem. K-State wasn't doing much in the way of corn borer research because of slow field testing. However, the seed companies were looking for ways to increase sales and saw a huge market in central and western Kansas. Suddenly, the producers had two players doing research on corn. The corn producers suddenly found the information doubled. However, the seed companies' focus on research was altogether different than the chemical companies. Their research was aimed more towards cultural, rather than chemical collection of data. This information was easier to understand and implement. Milo was generally planted in May after the ground had warmed up. So after a couple of generations,

May was considered to be the optimum planting time. Seed companies' data showed corn planting should start the middle of April, which was a month earlier than the producers were used to.

Old habits are hard to break, and the later planting date was no exception. By now, test plots had become fairly common. Both seed and chemical companies were aware that farmers were watching the test plots more and more. County agents began to schedule informational meetings at the fields where the test plots were located. Perhaps these field meetings did more to change the habits of producers than any other factor. Extension offices began mailing test plot yield data after the plots were harvested in the fall. The producers had all the pertinent information in one easy to understand source. It became very obvious that corn planted in April had a huge yield advantage over later planting. Much of the advantages were due to the fact that earlier planting interfered with the corn borer life cycle. Earlier planting meant a corn plant was physiologically mature when the borers were egg laying, and the young were hatching, thus not as attractive as a food source. Early planting plus early harvest of the grain nearly eliminated the corn borer problem. The early harvest part of the equation was the one solution to the borer problem.

Perhaps the biggest reason for the shift away from the Corn Belt which was made up of the states that lay south of the Great Lakes, the Dakotas on the west, and east to the coast was that this area received more rainfall, had fertile soils, and lacked the warmer temperatures of the high plains. These features made for ideal corn production. Most of the farms were smaller than those on the high plains and the farming practices were very different than Kansas, especially western Kansas. Until the introduction of mechanical corn pickers in the twenties, the corn was picked by hand. The weather make up was not ideal for cattle although the corn was ideal feed for the cattle and hogs. Because of the heavier soils and higher rainfall, mud was always a problem for livestock producers in the Corn Belt. When cattle are wet and cold their performance suffers and they can't gain weight efficiently. Much of the energy in their feed is consumed trying to stay warm and fighting the mud.

Corn harvested by hand and with the first mechanical pickers harvested the whole ear which left the corn kernels on the cob. The harvested corn was stored in corn cribs; wooden cribs of slat construction rather than solid sides were used to store the cobs. Ear corn stored in the slat sided cribs allowed air to circulate through the corn which allowed it to dry down. When the farmer wanted to feed grain corn he had to run the ear corn through a sheller which would remove the grain from the cob.

A corn sheller had two conveyers; one carried the grain while the second carried the cobs. The cobs were spread in the livestock pens as bedding to help keep the livestock out of the mud. The growing and feeding of corn was very labor intensive and required handling of each ear by hand, once when it was hand harvested, and then again when it was shelled prior to feeding or selling.

Corn production in the Corn Belt made dramatic changes in the early fifties when corn picker heads were adapted to combines. All of the hand labor was eliminated. The corn could now be picked and shelled in one operation right in the field. This change in harvesting methods also seriously affected the cattle industry in the Corn Belt. Farmers no longer had corn cobs for bedding as the cobs were left in the fields behind the combines. Corn yields were rapidly climbing as fertilizer use increased along with improved corn genetics. Shelled corn could no longer be stored in the corn cribs that dotted the landscape.

A new crop suddenly appeared in the Corn Belt. That crop was soybeans. Grain scientists had found soybeans were rich with vegetable oils. The oils were easily extracted from the beans and uses of soybean oils were used in many old and new industries. Although soybeans yields were lower than corn, the yields intensified the need for new grain storage systems. Manufacturing companies building metal storage and grain drying systems became common in the Corn Belt because the new harvesting and storage systems were very costly. The small inefficient farmer quit and their acreages were absorbed by larger neighbors. The small farms suffered the same fate as the small wheat farmers in the Midwest.

Because of the growing popularity of soybean oil, soybean production increased on the irrigated farms in Kansas. Soybeans are a popular food in most Asian countries so a huge market quickly developed. Since all of the equipment needed from corn production could be used for soybean production as well, beans began to reduce corn acreage. A side benefit of soybeans is that they are a legume and their root system manufactures and stores nitrogen fertilizer in the soil which following crops can use.

GRAIN STORAGE; TEST PLOTS; CHEMICALS; GENETIC MANIPULATION

Grain storage can't be attempted if the moisture content of the grain is above 15%. At 15% moisture, grain will spoil if it's carried over to the following year when the weather begins to warm up. This problem was addressed by more research -- this time however the research was carried out by the livestock division of land-grant colleges. They found that the nutritional peak of grain was around 32% of moisture content. This of course led to more research, namely, how do you store grain at 32% moisture and have a supply when it is stored at such high moisture content. Studies showed that grain could be easily stored for a year if oxygen in the grain was eliminated. The big blue Harvestore silos began showing up across the Corn Belt. This was shown to be the solution to the storage problem as they were sealed thus keeping oxygen away from the grain.

The problem was the cost of these units. Because yields were steadily increasing, the cost of enough silos to store a whole corn crop was prohibitive. The studies soon found that grain harvested at 32% moisture content, if processed and stored in bunker silos, was just as nutritional as that stored in the blue silos. At last the destructive corn borer problem was nearly solved. Irrigation and the solution to the borer problem caused corn production to explode across central and western Kansas. The acceptance of ag chemicals by new crop growers had brought about a revolution in the allied fields of corn production. The sprayer industry exploded with new designs and concepts. The nozzle industry suddenly were offering spray precision that only a few years before were unheard of. Planters were offered that made previous favorites seem antique in comparison. Ag chemicals had forever changed the face of agriculture.

In the middle 60's, Cliff Manry asked if he could invite some people from K-State to look at my plots. Erik Nilson, Rus Herpik , and a group of Kansas State University students arrived to question me about my plots. Erik headed the agronomy department, and Rus headed the irrigation department. They stayed two days taking pictures and asking questions.

Shortly after, K-State announced that a series of experimental farms were to be established across central and western Kansas. The first of these experimental farms was established in St. John. The facility was called Sandy Land Experiment Station. George TenEik was named the field director of the facility. I had met Rus and George several years earlier, when I began to study the feasibility of the new center pivot irrigation systems. The experimental field in Hutchinson focused on the dryland crops being grown in central Kansas, mainly wheat and milo. The Hays experimental station focused on livestock and livestock nutrition. The Garden City station, because of the different soils and higher altitude, was a combination of the three stations.

Because seed companies and equipment manufacturers were doing most of their own research the experiment farms eventually were no longer relevant. The Hutchinson and Garden City farms were sold to Pioneer Seed Company where they continue to do plant breeding research. Because the livestock industry was rapidly moving from the Corn Belt to the center of the country the Hays facility continues to do meaningful research.

In the seventies a new player in ag chemicals was starting to make themselves known. The company was Monsanto. Their business plan was a radical departure from the current seed and chemical companies. They kept a low profile in the Ag chemical business quietly focusing on one product while hiring the most successful lobbyists in Washington. These lobbyists were able to introduce and get passed changes in the U.S. patent laws. The new laws would allow patent work in the genetic field. They started buying up the best seed companies in the country.

The Monsanto rep called me and asked if I would include their herbicide in my test plot. When I asked what the name of their herbicide was, he informed me that as yet it was only a number and they were in the last phases of field testing. He wanted ten acres and assured me I would be compensated for any loss of yield if the herbicide killed or damaged the corn. I included his herbicides in my plot. He wanted me to apply it after I had planted, but before the corn emerged.

About a month later I called him and told him that I didn't think it was working as the weeds were nearly a foot tall in the corn. He thanked me and said that that was what they wanted to know. He also said I shouldn't try to use any rescue attempt with any other herbicide. By that time the ten acres had become a weed patch and any hope for any yield was gone. I tried several more times to reach him but he didn't return my calls.

I never heard from him again until October. He drove in, re-introduced himself, and thanked me for participating in their field trials. When I recovered my sense I began telling him what I thought of their herbicide and that they weren't ever to call me again asking me to do any research for them. He remained aloof and opened the trunk of his car and gave me a five gallon can of their herbicide as payment for my time. When I asked what they were going to charge for it he replied, "All the law allows." As I stood there with my mouth hanging open, he got in his car and drove off.

When he contacted me the first time he stressed that I was to keep it a secret and to place it as far away as possible from my other plots. I never mentioned the plot to Tom. After I had cooled down I told Tom about it and he said, "They are a very ruthless company." I made a decision that I would never use any of their products on my farm. As the years rolled by, Tom's description of their business practices was too kind. He explained that Roundup was a contact herbicide and it would be neutralized by contact with soil. When I sprayed the plot with nothing growing on it, it was completely neutralized as soon as it hit the ground. The only thing that the plot proved was that there was no residual effect. My introduction to international companies leaves a bad taste in my mouth even today. Monsanto's ability to recognize the potential market in Ag research is still amazing to me.

When Craig Venter isolated the genome and opened the door to genetic engineering Monsanto was quick to apply it to plants. They inserted the Roundup gene into most field crops being grown in the world thereby making them resistant to Roundup. Before the gene manipulation Roundup was deadly to nearly anything that grew in the fields. Suddenly, by applying Roundup before planting it would kill everything growing in the fields, then the fields were ready for planting. It took several years before farmers realized that a seedbed didn't need to look like a garden, but the dead weeds included grassy weeds. The dead weeds not only protect seedlings from blowing soil, but limits rain runoff as well. The following year Monsanto announced that they had added an insecticide gene into their corn and cotton seed, making them both resistant to the southwestern corn borer.

When a gene is inserted into a plant that gene is in the male pollen of the host plant. Any flower pollinated with that male pollen will also carry that gene thus perpetuating that genes' characteristics. Since corn and soybeans are primarily pollinated by windblown pollen it's easily seen how a gene carried by the majority of plants would soon become a part of the genetic base of all plants in the area.

The geneticists at Monsanto realized that any genes that carried certain desirable traits would eventually show up in all the corn and beans grown anywhere in the world. If it carried Monsanto's genes, a court of law would uphold that the grower had infringed on Monsanto's patent unless they could show that they had purchased their seed from a certified Monsanto seed dealer.

Prior to the early nineties, every farm community had a farmer or seed store that cleaned seed for the area farmers. Seed straight from a combine contains weed seed and a lot of foreign material that must be removed for a planter to accurately space the seed. The seed cleaners were kept busy getting seed for the next crop ready to plant. Nearly every soybean farmer saved seed for the following year from his previous crop. After his seed was cleaned, he would then plant it. Soon all the soybeans were carrying the Roundup gene. Monsanto put a small group of inspectors who started pulling samples from the seed cleaners' customers. Of course the Roundup gene was found in the samples. Monsanto then sued the seed cleaner and the farmer for patent infringement. The news of the suits spread like wildfire among farmers and seed dealers. Everyone was afraid to plant anything but Monsanto seed. The thing that Monsanto rep told me nearly twenty years earlier was beginning to come true again when he told me that they were going to charge all that the law allows.

In only two years they had eliminated not only the seed cleaners, but also the small independent seed producers and were then able to set seed prices. Farmers saw seed prices rise from around $100 a bag to nearly a nickel a kernel. The money Monsanto had spent on the lobbyist nearly a quarter century earlier to get the patent laws changed now seemed that it was money well spent. While my wife and I traveled New Zealand we saw fields of corn that were identical to the variety that we grew back home. In effect, Monsanto now controls the soybean, cotton and seed corn prices, as well as the insecticide market not only in this country but worldwide as well! As a farmer and author of this chapter it is unbelievable the changes occurring in the last half of the 20th century in agriculture production and consequently in the lives of farmers and their family.

KANSAS EXTENSION COUNCIL

In the late seventies Cliff asked if I would serve on the Kansas Extension Council Board. A board member had died leaving a vacancy. I had long admired the work and information the Extension Council had made available to the rural communities of the state, and I agreed. I had accepted thinking that the job might let me help shape what direction the Extension programs were heading. It had become obvious to me that many of the goals of the original concept of the department were going to have to be changed if the program was to survive. I had watched the research programs dry up and relevant information coming from the K-State schools falling behind as well. When I found out that a plane would come to pick me up for the meetings in Manhattan or Topeka, I looked forward to being a part of the overhaul of the Extension department.

At the first meeting I attended in Manhattan I was disappointed because it seemed to me the board and its director, Dr. Bob Bohanan, didn't seem to recognize that the council was faced with some serious choices. The nine board members seemed to be cheerleaders for K-State and basked in the light from previous programs. I flew home hoping what I had just witnessed was an aberration. The second meeting was a continuation of the first except for a

15 minute discussion by some department head. Dr. Bohanon then discussed the shortfall of funds from the state and a brief discussion of how to increase the state funding. At the next meeting, Dr. Bohanan laid out his solution to the funding shortfall. The board members were given a topic that they would present to the state legislature for more funding.

My assignment was to present a request for continued research for the corn borer problem for corn growers. K-State had continued research since the thirties into this problem with no workable solution in sight. I was scheduled to meet with a legislator from Wichita. When I was ushered into his office he was seated behind his desk with both heels hooked over the edge of his desk. He informed me that he had fifteen minutes allocated for my presentation. He said to me, "Before I hear your request for more funding, tell me how it will benefit my constituents in Wichita." The fact that he never put his feet on the floor indicated that no matter what I said he would never vote for more funding because of my presentation. I left his office with about six minutes of credit left on my 15 minutes that he so graciously allocated for my quest for continued funding. Before I left the capitol building I decided if my job was going to go to Topeka to beg for money for a failing idea, then I was going to resign as soon as I got home. My resignation was mailed the next day.

I had watched the number of research projects at K-State dwindle during the 60's as more and more of the meaningful research was performed by companies themselves or by consulting firms staffed by bright young K-State graduates. It took about five years until Dr. Bohanon and his board began to realize that while they were singing the fight song the department had died. When the time came for the funeral they grappled to establish a program that would keep the original intent of the Land Grant College alive. They chose to teach gardening enthusiasts the finer points of establishing and maintaining a flourishing garden. A new program called "The Master Gardner Program" was instituted. The program required the applicant to complete 40-50 hours of classes which covered soil types, fertilizer needs, horticulture, and flower selection. Upon successful completion of the course-work the participants are presented with a certificate bestowing the bearer the title of Master Gardner.

FARMING DAUGHTERS

After Sharon, our oldest daughter, finished her first year at college, she found a summer job in town with a firm that manufactured wiring harnesses. She hated the job, mainly because of office politics but I think she just missed farm life. We hated to see her so unhappy so after Jewel and I discussed it, we told the girls if they wanted we would give them all a job in the summers. The one requirement was that they would be doing men's work for men's pay. The girls decided they wanted to try our proposal.

At the time, we were putting up hay on a custom basis. I knew if I had another crew I could get enough hay to make our haying a full time operation. I left it up to Jewel and the girls to decide their schedules. They decided they would take turns doing the cooking and household chores while the rest worked in the field. I had bought a stack mover which came mounted on a trailer. I had a firm in Great Bend remove it from the trailer and mount it on one of our trucks so the stacks could be transported to the feedyard. The stack mover measured 10' wide and 20' long. It was obvious that the 10' width could cause legal problems because it exceeded the legal width by 2'. Before I bought the stack mover I contacted the State Highway

Patrol for wide load waiver, hoping that all we would need was a wide load banner on the front and rear of the mover. When I told them that loaded the width might be 20', but that we would only be crossing the highway and driving the rest of the way on country roads, they informed me that I would need a wide load notice car ahead and behind the load. They finally told me to ask our Sheriff about it and that the Patrol would go along with his recommendation. I had known Cliff Atteberry, our Sheriff, all my life, and I knew that the state had relaxed the laws for farmers, especially when hauling harvested crops.

After much discussion, he finally said that if we had someone come up behind us and we could get far enough over so they could pass, he would give us permission. But if anyone complained, he would shut us down.

Our youngest daughter, Carolyn, was drafted to deliver hay to the feedyard. Carolyn had tagged along with me all her life and she liked to be around cattle. She was always wanting to help feed and doctor the animals. When she was around ten she started pestering me that she wanted to do something, so I gave her a syringe and let her start giving shots to the cattle. We never worked cattle after that without Carolyn manning the needles.

We were using Hesston Stackhands stackers which made a loaf of hay 10' wide and 14' long containing four tons of hay. When retrieving the stack, the truck was

280

backed up to the end of the stack, the bed was raised until the rear of the mover was under the end of the stack. Six beams of the mover had chains that ran around the length of beams and when engaged, the chains slowly moved around the beams and pulled the stack onto the bed of the mover. It took about five minutes to drag the stack onto the truck. The bed was then lowered and a wind guard was lowered onto the top of the stack and it was ready to go.

Carolyn and I only moved a couple of stacks until she announced that she was ready and she flawlessly delivered hay from then on. She had no trouble with the law. Toward the end of the season she informed me if she would back into the side instead of the end of the stacks, she was sure she could haul two stacks instead of the one that she now hauled. The big problem was that instead of the 12' width of the mover, the hay would now hang over the side of the mover by about two extra feet on each side. She wanted me to come to the field while she showed me how she loaded the stacks. By this time she could handle the stack mover better than I.

She backed the mover to the wide side of one of the stacks and picked it up with no problems. She them moved to the second stack and moved the first stack back against the second stack and started the retrieval process again. The two stacks were tight together and loaded perfectly. We now had a load that looked huge and even I didn't think that we would get away with it. Thereafter she started hauling two stacks per load.

Shortly before she had to go back to school she had to cross the highway on the way to the feedyard. She just got across the highway when she heard the siren. I have always wished I had a tape of the conversation that took place at that moment when he confronted an attractive young girl hauling this humongus load of hay. He told her to unload it. She convinced him that it was simpler if she just delivered it. He finally relented and his parting words were "If I ever see you with another load like that I'm going to make you drive up to a tree and I am going to lock it so you will never get on the road again." After that she went back to the single stacks that she started with.

Jewel wanted to run the baler at night and I would run the stacker. The girls would run the swathers during the day as running them during the daytime would put enough hay down so the baler and stacker could run 24 hours a day. When jewel and I finished our shift in the mornings I would check our irrigation systems and start any that had stopped running during the night. Greg operated the irrigation systems during the days while Gordon and Bruce Rhea, who started working for us when he was in the seventh grade and continued working until he was in his early twenties when he finally quit and moved to Denver, ran the stacker. Dennis Urban did the same until the summer he graduated from college. Gordon ran the baler in the daytime while Bruce ran the stacker. The girls were always glad when their turn at cooking was over so they could get back in the field.

We ran seven days a week, only shutting down when it rained. A rain left everyone relaxed until it dried off. When the girls started running the swathers, I showed them how to grease all the grease fittings and told them that they must grease them four times a day. I don't think they ever missed a scheduled greasing. Today, 50 years later, they still fondly remember their days in the hay fields. As for me, my girls did as fine a job as any man could have done. They were a joy to be around, and their pleasant attitude was contagious.

After the girls went back to school I ran the stack mover delivering hay to the feedyard. But my farming operation had grown so much that I no longer could continue our custom haying as my own operation was taking all of my time. Those long summer days with my wife and family were the best times of my farming life.

MURDERS

In February of 1977 a friend had called Harold and said he had heard that the fish were biting in Lake Zapata on the Rio Grande in south Texas and wondered if it wasn't time to check it out. That was all it took for us to be on our way to Zapata. Harold and I and two friends were in Harold's plane, our tipster friend was in his plane along with three other fishing buddies. The landing strip at that time was the north/south main street in the small Mexican village of Zapata. This arrangement sounds strange today, but Harold had landed his plane on city streets in several other back wood towns while on cattle buying trips. We had encountered some bad weather over Oklahoma but it hadn't lasted long enough to make us land. We had made arrangements over the phone for motel rooms and guides with boats. It was late when we landed so we ate and went to the motel. The guides were going to pick us up at 6:00 AM as it was about 30 miles further where we would put in the boats.

When we hired guides for the day it meant you were on the water at sun up and you quit around 4 PM. We fished hard that day but didn't catch much, which was rather typical for us. Our trips were fishing trips and if we caught any fish it was accidental and a surprise bonus for us.

The following morning after we ate breakfast one of the group called home to check in. When he hung up the phone he looked like he had seen a ghost. He told us a terrible thing had happened at home the previous night. He said someone had shot and killed my cousin Joe Wurm, his wife, Diane, and their nine year old son, Jimmy while Mike, their 16 year old son, was at a school dance. I immediately called Jewel and she said no one knew any more than that. I told her that we would head home right away. The guys in the other plane would gather our gear and settle up with the motel so we could leave as soon as possible.

We landed at Larned just after noon. Jim, our youngest child at 13 years and only child remaining at home, had loaded my guns and laid them out on the kitchen table in the event they were required to defend themselves from the murderer. When I walked in the house, Jim and Jewel were scared to death as Joe and Diane's home was only two miles from our home. No one had any idea what had happened other than all three were dead.

Rumors and speculation were rampant for a few days. Everyone had their own opinions as to what had happened. When the details finally emerged that Mike had shot all three, friends and neighbors were stunned. Mike was a student at Macksville High School and was well liked by his friends and teachers. In the ten years of school at Macksville nothing had indicated that he was a troubled youth. Some people felt that he was accused simply because he was handy. Some were blaming the Sheriff of being too quick to charge him with a crime he couldn't have committed with many potential criminals at the ready at the Larned State Hospital, a state mental institution for the criminally insane, only 15 miles away.

He was charged after he confessed, but people still felt he was innocent. My cousin Vernon and his wife Mary Ann were close friends with Joe and Diane. Vernon confided in me that Joe was very hard on Mike. Vernon felt that the animosity between Joe and Mike stemmed from the fact that Mike was nearly deaf and hadn't been diagnosed until Mike was nearly out of grade school. Joe felt Mike was surly and didn't pay attention to what he and Diane said. Because Mike was a juvenile, none of his trial was published. He was sentenced to the Menninger Clinic in Topeka. The Menninger Clinic had a division for troubled youth. Mike was paroled when he was eighteen. Several years after he was released he contacted Uncle Leonard and Aunt Lucy, his paternal grandparents and asked for a meeting with them. They reluctantly agreed. Mike expressed his sorrow for what he did, and asked if he could be buried next to his mother, father, and brother when he died. After several weeks they reluctantly agreed. In a matter of weeks he had his headstone installed next to his families' graves.

Diane's parents sold their farm and retired about ten years after the murders. Her father died shortly after. Several years later Mike was charged with stealing all of his grandmother's money. It seems he had convinced her that he could manage her money better than she could and she gave it to him. He promptly lost or spent it. Nothing more was heard of Mike until about 2006 when the Kansas City Star ran a headline that a construction company in Kansas City was being charged with, among other things, the embezzlement of money from a bank in Kansas City. Mike Wurm was listed as a co-conspirator in the charges. I am sure that many of those who felt that Mike couldn't have been guilty of murdering his family are beginning to wonder if they might have been wrong.

Anyone who knows anything about sheep knows if you have a flock of white sheep, sooner or later a black sheep will appear. The Mike Wurm episode was the first of two black sheep that showed up in the Schartz flock. Dad's sister, Mathilda, married Leonard Komarek from Ellinwood. After they married they moved to Spearville, Kansas to the farm that Mathilda had inherited from her father. They had four children before he died unexpectedly at the age of 45 from a heart attack. The oldest was Louise and a year later Mark was born. Several years later Bobby was born. About five years later Clinton was born. Clinton was only a year or so old when his father died.

Aunt Mathilda tried to raise her family as her sister Flora had raised her and her siblings. She and her children stayed on the farm and she, Louise and Mark, ran the farm as best they could. Shortly after the oldest kids had just started high school Aunt Mathilda remarried. According to family lore Tony, her new husband, was an alcoholic. He had two sons about the same age as Louise and Mark. Everything was in place for some severe problems to develop.

Mathilda's kids had pretty much grown up fatherless and Tony's boys had grown up motherless and raised by an alcoholic father. If ever there were two families destined for failure these two were it. By the time she remarried her two older boys were running wild. Clinton had always been very small for his age and his older brothers teased him unmercifully. Because they lived 75 miles away we never saw them but a few times while we were growing up. Louise had married right out of high school and had moved away.

Mark and Bobby didn't get along with their stepbrothers and Aunt Mathilda couldn't control any of them. Bobby and Mark drank too much and I am sure they both became alcoholics. I am not sure what Clinton turned into until one day, it must have been in the late 60's that we saw in the newspaper that Clinton had been arrested for the murder of Bill Polkinghorn, an owner of a trucking company in Dodge City. It seems that Clinton had thought that Bill's secretary was his girlfriend, and Bill had thought otherwise, or maybe Clinton just thought Bill might be a competitor. He was convicted of murder and sentenced to the penitentiary. He served 15 to 20 years and was released. He died shortly after his release.

IRRIGATING; VALLEY WATER DRIVE MODIFICATIONS; INVENTIONS

Soil scientists have classified the soils south of the Arkansas River as windblown sand. This band of sandy soils was mostly about 10 miles wide and included the lands which made up our farms. A unique factor of the soils south of the river was that immediately south of the river and extending south for two or three miles was a band of very sandy dunes and hills. They were considered as being too rough to be farmed, and were not broken out until the advent of sprinkler irrigation in the seventies.

When I bought my first Valley Center Point Irrigation system in the early sixties I had no idea where the path would eventually lead me. I was quickly caught up in the increased work load and hurrying to learn the art of irrigation. The increased yields quickly put to rest the idea of changing professions. One of the features of center point irrigation systems that appealed to me was that according to the literature they could be moved easily from field to field.

They could in fact be moved from field to field but I was never able to discover the easy part of the task. My farm consisted of three quarters, each comprising of 160 acres and one quarter which contained the farmstead and shelterbelts. A 13 tower system was purchased for the three open quarters and a seven tower system which watered 40 acres for the home quarter. A water well was drilled in the center of the section and an underground pipe line radiated to the center of each of the three quarters. The same configuration was used for the seven tower system on the home quarter.

When you wanted to move the system you would run the system until it was pointing at the pivot point on the quarter you wanted to move to. The system was shut down and from here on, the easy part always eluded me. The 26 wheels had to be turned so they faced parallel to the pipe which carried the water. To change the wheel direction the tower was jacked up so both wheels were off the ground. A safety pin was removed from the end of the axle and the wheel and axle were pulled from tower and reinserted into retainers welded on the base of the tower. Meanwhile, the wheel had been running in mud so the wheel and axle assembly was caked in mud and the tower itself was standing in mud. Of course the system itself was always in a growing crop which made the job more challenging.

When all the wheels had been changed to the transport position the center point was unbolted from the restraining pad and a long cable was bolted to the overhang end of the system. A tractor was hitched to the cable and it was ready to move. It was very hard to move the system at first because all of the wheels were in the tracks left by the system as it rotated around the field. But once moving it pulled rather easily.

When the system was being towed to another location it was exciting because you were hooked to a machine that is 1,300 feet long and you can only hope that it is following. When you got it to the new location it was much easier to change the wheels back to the running position because most of the mud had fallen off the wheels and you were working on dry ground. The first time we moved it my dad helped me and it took a full day to make the move. I decided that if we were going to move it I wanted to change the way the wheels were rotated.

I had purchased the systems from Bill Conrad so the next time he came by I expressed my opinion of how I hated the way the wheels were turned. Bill told me that all of his customers complained about this feature. I told him I was going to make some changes to make it easier to move. He became very excited and said that all of the Valley salesmen wanted an easier way to move them, but when they asked Valley to change the way the wheels were changed, the Valley management told them it couldn't be done. I had planned to spend the coming winter building a swivel to change the wheels.

That fall I started building a prototype. To install the swivel it was necessary to modify the base pipe to which the axles bolted. I was a bit reluctant to take a torch and welder to the base pipe because once that was done if my idea didn't work I would have to buy a new tower. I built the second swivel and mounted the two swivels on a tower and was very pleased at how they worked. I immediately started on the 24 that would let me convert all of the wheels on the system. When Bill Conrad saw how easily the wheels could be changed he asked me to go to the Valmont factory in Valley, Nebraska to show them to the management of Valmont.

Bill set up a meeting with the head of Valmont and the following day we flew to Nebraska. A driver picked us up and took us to the factory. Bill and I were ushered to their conference room where we were introduced to the engineering team in charge of the irrigation division. We were told to take a seat at the conference table which was at least 25 feet long.

When the four engineers arrived they all sat at the other end of the table. It was about this time when I realized the futility of the meeting. The four engineers at the other end of the table reminded me of vultures just waiting for Bill and I to quit twitching before they would descend on us for a feast. Bill was asked what his role was in the presentation and he explained how many more systems he could sell if it wasn't so hard to change the wheels to the towing position. Then I was asked to show my swivel. (When Bill realized that I might be able to build a swivel he suggested that I patent the idea because he felt that Valmont would embrace the idea, and thus started my experience with the patent process. At the time of the meeting I had been awarded a patent applied for certificate which protected my idea just as a patent did.)

When I finished explaining how the swivel worked the only question they asked was whether I had applied for a patent. They never even came to our end of the table to look at the swivel. The engineer who I thought was the head of the engineering team told Bill and me that they weren't interested because they would have to change the manufacturing process to install the swivels but if it could be modified so that it could be bolted on they might consider offering it as an option.

This was the beginning of a long and tumultuous affair with Valmont. Bill and I had a long quiet flight home. Bill never lost his enthusiasm for the potential of the swivel. He asked me if I thought it was possible to build one that bolted on instead of having to weld it on. I told him I didn't know but I would find out. The let down of Valmont's rejection of the swivel allowed me to look at the problem of towing a system from Valmont's perspective. If I were in Valmont's position I would have done exactly what Valmont did. A first time buyer would like the potential of the possibility of watering 2 fields with one system, but after moving it a few times, the labor and time involved would convince a buyer to purchase a second system thereby using two systems to their full potential. When I realized that this was Valmont's business plan, I started on the bolt-on model with considerable less enthusiasm than I had on the first model.

Bill's visits were becoming more frequent as he checked on my progress on the bolt-on model. When I tried to discuss what I felt Valmont's position was Bill strongly rejected my idea. He felt that moving a system was one of the best features of the system. Since the swivel idea was proven in the first swivel it didn't take long until I had a bolt on model. Planting season was nearing and I was pressed for time and I was sure that Valmont would reject the second swivel as well. When I showed the bolt on model to Bill he was ecstatic. I told him I had neither the time nor facilities to manufacture and sell the swivels, but if he could find a manufacturer I would license the swivel to him and he would give me $1.00 for each one he sold. Bill left with renewed enthusiasm.

His first stop was Valmont where he was greeted with the same skepticism that they had exhibited on our first meeting. Bill found a small manufacturer in Dodge City who would custom build the swivels for him. Before he was able to get into production the dealer for Valmont, who Bill worked for, received a letter from Valmot which stated that any Valley system that had been retrofitted with the Schartz swivel, the Valley warranty would be void!

Bill was devastated and I wasn't sure how I felt but I hoped I could get even eventually. Because the Valley water drive had proven the concept of center pivot irrigation it wasn't long until a new pivot system hit the market. These new systems were electric powered on rubber tires and had a bowstring truss method of suspending the water pipe between the towers. The ground to pipe clearance was also increased from 7 feet to 10 feet which made the new systems much more efficient for growing corn. Everyone knows electricity and water do not mix and it wasn't long before reports of deaths attributed to electrocutions while the servicemen worked on these new systems.

The old Valley water drives remained popular even though they were very labor intensive to keep operational. After a couple of seasons of operations, wear on the water drives began to become apparent. As more and more systems were being installed in our area customers were complaining about having to go to Dodge City for parts. Fred Casterline, the Valley dealer in Dodge, called one evening and asked me if I would agree to open a parts depot for his customers in my area. He said I could use any parts in the depot for free if I would open the depot. I quickly agreed to his offer.

Because my systems were a couple of years older than any of the systems in the area I knew which parts were going to be in demand before the other owners did. This arrangement between Fred and I lasted as long as I ran the water drives. The first parts to wear out were the Trojan bar dogs and brakes. The steel wheels had angle iron lugs every 8" around the wheels. The lugs extended past the edge of the wheels by 2". This lug extension was where the power to move the system was applied by the Trojan bar dog. The Trojan bar dog would move back and forth sliding over the extended wheel lug. Because the wheels were running in mud all the time, the sandy wet soil would abrade the lug and Trojan bar dog as the system circled the field.

The Trojan bar dog made four strokes a minute thus moving the system 32" a minute. This was the speed on the outer end of the system while the drive unit next to the pivot only moved about eight inches every ten minutes. As you approached the end of the system the wear was much higher. As the wheel advanced eight inches a spring driven brake engaged a wheel lug so the wheel couldn't roll backward. There were 32 lugs on each wheel so the Trojan bar dog and brake would slide over a wheel lug many thousands of times in the course of one circle of the field. If the Trojan bar dog or brake were worn out it would cause the system to shut down. It was rare to make a full circle without a shut down because of a failure of one kind or another.

The most dreaded shut down occurred when an intermittent short occurred in the electric shutdown circuit. The shut down devices consisted of a cable which ran from the pivot to the end tower which when activated would cause the whole system to stop moving. When activated the pump engine would continue to run but the system would not move. When a tower stopped or got too far out of line it cut off the water supply to the end tower so the system could not move.

The engine kill switch was the primary safety. An electric wire ran the length of the system and consisted of a mercury switch at each tower. If any of the towers got ahead or behind, the mercury switch on that tower would break the electric circuit which would kill the engine. This type of system shut down was the most common. The safety system was activated by an ingenious method by the way the safety wires were routed along the pipe that held the sprinklers. If the system was shut down the operator could sight down the length of the system. If a tower was out of line that was where the problem was. If the operator had any experience he would get the repairs and the tools to install them and walk through the crop and install the parts and then restart the pump and watch the repaired tower move back in line. Repairing and restarting could take anywhere from an hour to a day depending on how many trips back to the parts supply store were needed before you got the needed parts.

It was only a couple of years until my brothers and I were operating 13 center pivot irrigation systems. Generally the systems were started immediately after planting to get the crops up. They were then shut down for a couple of weeks then restarted and then ran continuously throughout the season. We would average about 30 revolutions per system throughout the season. My original plans of using the systems only during periods of low rainfall were quickly replaced by full watering of the crops. The water sprinklers would supply about ¾ inch of water every four days. If the systems weren't kept running the crop would become stressed and it was impossible to catch up and the yields would suffer. While the overall design of the system was ingeniously simple there were many mechanical parts that had to work flawlessly if the system was expected to perform as designed.

One day while replacing a trojan bar dog which had worn out I began to study it. It was a welded part made up of seven individual pieces of iron all welded together to make the part. The trojan bar dog was the most apt to need replacement than any part on the system. There were 26 of these parts on each system. The operator's replacement cost was $15 each. As I studied the part it became obvious that the part could be made of two pieces of iron instead of the seven that Valmont used.

I went back to the shop and built the model of my own trojan bar dog, took it back to the field and installed it. I checked it daily and while it performed as well as the $15 model it was apparent that the Valmont model would last twice as long as mine. I found that to fix the rapid wear I needed to know much more about metallurgy than I now possessed.

While browsing in a bookstore I came across a book entitled, *The Machinists Handbook.* I have spent many evenings enjoying this wonderful book. It contained chapters on every conceivable topic that a machinist could encounter while working with iron. The book stated that under high wear due to running under abrasive conditions parts needed to be heat treated. I asked a blacksmith friend if he knew where I might find a heat treating company. He said that he thought there was such a firm in Wichita. I picked up the phone and called information and asked for a heat treating company. She connected me to Batson Heat Treating on West Street. As I write I am amazed at how often my introduction to wonderful people began with a simple phone call.

Dale Batson's secretary put me through to Dale. I introduced myself and explained that I was having a wear problem and I was looking for a solution. He told me he thought he could fix the problem. He suggested I bring a sample and visit his facility. I left immediately for Wichita. This was the first of many trips we would make to Wichita for the finishing touches on the parts that we would eventually make for the Valley Water Drives.

PATENT APPLICATION

I had no idea about how to apply for a patent, so I resorted to what I had learned before, and that was to start asking questions until I found someone who knew the answer. Fortunately, the first person I asked was my attorney. He said he had no experience in patent law but he knew an attorney in Omaha who was a patent attorney. He gave me his phone number and suggested I call him. I called him and after he got done with his questions I had nearly given him my life story along with about six generations before me. He agreed to represent me in my quest for a patent. He warned me that a patent was very hard to get and in the event that I did get one he hoped his firm could also handle my infringement cases if necessary. He had informed me that I could expect to pay a minimum of $20,000 to get a patent. Two days later I received a bill for the time spent on our opening conversation. His billing rate was $200 an hour. Had I not been such a slow learner I would have sold my farm, gone to school, and became a patent attorney. The patent attorney sent me a letter requesting a full disclosure of my invention and some photos or sketches of how it worked. Suddenly my being able to draw was an asset.

After I had assembled everything he wanted, I sent it all to Omaha. I heard right back from him. He needed a thousand dollars to hire a patent draftsman and a patent writer who knew just what the patent examiners needed to start the search. He said as soon as the patent search was started I would need to forward $5,000 to cover the expenses to date. When he sent the drawings and abstract for my approval, they appeared to be photo copies of what I had sent him. I called and complained about the cost and appearance that they had been copied from my own sketches and description. He immediately congratulated me on the work that I had submitted. When I received the copy of the abstract for approval I was appalled. The abstract had almost nothing in it that would correctly allow the reader to understand the function of my design or what its purpose was or what I wanted the patent to cover. A phone call describing my displeasure with the abstract got an explanation that it might take the writer up to ten revisions before an applicant felt the abstract was concise enough to fully cover a device. I was beginning to get frustrated with the whole procedure. There was no doubt that my original drawing that I sent had been photo copied and the author of the abstract had absolutely no knowledge of how a system worked. After I listened to his lame excuses I said I would write the abstract and his writer could add any legal terms that may be needed. When I finally ok'd the drawings and

303

abstract I asked how long the search would take until the patent was issued. He replied that it normally takes about a year but it could take up to eighteen months. He hastened to add that for an extra $5,000 I could get what he called an expedited search which would only take about a month to complete. It quickly appeared to me that the cost of obtaining a patent was rounded to the nearest thousand. If I hadn't already invested so much to this point, I would have just said to hell with it. I should have realized that the patent process was just another governmental process and was designed to confuse an applicant more than protect him. It slowly became obvious that I needed to add attorneys along with the government to my most disliked list.

I should add that the correspondence that flowed back and forth surely helped reduce the deficit that the Postal Service reported for that fiscal year. If I was displeased with the abstract writers inability to comprehend anything mechanical compared to the guy who conducted the original search, the abstract writer was a genius. When the application was handed to this clown all the frustration up to this point seemed trivial. In earlier days of the patent process an applicant was required to submit a working model of whatever he wanted to patent. I think this proves that the founding fathers of the patent process suspected that to fully understand a new idea a working model was required. After the application reached this point it was handed to the patent examiner who checked the application against all of the millions of previously issued patents, at least that is what I was told. A whole new round of correspondence between the examiner and me ensued. He would send me a copy of any patent which he felt my submission even remotely infringed upon. Mostly the infringement could be eliminated by just changing a word or claim. Other times it required rewriting a whole section of the application or maybe it would require a new drawing of a particular detail. Before the process reaches this phase however the applicant receives permission to label his invention with a Patent Applied For, notice. This notice protects the inventor from anyone submitting a patent for the same idea before a patent is granted.

A patent gives the inventor sole right to build and sell his patented product for seventeen years, a period of time the writers of patent laws felt was sufficient for an inventor to recapture the costs involved in the perfection of the idea. However, any costs involved in protecting the stealing and selling of a patented idea must be borne by the patent holder.

Through the years I applied for 12 patents and was granted five. On several patents that were refused I felt the grounds for refusal was the examiners not fully understanding exactly what I had achieved. About six months after I got my last patent I received a letter from the US Patent Office stating that they were instating a yearly maintenance fee on all patents and to send $1,250 per patent to cover my patents for one year. This request only deepened my disgust of the whole process, and I did not comply thereby making all of my patents null and void. I decided the best course to protect oneself was simply, "be there firstest with the mostest." More simply stated before you release your product to the public, have a huge inventory on hand so you can take care of demand. It appeared to me that infringement was driven more by the designer not being able to satisfy the demand for his product, than any other factor.

JAY HUNGATE; PICKLE CREEK MANUFACTURING

It soon became apparent that I had to make a choice between being a farmer or a manufacturer. Jay Hungate, Jewel's brother-in-law, had quit his teaching job and was wanting to get into something else. I approached him with an offer as part owner and manager of Pickle Creek Manufacturing, the company I had developed to create replacement parts and improvements for my farm machinery and irrigation equipment. He became the manager of P.C.M. Jay proved to be a real asset to the firm. We decided to buy an RV and he would call on all the Valley dealers twice a year. I had learned that name recognition, along with a quality product, took a long time to establish with potential customers.

Jay was a very personable type of a person and was a born salesman. He quickly found which contractors most irrigators were hiring to repair and operate their system. These contractors had no allegiance to Valmont because Valmont would not discount their repair prices to them. The contractors quickly became our customers, some of whom placed huge orders with us and remained loyal to PCM. I had noticed that the lugs on the wheels which the trojan bar dogs slid back and forth on were starting to show signs of wear. I began to try to figure out how to repair those lugs.

When I designed our trojan bar dog it became evident that I would need some equipment that I didn't have. I would need an iron shear, a big press and a hole punch. All of these items could be purchased from manufacturer's supply houses. But at $15,000 I felt the price was too high. So I built an ironworker patterned on a brochure that I had requested from an ironworker manufacturer. I had lost my homemade ironworker in a shop fire a year later and replaced it with a Metal Muncher, a commercial iron worker. This piece of equipment was the backbone of our shop, and I always marveled at how versatile and reliable this machine is.

The original wheel lugs were made of a piece of angle iron welded across the 8" wide face of the rim of the wheel and extended about 1-1/2" beyond the edge of the wheel. This extension was the area that the Trojan Bar moved over as it pushed the wheel forward once the wheel moved ahead 8". A brake would engage the lug while the trojan bar dog slid back to engage the next lug.

Since there were 32 lugs on each wheel and a standard system utilized 26 wheels, that made 832 lugs on each system that needed repair. Jay told me that a dealer in Texas was welding a 1" piece of rod to the lugs as repair and suggested that we start making and selling these 2" long pieces of rod as repairs for the wheel lugs. I told him before we committed PCM to this means of repair I wanted to try an idea that I thought would be much cheaper than hiring a welder to weld on 832 pieces of rod.

I went to a plumber in town and purchased a 20' piece of 2-1/2" diameter pipe. The first step was to cut a 2-1/8" piece of pipe which was the length of the lug on the wheel that was encountering the wear by the trojan bar dog. The lug was made of a piece of 1-1/2 x 1-1/2" angle iron. The lug end was formed by bending the top of the angle. Since the wear was only on the top of the lug, my plan was to use the bottom part of the lug which had no wear to anchor the repair by friction to the unworn part of the lug.

Since I wanted to anchor the repair by friction the repair was going to require extreme accuracy during its fabrication. It would also mean I was going to have to build tools and dies to make the bends required. I set to work on the tools and dies I would need. It wasn't long until I discovered to achieve the correct shape it would take two stages of forming to achieve the results I wanted.

After several days and hundreds of errors I finally achieved success. I began cutting the rest of the pipe into the 2 -1/8" lengths to be sure I could replicate my original design. After fine tuning the dies I found that the tolerances needed were easy to maintain and replication stayed dead on. I had achieved exactly what I wanted and Jay and I called it the "lug gripper."

I ordered a semi load of 2-1/2" pipe. My metal saw was a cheap band saw that I had purchased in a farm supply store and was designed for light farm use. We had a semi load of pipe ordered and it all needed to be cut into 2-1/8" lengths. That was going to require at least one man to do the cutting. As I was cutting the pipe I saw that with a little work I could automate the saw to the point that the only labor required would consist of placing a piece of pipe on a table, turn on the saw, and it would automatically cut the entire 20' length of pipe into the required lengths.

A week later I had the saw remodeled and it worked well. I had designed the table that fed the pipe into the saw to hold six joints of pipe stacked one on top of each other. It took about seven hours to reduce the 120' of pipe into 680 lug gripper blanks which would be enough blanks for 2/3 of a system. After I had made the first 50 I noticed my tolerances began to vary. I checked my tooling and I could see some wear. I made a call to Dale Batson in Wichita and he explained that unless the tooling was heat treated I could expect to spend all of my time building new tooling. His advice was correct and his heat treated tooling was still in use on our last batch of lug grippers.

We took delivery on our first semi load of pipe and we started sawing it up. When I took the first blanks to the metal muncher to start the forming process, the first blank broke on the final bend – it went into the scrap barrel. After the fifth failure in a row I began to worry because once my tooling had been finalized I hadn't had a failure in the fifty or so that had been made from the pipe from the plumber. I ran a few more blanks with the same results. Finally I knew I had a problem.

I took a few of successful lug grippers along with the failures and headed for Wichita and Dale Batson. Dale looked at my samples and said that although the pipe from both samples looked exactly alike they obviously were not the same. He gave me the names of several metallurgy labs and suggested I have an analysis run on them to find out what the makeup was of the two samples. We waited for the reports from the three labs that were studying the samples.

The reports all said that the samples were very similar, but the ones that hadn't broken showed about 2% more chrome than the broken ones. Two of the labs also said that it was impossible to make the shape that I wanted by cold bending. I couldn't figure out how they felt it was impossible to achieve the shape via cold forming when they had a sample of the cold formed lug in their hand. The solution to my problem, I felt, was to find the mill that put chromium in their pipe.

On one of his trips calling on Valley dealers Jay had seen a set of reference books for manufacturers. It consisted of three large volumes that named and gave addresses of almost anything that a manufacturer might need. The name of this vendor list was "The Thomas Register." We quickly added the volumes to our library. I checked The Thomas Register for tubing manufacturers and started calling. After two days on the phone I was about to give up on finding the mill that had made the pipe. I had tried to narrow the call list down to mills in the central part of the country thinking that the plumber's supplier would try to keep his shipping costs as low as possible. I had called all the mills in the central US whose names had started with the letter A and was about half way through the mills who started with the letter B when I got to a mill with the unlikely name of Bull Moose Pipe and Tubing Co in St. Louis, Missouri. The phone was answered by a gruff and very profane old guy by the name of Sam. When he was talking he was constantly yelling and giving orders to his employees. In between order and commands he asked what the hell did I want. I nearly hung up. I asked if his company made tubing or pipe with 2% chrome, and he said yes but what in the hell did I need it for. When I was able to talk between his shouted commands, he asked where I got a sample of his pipe from.

When I told him that I had gotten it from my local plumber he calmed down a bit and said they only made that pipe on special order and By God he would like to know how it could possibly wind up in a plumbing shop in Larned, Kansas. Sam suggested I send him samples of the good lug grippers and they would run them through their lab. I figured that was going to be the last I heard from old Sam.

About a week later Sam called. He told me that my samples had indeed come from their mill. He went on to tell me that there was no way that I would be able to make the bends I wanted by cold forming. When I told him that the samples I sent him had been cold formed, he said, "You're shitting me, right?" When I asked if I could get him to send me a six foot sample so I could try to make sure it worked he said yes.

When I got the sample from Sam I quickly began preparing it for bending. The sample ran perfectly and I quickly called Sam back. My first question was how big an order did he need to run a special order. He said that if I was sure that this was what I needed they would run a twenty ton order. This was a semi load. I placed an order for a semi load. Sam told me he hoped I didn't try to bend the pipe to the configuration of the samples that I had sent him because it couldn't be done. I told him to ship it anyway.

After I had run our first load from Sam I called him back and ordered another semi load. Sam seemed pleased and after a long conversation interrupted several times by shouted orders Sam laughingly told me not to try to cold bend his pipe because it couldn't be done. We both laughed and hung up. As soon as we had enough lug grippers made and had them hardened we installed them on one of my systems to test them. They worked perfectly and we began full-scale production immediately.

The first thing when we arrived at work we would stack six pipes on the saw table and start the saw. It would run until about 4 p.m. when it would finish cutting the blanks for the lug grippers. One man would then start the bending to the final shape. We ran on this schedule for several years. We had watched several other parts on the systems that were obviously going to have to be replaced because of wear, and started building those parts as well. Eventually our inventory was made up of over 20 parts for the Valley water drives. We learned from dealers and contractors that Valmont was not happy about us although we never heard from them directly.

I had started advertizing in the High Plains Journal, a weekly farm paper published in Dodge City. The paper had a huge subscriber list and most farmers in the high plains subscribed to it. Jewel and I had decided on Pickle Creek Manufacturing as the name for our new business. We

314

introduced our PCM trojan bar dog in the High Plains Journal priced at $2.49 compared to $14.99 which was Valley's retail price for their Trojan bar dog. The response from Valmont was immediate. A letter was sent to all of their dealers forbidding them from buying or installing our repairs on their customers systems. Bill Conrad made a trip to PCM just to show me the letter his employer had received. He wanted to know how committed I was to making and selling parts for the irrigation systems. When I explained that I planned to manufacture all of the high wear parts for the systems he was enthusiastic because he felt that Valmont had snubbed us both when we showed them the wheel swivels.

I knew from the beginning that we were in a maturing market with the Valmont repair business because the old water drives were being replaced by the newer electric models powered by oil hydraulics which eliminated the dangers imposed by the electric powered systems. The best known of these hydraulic systems was offered by T&L, a firm in Hastings, Nebraska. Pickle Creek Manufacturing was ripe to branch out into other agricultural avenues.

FERTILIZER PLACEMENT TUBES; FLEX KING

My interest in fertilizer placement had been ongoing through the years of expanded irrigation development and starting the manufacturing business. Pickle Creek started building and selling some of the equipment that I thought held the most promise. After my initial foray into irrigation system replacement parts, the next development was fertilizer delivery tubes that bolted onto a sweep plow. The most popular sweep plow was the Flex King, a tillage machine built in Quinter, a small town about 50 miles west of Hays. The idea of these tubes had been around for years being built and sold mostly out of small farm shops. Replacements for them were very hard to come by as most of the builders of the tubes disappeared after a few years, and many times you either had to make your own or quit using the sweep plow as a means of applying fertilizer. Pickle Creek began building these tubes. We had been attending and displaying our irrigation repairs at the 3i show in Kansas and at the Husker Harvest show in Nebraska ever since the start of Pickle Creek. These shows and placing our advertisements in the High Plains Journal and Irrigation Age had given Pickle Creek a lot of name recognition and we always had a crowd at the shows.

Usually we had two of our people at the shows to answer questions about any of our products.

After one of our 3i shows we got a phone call from Jim Boone, the owner of Flex King, who wanted to come visit with us. When he got to the farm I immediately noticed his black flat brimmed hat and neatly trimmed beard. His black pants had a strange cut as well. I had found that when you visit manufacturers the visits always started with a tour of the facilities. Jay and I gave the tour to Jim. Jim's story started very similar to Pickle Creek's in that he and his brother Gary thought they had a better idea than what the market offered, and before they knew it they were in business. Jim never brought up his religious conviction nor did we ask. Jim finally said that he had heard of our fertilizer tubes from his customers who had all recommended our tubes to him. He said that his firm was working on using his sweep plow as a planter and wondered if it would be possible for us to fabricate the tubes he needed to build his first prototype for testing. We assured him we would like to try. When he left I knew that he would be on my list of most favorite people that I had met. When we started building the fertilizer tubes I had to build a hydraulic tubing bender because I felt we must be able to replicate the bends required for the tubes. A gauge was built for both the right and left tubes and because there were 4'-5'-6' tubes necessary for different size plows we had quite a few gauges hanging on the wall behind the tubing bender. We had a young man named Joe who was our first employee and as he gained experience he became an artist at operating the tubing bender. When I needed a new size fertilizer tube I merely asked Joe to build it for me and generally by the end of the day Joe would have the tube made plus the gauges necessary to duplicate them. The fertilizer tubes we were selling were fabricated from ¼" plumber's pipe. The tooling I had built was made to accommodate ¼" pipe. Flex King wanted their seed delivery tubes fabricated from ¾" pipe which meant I would have to build all new tooling for Jim's new seeder.

Our fertilizer tubes consisted of a tube that started at the top of the standard which was bolted to the plow frame and ran vertically down to the V shaped plow. The width of the plow was determined by how many of the V shaped plows were bolted to the plow frame. For example the 42' Flex King plow, which was the largest plow they built, consisted of seven six' plows on a 42' frame. The tubes required consisted of seven right angle and seven left angle tubes. The fertilizer went into the top of the tube near the top of the frame down to the back of the V and then along the wings of the V. Holes were drilled at 1' intervals for the fertilizer to exit the tubes. Jim's design required a tube for each row of seed. To achieve a 12" row spacing would mean that there were going to have to be a minimum of six tubes on each of the blades of the plow. The blades of the plow lifted the soil about 2-1/2" before it left the blade and we had to make the tubes to fit in the 2-1/2" cavity directly behind the blade. Since the tubes had to be stacked behind the standard that carried the sweep fitting all those tubes into that space was going to prove difficult. Jim delivered a sweep bottom to us so we could fit the tubes correctly. I talked with Joe about the feasibility of the project and he felt that, if I could build the tooling, it might be possible. I went to my Machinist's Handbook and found what the maximum bend was for ¾" pipe was and built the tooling. Joe started bending the tubes and building the gauges needed. When Jim picked up the first batch of tubes he was very pleased. Jim had contracted a Canadian manufacturer for seeding equipment to build the seed bin and everything needed to get the seed to our tubes. By the time the seeding equipment was installed on his sweep plow it was a very impressive piece of equipment.

When Jim had approached me with his idea I was skeptical as to whether it would work as he had planned. There was no doubt that he could seed wheat with his idea. I felt the thing that would doom it was the depth and scattering of the seed as it exited the seed tubes. Since Jim had not asked for my advice I kept quiet. Joe was kept busy all of the early summer building tubes for Jim. Jim asked his best customers to field test his seeders. The bulk of his test farmers were in the eastern part of Colorado and east to the Garden City area in western Kansas. Most were on his largest plows which were 42'ers. We shipped our first truckload of tubes around the middle of July. Jim's crews were busy mounting the Canadian hopper seed metering devices and our seed tubes to new plows that were being built at Qinter. A 42' plow equipped to seed was quite an impressive piece of equipment and I guessed that they would retail at over $100,000.

Wheat seeding generally began in eastern Colorado around the middle of August while in western Kansas seeding date was early September. Jim sent a plane to pick me up so we could watch his first seeder make its debut in the foothills of the Rockies. I took Joe along as a bonus since he did such a great job on the seed tubes. It was quite a sight when they pulled into that field with Jim's seeder behind a new four wheel drive tractor. We watched it as it circled the huge field. We estimated that it was seeding around 50 acres an hour. (With the traditional seeder I had, seven acres an hour was the best I could hope for.) If performance was Jim's goal he had hit a home run!! As we checked the seed placement my concerns were confirmed. I never mentioned the potential seed scattering issues to Jim. A sweep plow slices through the soil about 2" deep when being used as a seeder. The soil going over the blade of the plow is then dropped back down on the soil where it was cut, leaving the cut soil loose and fractured. The seed is placed under the loose soil made by the blade as it cuts through the soil. Ideally seed should be placed in firm soil so the seed is surrounded by firm soil to promote germination. With Jim's seeder the loose soil completely surrounds the seed and a few hours later the loose soil has dried out. Conventional seeders have an opener for each row and can move up and down depending on how smooth the soil is. Jim's seeder had none of the flexibility of the traditional seeders plus the seed bed was loose and would be prone to drying out which would result in poor germination. I was sure Jim's hope for a new use for his sweep plow was doomed. As the season progressed Jim was sure the poor stands behind his seeder was caused by the dry weather that had settled over the high plains after the wheat was seeded. He forged ahead so he would be ready for milo seeding in the following spring.

If I remember correctly it was in November when he asked if I thought it was possible to build a fertilizer pump that had the capacity to apply fertilizer with the seed behind his planter. Jay and I had discussed this idea for some time and I thought it might be possible. I had decided that the pump design that showed the most promise was a peristaltic pump. A peristaltic pump operates by a rubber tube with a roller which rolls over a tube filled with liquid. As the roller rolls over the tube it forces the liquid out of the end of the tube. The concept had been proven by several manufacturers of pumps of this design; most notable was the pump which is used as a heart substitute during heart surgery. My design consisted of several parameters. Because liquid fertilizer is very corrosive, I wanted the pump to be built out of materials not affected by an internal leak of fertilizer. To achieve this design goal the pump would have to be built of aluminum or plastic or a combination of the two. After a couple of weeks at the drawing board, I felt that I could start building a pump. My design had 24 outlets which was twice as large as anything on the market at that time. It would require several aluminum castings along with four plastic gears. The rollers that squeezed the fertilizer out of the tubes would be made of stainless steel pipe.

I found the address of a foundry in The Thomas Registry. The foundry was in Wichita, not far from the Batson heat treating plant. On my next trip to Wichita I stopped in at the Wichita foundry. I was met by a man named Frank, the owner of the foundry. After he had made the usual tour of the foundry we went to his office with the plans for the parts that I wanted made. Frank was an older guy who had been a B24 pilot in WWII, and because I loved stories about pilots in WWII I spent nearly all afternoon listening to Frank's exploits as a pilot. I finally was able to explain to Frank that I knew nothing about casting aluminum but felt because of its resistance to corrosion it was a good candidate for a pump. Thus began my education in the art of aluminum casting. Frank had started his foundry after WWII and because Wichita had so many aircraft plants he quickly found all the business he could handle. Maybe it was because I knew so little about casting aluminum that he recognized himself in me, or maybe he just liked to have a captive audience to tell his WWII stories to. I'll never know for sure but I quickly added him to my list of Most Liked People.

Frank explained the first step to having a part made was to have a pattern maker make a wood pattern of each of the parts so they could cast the parts. He gave me the name of the pattern maker who made most of his patterns. I went to the pattern maker and I listened to his explanation of how hard it was to design a pattern for a casting. Because of the complexity it would run about $3500 for each pattern plus any changes that may be required. I decided that the pattern maker could become a bottomless pit that I would try to fill with dollars. I was ready to tell Frank that I was going to give up on the aluminum casting idea, when I wondered if the patterns could be made of iron instead of wood. When I asked Frank if they could be made of iron he got a strange look on his face and replied, "Oh no, they must be made of wood." When I pressed him further he had no reasonable answer. I explained that I had all the facilities to make them of steel and I didn't want to be held up while the pattern maker made some small change to the patterns. It wasn't long before he relented and we chose the simplest part for me to make the pattern out of iron. Two days later I was back at the foundry with my first pattern. The three men on the foundry floor were Frank, his son Jack, and a huge Asian man. The procedure was to take the pattern and place it in a box that was half as thick as the part to be cast and then fill the box with a black sand leaving half of the pattern sticking out of the sand. After the sand was packed down the pattern was removed and the top half was put into another box and black sand was packed around the top half of the pattern. When the pattern was removed the two box halves were then placed face to face leaving a perfect imprint of the part in the black sand. A sprue hole was dug out of the packed sand so the melted aluminum could be poured into the cavity left in the mold made by the pattern. After the aluminum hardened the black sand mold was broken and the piece was duplicated perfectly. Frank's son Jack gave the impression of a person who all his life he had gotten up in the morning and hadn't yet figured out how to get away from this hellish job. Obviously the only thing he had learned was not to stick his hand into the cauldron of molten metal.

When our first casting was removed from the mold Frank slapped me on the back and said it was the first

324

casting he ever poured from a pattern made of iron. I started on the other two patterns that afternoon. My design called for four gears made of plastic – the pump design was basically two pumps placed face to face connected by a frame that had the four bosses that held the stainless steel rollers that squeezed the fertilizer out of the rubber hoses on the inside of the pump. I found the name of an injection molder in Algonquin, Illinois and sent them the drawings for the required gears. I received a call from the molding company that the molds were finished. We were ready to run some samples. The next six months were spent tweaking patterns and building fixtures and jigs to assemble the pumps. We spent weeks testing different hoses and hose fittings.

About a year after we had decided to build a pump, our first pump was running on the test bench. I was anxious to begin field testing. The first pump was mounted on a sweep plow. After about an hour in the field the pump failed. Back in the shop I could find no reason for failure. I built the second pump and got the same results. Our first pump was still running on the test bench after 30 twenty-four hour days. I eventually figured out that the failure was because the dusty field conditions affected the pump. As long as there was no dust the pump performed flawlessly but with just a little dust it wouldn't last an hour. I had invested two years, thousands of hours and a bunch of money, only to be defeated by a little dust. I hated the long drive to Quinter, but most of all I hated to tell Jim that I was going to give up trying to build the pump. During the design and prototype testing Jim was always enthusiastic and a great source of encouragement.

We were in Jim's office when I told him of my decision to abandon any further work on the pump. He leaned back in his chair and said, "Since it seems that this is the morning of bad news, I have decided to drop my seeder project as well." The worst time in the manufacturing business is when you realize it is time to abandon a project that you felt held great promise. As I drove home I hoped Jim had felt the sense of relief that I felt by sharing our failure that morning.

When I got home I immediately started on building a paint machine which had been put on hold while I was working on the pump. We hadn't been painting the parts we built simply because we didn't know how to paint the parts we were building. Spray painting wouldn't work because it wasted too much paint, and brushing paint on those small parts wasn't an option either, so we had been shipping everything unpainted. While reading The Thomas Register I had come across a paint that you simply dipped a part into and when it was removed the paint dried nearly instantly. A paint manufacturer in Wichita was making this paint and a call to Wichita confirmed the advertisement. On

326

the next delivery of parts to Batsons we brought home a five gallon can of this new paint. It worked great. The only drawback was the time and labor required to dip the part and then hold it while the paint dried. I visualized a machine that could solve this problem. The machine would consist of an iron frame which would hold a 25' chain that resembled the letter D. The straight side of the D would be the top while the curved side would be at the bottom. At one corner of the D would be a drive sprocket while an idler sprocket was at the other corner of the D. The chain would have hooks welded at 6" intervals. The bottom of the D would pass through a pan filled with paint. I geared the chain so it took 10 minutes to make one revolution. The paint machine was mounted on wheels so it could easily be moved outside when we painted. There were 50 hooks on the chain so 50 parts could be painted in 10 minutes. A barrel of unpainted parts and an empty barrel would be set at the end of the machine. The operator would start the machine, take a part out of the barrel, hang the part on the hook and continue hanging parts as the chain moved by. The parts would then be submerged in the paint pan and be lifted out as the chain moved up to the drive sprocket. As the chain moved past the second sprocket the paint was dry and the operator removed the painted one and put it in the empty barrel, got an unpainted one and put it on the vacated hook. We didn't paint the lug grippers or any of the many bushings we built, but everything else was painted.

Our testing of minimum tillage pointed to a need for a way to increase the amount of liquid fertilizer that was carried by the tractor and planter. Saddle tanks for tractors had been on the market for several years. They were mounted on either side of the engine and between the front and rear wheels of the tractor. This mounting method made it hard to service the tractor engine and difficult to get on and off the tractor. I devised a way for the tanks to be carried on extensions on the rear axle of the tractor. Mounting the tanks on the rear axle made for a neat mount and completely out of the way of the operator. I applied for a received a patent on the tank mount. Because it would require so many different configurations of mounts for different tractors we never offered them for sale. Twenty years later after my patent had expired a firm who specialized in fertilizer equipment offered axle mounted saddle tanks for several tractors.

SKIING AND RECREATIONAL ACTIVITIES

While I was in town one day, an acquaintance who farmed north of town happened to mention that a group of friends from Larned were putting together a ski trip to Breckenridge and wondered if Jewel and I would like to go along. I had always wanted to try to ski but Jewel had never shown much interest in it. Our winters had always been busy with our kid's school activities but since Jim was the only one still in school we found ourselves with much more free time during the winter months. We decided that we would join the group for the ski trip.

The group was going to Breckenridge on the second weekend in January. Any new activity was traumatic for Jewel because she was so fashion conscious. Since we had never been to a ski area before she was sure she would need a bunch of new clothes. She spent the early part of that winter shopping for the appropriate clothing.

Our trip to Colorado was off to a bad start because the rest of the group had left town an hour earlier. Jewel and I had arrived at our travelling companions' house at 8:30am and stood by helplessly watching them darting around the house without accomplishing much. At 9:45 they announced that they were ready to leave after checking the house one more time. By the time we were on our way the weather had turned sour; the snow was coming down hard and the wind was really starting to blow.

When we got to Lacrosse, 40 miles away, one of our passengers wanted something from her purse and she couldn't find it. We stopped and nearly unloaded the trunk looking for the purse. As we reloaded the trunk she decided she left it home on the table. Since all the cash they needed was in her purse we had to go back to Larned to get the purse.

I was a basket case by the time we retrieved the wayward purse and finally arrived in Hays where we got onto I-70 and headed for Colorado. After about 70 miles it had become obvious that Jewel's and my trip back home would probably be in the back of a hearse. The idiot driving the car had no idea of how to drive on a snow covered road. He obviously thought of this trip as an adventure and each near mishap was to be enjoyed to the limit. At one point he stomped on the accelerator and we made a complete 360 degree skid across both lanes of the road. He seemed to think that because the speed limit was seventy you were supposed to drive seventy. We would come up behind a semi and as the snow and slush was being thrown up by the truck he would ease into the slush and when the windshield of the car was covered by a foot of slush he would slow down and drop back only to try again.

It soon became obvious that on every semi there were three of these plumes of ice and slush. The first one thrown up by the rear wheels of the trailer, the second one thrown up by the rear wheels of the tractor, and finally the third one from the front wheels of the tractor. With every semi we passed we would be driving with a foot of slush on our windshield or so it seemed to me. We drove across western Kansas like this and it seemed our driver relished every mile. I was so scared I didn't even notice if I had wet my pants or not. Several times when it seemed that there was no way we could possibly survive I had nearly suggested that I should drive.

By the time we reached Eastern Colorado it had gotten much colder and the snow was increasing to the point that each lane was just a track and all vehicles were only driving 50 miles per hour. Thus we continued on to Breckenridge. The other eight in our party had arrived in time to rent their boots and skis. We would have to wait until morning to rent our gear.

While we were renting our stuff the rest were hiring an instructor. Only two couples had skied before and the rest were beginners. We found our group on the bunny slope with a bright and cheery young college aged girl who was trying to convince this bunch of flatlanders that skiing was the best thing since sliced bread.

After a morning of falling down, trying to get back up, and trying to untangle skis and poles our instructor announced that we were ready to take on the mountain. She told us that the ski trails were marked, green for beginners, blue for advanced, and black for only the best skiers. She warned us to stay away from the black runs unless we had come to Colorado to commit suicide. Needless to say her description of the black runs didn't help the confidence of our beginners. John Haas, one of our group, had learned to ski while in high school and was so taken by the sport that he had spent his first winter out of high school working as a busboy at Breckenridge. John immediately became our mentor.

It soon became apparent that the skiers fell into two groups. The first group skied only for fun and the second were there to make a fashion statement. This was in the early seventies and the general public had only recently been introduced to the sport. John and I fell into the first group. John is a short man built like a watermelon. His attire consisted of a half-smoked cigar tightly clamped in his mouth, a long fur coat whose bottom came to his boot tops, soft leather ski boots, and the longest skis he could buy. If John was walking through the parking lot and saw anyone with longer skis than his, he would try to buy them. My attire meanwhile consisted of a sweatshirt and sweatpants encased in a pair of insulated coveralls. I had chosen this wardrobe so I could carry my pliers with me. I had learned on the farm that a good pair of pliers could rescue a person in all but the worst situations.

On our first afternoon, John got all of us beginners on the lift for our first run down the mountain. Getting on the lift was easy because the ground was flat which made it easy to control the skis. Getting off was a whole different matter. The top sloped away at a steep angle and it was obvious that we would almost immediately be approaching Mach I before the first scream left our throat. When Jewel and I got to the top I took her hand and as I got off I pulled her screaming NO-NO-NO. We both wound up in a pile.

When John and his wife Carolyn arrived, we were trying to untangle ourselves while we told John what we thought of him. The experience of getting off the lift nearly stopped Jewel from ever skiing again. It was three more visits to Colorado before she left the bunny slope. John and Carolyn began putting together ski trips several times each winter and we went along every time. Because John had taught us all to ski we started trying to emulate John's style. Only on the coldest days did he ever button the top button on his ridiculous fur coat. When he came down the hill he would swing his poles around his head resembling a helicopter in mid-crash, the tails of his coat streaming behind him, yelling at the top of his voice. I have never seen an example of such exuberance and joy since those days on the mountain with John. On every trip we heard rumors of skiers who had hit a tree and were killed. I believe these rumors had a profound effect on Jewel's reluctance to leave the bunny slope. The trees on either side of the runs down the hill represented a potential death opportunity.

After a day of going up and down the hill and stowing our ski gear it was time to party. The Larned group always arrived at our chosen ski area with our cars packed with huge pots of soup and plenty of booze. Usually the soup was all consumed by the second night and hunger forced us onto the streets looking for a pizzeria or hamburger joint. After we had eaten and returned to our condo most of us were so tired that we all went to bed leaving the partying for the next night.

Two years after our first ski trip I had a flat tire on the rear of one of my tractors and because the tire was filled with a new heavy ballast powder it was necessary to get a tire firm from Dodge to repair it. Elmer Kliesen, the owner of the tire firm, came to repair my tire. Elmer was a big man who had spent his entire life in the tire business and knew how to convince a potential customer that Kliesen Tire should take care of all his tire needs. Elmer was a gregarious person and talked all the while he fixed my tire. He casually asked if I had ever skied and when I told him we had been to Colorado a few times he said that his son,

Gary, was president of the Dodge City Ski Club and he would call me and get Jewel and I to join the club. That night Gary called and invited us to come to Dodge and meet most of the members of the club and to discuss their annual fly-in trip to Snowmass in Aspen.

Gary was obviously Elmer's son as soon as we met him. He apparently never met anyone he didn't like and made you feel at ease immediately. June, his wife, was a teacher at Dodge Juco and was a pleasure to visit with. As soon as Jewel told June that our oldest daughter, Sharon, was a student at Dodge Juco the die was set. Gary's job as president was to plan all the trips to Colorado and as the coordinator he and June got a free pass on all of the trips. At the meeting he announced he had chartered a 54 passenger plane for the trip to Snowmass. He had also rented condominiums that could accommodate the entire ski club right on the slope so we could ski to the main lift. He had also gotten almost a half price reduction on our ski rentals and lift tickets. Gary had worked at Snowmass as a ski patrolman for two winters right out of high school. It was obvious that he knew his way around the ski industry. We were so impressed with the organization that we signed for the trip that night. We were to make a whole new circle of friends because of a flat tire on a tractor.

The club consisted of feedlot managers, bankers, large farmers, cattle buyers, and all manner of business people. Their ages ran from the mid-thirties to mid-sixties. When we told Gary and June that we had reservations because we were rank beginners, they quickly pointed out that the club also had beginners and we would have no trouble fitting in. Frequent phone calls from Gary or June kept us up to date on the plans.

Jewel and I arrived at the Dodge City airport at 4:45 A.M. the day of departure. Gary had made arrangements with the airport restaurant to be open for breakfast and coffee. Our departure time was 5:30. Gary and June were worried that they might not fill the plane causing an increase in price for the rest of us. But all 54 seats were full when we left Dodge. As we got closer to the Rockies it started to get cloudy. When our pilot informed us that we would be landing in ten minutes all I could see was mountain tops sticking up through the clouds and all I could think of as we descended through the clouds was those mountain tops sticking up through the clouds only minutes before. We broke out of the clouds and the runway was dead ahead. We taxied to the terminal where a car was waiting to take Gary to check the lodgings and then to purchase our tickets. June directed us to the terminal where we would get our bags and board the two buses that would take us to our condos.

We had never seen a better organized operation than the one we witnessed that morning. Gary met us at the entrance to our condo and gave each of us our three day lift tickets. We went to our rooms and changed into our ski clothes. It was snowing hard as we left the condo and headed for the lift less than a block away. June and Barb who owned a dance studio in Dodge and taught cheerleading classed to most of the cheerleaders in the high schools in Western Kansas were waiting for us when we left the condo. They were in charge of Jewel and I on our first morning in Snowmass. Jewel argued that she wanted to go to the bunny slope. But the gals from Dodge insisted that the run we would take was as easy as any bunny slope.

When we left the lift it was snowing so hard that we couldn't see the trees on either side of the run. June skied backward in front of Jewel and Barb behind. We skied that run until noon when we had a hamburger in the lodge. It had stopped snowing when we got on the lifts after dinner. When we got to the top Jewel announced that she wasn't going to ski on that steep a slope and asked June to get a ski patrolman to take her back down. June and Barb then had to convince her that she had skied that run all morning. They were finally able to convince her that because we had skied in white out conditions all morning it wasn't dangerous now. After we made it down it became obvious that Jewel had finally conquered her fear of going down a hill. By the third day she was skiing with the best skiers in the club and having a ball. Jewel had hidden my coveralls that I had worn on our first ski trip because she said I looked "dorky." John Deer had just began selling snowmobiles and offered a line of snowmobile clothing. Ken Fenwick, the manager of our dealership convinced Jewel that a snowmobile suit was just what I needed. In my green and yellow suit I stuck out like a centipede on crutches on the slope.

John and Carolyn Haas, who were with the Larned group, had convinced me that if I was to be recognized as a skier I had to have a bota slung over my shoulder. A bota is a goatskin container that holds wine so if you get cold the wine will warm you up. John had told me that wine was for sissies and if you were cold Schnapps was the only thing that would warm you up. My bota was filled with Schnapps. Gary, who felt responsible for everyone from Dodge was constantly making sure that all of the groups' equipment was properly adjusted. The first day or two he would flag me down to use my pliers to adjust bindings and make sure that my schnapps hadn't gone bad. After most of the group found out that I had a pair of pliers I was constantly being stopped so they could use my pliers and of course to check out the schnapps. My pliers were used to adjust not only bindings but sunglasses and goggles as well. It was hard for me to get much skiing done as I constantly had to go back to the condo to refill my bota. But damn we were having fun. It wasn't long until the Dodge group realized that Jewel and I were true greenhorns and they took it upon themselves that we must be educated on how best to get the most from a ski trip.

A large group of party animals from Dodge had rented cars so they could enjoy the night life in Aspen which is about five miles from Snowmass. The first stop on our educational tour was the huge gay bar in downtown Aspen. Even though we were with a large group, we found ourselves very uncomfortable in this setting. We couldn't get out of there quick enough. Someone in our group had made reservations at a dinner club for our evening meal. We again found that our group had been shown preference in seating and service. Obviously the Dodge City Ski Club had been here before. We took four of the fly trips with the ski club before petty jealousy finally ended the club's existence. We remained friends with most of the club. We would make three or four ski trips each winter with either a group from Larned or Dodge.

It was around this time we had an irrigation system destroyed by a wind storm and I was able to buy the destroyed system from the insurance company. It had long been my plan that if I lost a system to a wind storm I would salvage the system and build a shed to house some of my farm equipment. The damaged system was declared a total loss and I purchased it for next to nothing. We tore it down and designed a shed using the main pipe for the main structure. We were able to build a shed that was 96' long and 36' wide with the salvaged pipe. While we were building the frame of the building a 32' pipe fell 18' and pinned my leg to a ladder. I had no broken bones but my knee was crushed. I spent the next six weeks in a full leg cast. When the cast was removed I asked the doctor if I could ski again and he said, "Of course, but if you hurt that knee you will have a stiff leg for the rest of your life." I haven't skied since. But I did have a nice shed once we finished it.

Jewel's Continued Musical Accomplishments

As the kids left home, Jewel began looking for new musical challenges. It seemed that the local churches were always in need of organists, so Jewel decided she needed an organ. She found a music store in Hutchinson that had recently traded for a church organ, so we bought it. The organist at the Methodist Church, who had a master's degree from KU and was widely respected as an organist, had agreed to give her lessons. This turned into a love-hate relationship. Dorothy organized and coached any and everything musical in a hundred mile circle of Larned and no one challenged her vision of how music was to be performed. That is, until she agreed to teach Jewel. Most of Dorothy's organ accompaniment duties were involved with accompanying vocals, while Jewel's idea was that organ music was to be performed for the lovers of organ music.

When Jewel was asked to substitute for an organist she would only agree if she didn't have to accompany the choir. She was then free to give her rendition of how the composer had intended it to be played. She had explored the very limits of what an organ could be expected to do on her organ. So when she sat down at a good organ, most of her listeners were blown away by what they heard. She would rattle the windows and the plaster on the ceiling with her use of the many stops, foot pedals, and volume pedals of the organ. When Jewel first substituted for Dorothy at the Methodist Church, Dorothy immediately called Jewel and said that she heard Jewel was playing too loud. Jewel told her the music showed that some passages were to be played loud. And she would play it was the composer intended. I always loved watching her at a good organ. When she finished a passage and her hands started dancing on the stops, you had to prepare yourself for what was forthcoming. She was always aware of what composer wanted and how he expected his masterpiece to be performed. She had a dedicated group of fans who followed her wherever she played and I enjoyed how dedicated they were to her mastery of an organ. Most people think of church music when listening to an organ, but in the hands of a good organist, it can be a new musical experience!

AVI

In 1974 the John Deere dealership in Larned came up for sale. Harold Koehn and I discussed buying it if we could find a manager. We had watched a young man who came to Larned and started an auto parts store. We approached Ken Fenwick with an offer of the three of us forming a partnership and buying the dealership. Farm equipment had started to get much larger and there were no buildings in Larned large enough for a dealership. A 20 acre tract of land was purchased on the west edge of Larned and a new building was erected. After signing a contract with John Deere, we were in business. We called it Ark Valley Implement -- AVI. Ken quickly proved that he was a good choice for a partner. After only a year or so he had established the dealership as the #1 dealer in tractors in the Dodge City branch. He faced a couple of formidable dealers for combines in Greensburg and Kiowa. The prices Deere sold their equipment to their dealers were based on the number of units sold previously by the dealer. Kiowa and Greensburg had long ago established themselves as the leading combine dealers in Kansas and the high plains as well. They were able to buy combines cheaper from Deere because of volume buying than Ken could. Not being able to sell high profit combines was a challenge at our dealership. At the start of a new year Deere announced its bonus trips for dealers who exceeded Deere's forecast of sales for the coming year. Ken's tractor sales performance was responsible for trips for the three of us and our wives to the Bahamas, Australia and New Zealand plus shorter trips to Kansas City and Minneapolis, Minnesota.

In 1993 Deere began restructuring their dealer network. They set sales goals that dealers could not achieve simply because of the lack of customers. Meetings for dealers and customers were held in all the towns where dealerships had been a huge part of the local economies. When the Deere reps met with us their goals for AVI were preposterous and we decided to close the business. Nearly 75% of Deere dealers across the high plains closed as well. Dealerships in third generation hands whose families were the pillars of their communities closed.

Deere's assessment of the new farm program instituted in 1985 would impact the implement business in unbelievable ways. Pawnee County, my home county, had enrolled over 25% of its tillable acreage. Farm acreage across the U.S. was removed by similar amounts and even more in many instances. If there was ever an example of government run amok, this program would win first place. The change in the society of farmers was unbelievable. I had decided when the first informational meetings were held that I would not participate. The first meetings declared that participation was mandatory, but this was later changed to voluntary participation. Farmers no longer visited about their crops and livestock but how to increase their government payments by participating in programs hidden in the farm bill. This farm bill will go down in history as having introduced the most adverse effects on agriculture in all of its previous history.

Shortly after we purchased AVI, Ken started looking for a center point irrigation system to add to our list of ag machinery. He finally settled on a system called T&L which was manufactured in Hastings, Nebraska. The thing that made it a bit different than all the other systems on the market was its unique means of how it powered its drive wheels. The use of pressurized water had been dropped by all of the manufacturers in favor of using electricity to power the systems. T&L was using oil hydraulics as their choice to drive their systems which eliminated the danger of electrocution that was inherent on all of the other systems then on the market. When we acquired the dealership for the T&L line I purchased two of the T&L's. The T&L's had one shortcoming and that was that the hoses that carried the oil from the hydraulic pump at the wellhead to each of the towers had to be wrapped around the pivot point and as the system circled the field the hoses uncoiled. After they fully uncoiled the system was shut down and the hoses were rewrapped at which point it was then ready to make three more revolutions of the field.

Ken had talked with T&L about this feature and asked if it was possible if an oil swivel could be installed so the wrapping of the hoses could be eliminated. The management at T&L said they had four hydraulic firms working on a swivel but none were ready to market. Ken had sold a system to a customer with a swivel that T&L thought showed promise and were considering it to be placed on all of their systems. This swivel proved to be so unreliable that Ken had to remove it from the system. Ken then asked if I thought I could build one that worked. I had been thinking about a swivel since I had purchased my first T&L the previous year and I felt I pretty much had it worked out in my mind. The one drawback that I faced was that it was going to require a good lathe and mill to do the required machine work. We had purchased a small light lathe a few years earlier but it would not be big enough for what I had in mind.

We contacted a machine tool broker we found in the Thomas Register. He said he had several lathes for sale that would be just what we needed. Greg had worked with lathes and mills while attending trade school so he would be the one who would build the prototype. We purchased a large lathe and milling machine plus an industrial drill press. I finally had the machines I had dreamed of for so many years. It only took Greg a week to build the first swivel. After studying the prototype I made a few changes in the design. As soon as we settled on the physical design we started researching the seals that would be required to make it leak proof. The challenge of the swivel design was the slow speed that it would operate at since the top speed required was one revolution every three days. Most seals were designed to operate at higher speeds and used the higher speeds to maintain the forces required to seal effectively. After many phone calls to seal companies we had numerous seals to test on our working prototype.

Testing would be done on a test bench as it was fall and too late to field test it. Once on the test bench and running we tried several different seals until we finally settled on the best ones. The seals we settled on were manufactured by Chicago Rawhide, one of the largest seal companies in the country. I had furnished them with drawings of the swivel so they knew what we needed. They gave us the seals for the prototype. Our design for the placement of the seals showed that to install the seals was going to be problematic. This was solved when I designed and built a special seal installation tool. When we ordered seals for our first production run we received a phone call from the engineering department of Chicago Rawhide. They explained that the seals we wanted could not be installed as our drawings indicated. I told them to send them because we had figured out how to install them without ruining them. They told me that it was impossible to install them according to the drawings. They agreed to ship them with the understanding that they would not guarantee them not to leak. I told them to ship them anyway. About ten days later we got another call from them and asked how we were getting along with their seals and warning me again that to install the seals according to the drawings would ruin them. When I explained that our first swivel had run nearly two months on the test bench and had not leaked they said they would call back. Two hours later they called back and asked if I would show them how we had installed them without ruining them.

The following day I picked up four engineers from C.R. at the airport. They acted a bit surprised when they saw the test bench that we had built to test the swivel. We had used a small gearbox that we had lying around the shop salvaged from some piece of equipment that gave us the first step in achieving the one revolution every three days. The final step was achieved by a 6' sprocket that I had built out of an old wheel from some piece of salvaged farm equipment. While the test bench was rather unorthodox it performed well. They seemed impressed with the installation tool that we had devised and complemented us on the design of our swivel. Our prototype ran all winter and by the early spring we installed our first swivels on two of our T&L systems.

I had lost all confidence in the patent system and had decided not to apply, but Ken and Jay had argued that they thought it should be patented. I prepared drawings and wrote the abstract in preparation for application for the patent process. I mentioned earlier how important the Thomas Register had become as a source to find vendors for nearly anything we needed. We decided that we would try to get the swivel into the hydraulic section of the Thomas Register. As the yearly update to the Thomas Register was nearly upon us we were able to be included in the latest edition.

Within a week after the latest Thomas Register edition was on the market I received two phone calls that surprised and pleased me very much. Boeing Aircraft Engineering department called and asked about the swivel. As their questions became more technical and as I asked for more details the engineer finally told me that the intended use was highly classified and he couldn't be any more specific than he already had been. I finally told him that we would send him a swivel they could then evaluate and let me know if they needed any changes in the design. I received several phone calls back from Boeing on several small changes that they would possibly need. The last call I received was several months later from the engineer that had first called me. He told me that the intended project had been declassified and that he could now tell me what they were working on. It seemed that NASA had asked several defense contractors to bid on the robotic arm on the space shuttle. Boeing wasn't selected as the prime contractor for the space shuttle robotic arm and they were no longer involved in the project. He said the swivel would be placed in their vendors' sample inventory in the event that a need arose for a swivel.

We had also received a call from Chrysler asking for drawings because they were working on an update on the Abrams Tank. A thank you letter was the last we heard from Chrysler.

Ken was very excited about the swivel and following my experience with Valmont on the wheel modification I held no hope of selling it to T&L. My experiences had taught me if you developed a marketable improvement the only way to succeed was to market it yourself. This meant that a huge amount of money was required for advertisement plus a large amount of money tied up in inventory. If your project proved successful you had to be able to satisfy customer demand or you may lose those customers to copycat manufacturers.

I gave complete control of the marketing of the swivels to Ken and he immediately contacted T&L after I was granted a patent. He asked me to go to Hastings with him when he made his presentation to T&L. These trips had all become very familiar. Management was usually represented by several white shirt and tie types. There were also a couple of engineers present. Usually the oldest and scruffiest of the engineering group was the brains behind the entire bunch, and it was he that you had to prove that your idea was better than his. Everyone present at those meetings deferred to him.

We knew that T&L had spent a ton of money on outside manufacturers to produce a swivel, but had been unsuccessful. Leroy Thom, the president of T&L, introduced us to the guy (whose name I don't remember) who made the hydrostatic drive work on their systems. I have always wished that we had met under different circumstances because he hadn't spoken a dozen words before I knew that this man knew hydraulics. But the only reason he was at the meeting was to protect his baby from these guys from Kansas.

The younger engineers expressed genuine interest in the design and operation of the swivel and the sales department also showed a lot of interest while management deferred to the engineering and sales departments. Before the meeting was over it appeared the old guy had decided that a swivel working under the conditions required was an impossible goal. When we made our presentation to them my first two swivels had run two seasons on my systems without any problems and we had installed another seven on other customers' machines.

When the old guy finally spoke up he said they wanted a swivel that they could test on their own systems. I agreed and we gave them a swivel to test. I had not told them about the special seal installation tool required to enable us to assemble the swivel. Two weeks later I got a phone call from the old guy wanting a set of seals. I asked him what he wanted them for and he said that the swivel had developed a leak. When I asked for details he would only say it was leaking. When I explained that only two things could cause exterior seal leakage, one was trying to disassemble the swivel, and the other was destructive testing. He became very defensive. I asked him to send the swivel back and I would then replace it with a new one. I never heard from him again.

The only drawback of the swivel was its cost. Field installation required a full day for two men, and involved welding new parts on the pivot point. Field installation plus the swivel cost nearly $1,000 but if the modifications were performed during manufacturing the cost would be about $250. Before I retired we had sold and installed about 25 swivels. When Jay took over PCM, he never pursued the swivel. While looking at a T&L sales brochure I see that the swivel they now use resembles my design almost exactly. This pleases me almost as much as if I had sold it to them.

THOUGHTS ON GOVERNMENT FARM SUBSIDIES
AND OTHER GOVERNMENT PROGRAMS

Farm productivity doubled after WWII to the point where we were faced with a surplus in productivity and products. Part of the surplus problem was caused by the change in weather cycles which were broken by the return of more rainfall. At this point in ag history farmers were becoming introduced to a form of socialism as the government started convincing the farmers that Washington could solve the problem of the surpluses. The government used the surplus to keep the foreign countries in line. Those countries bought our surplus grain to feed their people. If they refused to do what Washington wanted the government refused to sell them grain. Suddenly our grain became a huge political blackmail tool. All a farmer had to do in exchange for a welfare check was to do what Washington told them to do. Bureaucratic offices were opened in all county seats that allocated the number of acres of wheat that could be planted in each county. This created a lot of problems when a farmer felt that he hadn't been allocated enough acres compared to a neighbor across the road. This friction did more to ruin the neighborliness of the ag communities than anything seen in ag history. No one trusted anyone any longer. But in six months they would receive their checks from Washington. If a farmer refused to comply he was fined by a reduction in his allotted acres and he would not get a check. This ploy worked so well it became the pattern still used today. The welfare state is alive and well thanks to what the government learned at the farmers' expense 70 years ago. Many farmers simply gave up rather than fight for the independence that they had enjoyed for several generations. They moved to the cities looking for their freedom lost. Their lands were quickly taken by those who remained. The wheat allotments from the lands of previous farmers put the survivors wheat acreage back to what it had been before the takeover of the wheat production by the government plus the government subsidy check made the farms once again profitable. Farms had unplanted acreage since the wheat acreage had been slashed by the government.

It wasn't long until farmers started planting this excess acreage to milo as a cash crop. Previously milo was grown as a feed for a farm's chickens and livestock, so acreage was dictated by each farm's livestock needs. Since the use of milo was low the government didn't impose production controls on the crop. But as milo production started increasing the Department of Agriculture began eyeing this increase in acreage as dangerous and talk of placing controls on milo as well as wheat was being heard in Washington. Farmers started planting milo fencerow to fencerow. With wheat a farm's wheat allotment was derived from the farm's wheat planting history. If a farmer had practiced good husbandry and had left some of his farm fallow, that farm's wheat allotment was slashed more than his neighbor who didn't try to improve his skills by good husbandry.

As a good argument against government controls one only has to check the livestock industry. For some reason the department of agriculture never threatened the livestock sector. When meat production got too high and less profitable, farmer's culled cow herds until the demand for beef stabilized and then started back up when profit margins began building again. This plan has worked well for hundreds of years without government intervention and livestock producers have learned to live with it without many changes in their programs.

As the years passed and administrations changed, so did the farm programs. They became more complex and the rules were being interpreted differently by each county ag office. The rules and penalties for failure to comply often were not recognizable from county to county. Rules and regulations were continually changed and added.

The crowning glory of farm programs was instituted in the late eighties. It was formulated and pushed by another government agency, the Environmental Protection Agency, or the EPA. The EPA was a watchdog group that felt that it would be better if its agency was put in charge of how the agricultural lands were used or, in their words, abused. The agricultural department had recently mapped all the soils involving food production in the U.S. The EPA then exploited these new maps, which identified the soils according to different types. Some of the categories included wind and water borne soil types. The EPA then decided which of these soil types needed expert managing from Washington. The program made all soils types available for the program, but focused on the wind and water deposited soils. Participation and acceptance into the program was a nightmare. First the landowner had to check with the county office to see what category his soil type was. If it was made up of wind and/or water borne soils, his land went to the head of the list of soils that the government wanted retired from crop production. Then the farmer submitted the number of dollars per acre per year he would take to remove his acres from grain production for a period of ten years (the years the program was to run). The entire country was invited to participate. If a farmer bid $20 per acre to participate that would amount to $200 he would receive per acre over the life of the 10 year contract. At the end of the contract he still retained ownership of the land and could then farm it again. Most of the soils that were bid into the program were selling for $150 to $200 per acre, which meant the government was going to pay for the land but in the end not own it. No one has ever been able to explain the economics of this to me. How can you pay a fair price for anything and at the end of ten years give it back to who you purchased it in the first place?

Needless to say the program was riddled with loopholes that were exploited by many, if not all. Land prices jumped because in the end the government was going to pay for the land. Farmers who rented farm land were suddenly without land to farm as landowners bid their farms into the new programs and thus no longer needing renters to farm their land. New rules and regulations were being delivered almost daily and county offices were swamped by land owner fighting for a place at the trough. Generations old friendships and alliances were torn asunder. Because of the reduction in tillable acres many equipment manufacturers shut their doors or failed. Many farm equipment dealerships closed their doors. Banks suffered as well because fewer farmers needed credit to plant another crop. The turmoil was unbelievable. The ag community was in a state of turmoil of epic proportions while our city cousins were unaware that anything was happening in the countryside. Small equipment manufacturers, which had sprung up in years previous to this fiasco, closed their doors and their employees left for Topeka and Kansas City to find work. Home construction boomed in the cities setting the stage for the housing bubble collapse that would contribute to the 2009 recession.

To participate in the windfall a landowner had to agree to discontinue growing banned crops on their farms. They had to plant their farms to grasses that the government approved of. They also had to mow the new grass once a year for two years to eliminate any weed pressure to the new grass seedlings. They could not graze or hay the grass for the 10 years of the program. There were several grass seed firms in the state at that time and they were able to take advantage of the grass seed bonanza caused by the new farm law.

It wasn't long until grass seed shortages began to show up. The seed companies began contracting with farmers to harvest grass seed from their pastures. If the farmers and ranchers contracted their grass seed to the seed companies they had to keep livestock off the grass so the grass could set seed. Suddenly the cow calf operators found the markets being depressed because the cattle were being sold as the grass supply vanished for grazing. This was another consequence of the new farm program that no one had foreseen. The ag sector remained in turmoil that still resounds today. One industry that saw a potential was the building and sale of planters for grass seed. None of the conventional planters could be used for grass seed planting. Grass seed does not resemble any seed a farmer had ever seen because the rules dictated that a mixture of grass be established on the program acreage. The seed ranged from almost invisible fly spec size to seed half the length and size of match sticks and weights that ranged from pounds to ounces per bushel. The ability to accurately plant these seed called for sophisticated planters never before seen.

By the time manufacturers had finally designed and built a planter farmers had nearly finished planting their acreage. Early on at the start of the program the government hired inspectors to make sure the mix of new grasses met the criteria that the government wanted. These early inspections rarely were approved by the inspectors. This caused a firestorm of protests from the farmers who had planted and thought they had complied with all the rules the government had required. The rules were sometimes bent by the inspectors who were mostly farmers displaced by the new program. More protests followed as a farmer's neighbor might have been inspected and approved while his failed the inspection, because his inspector would not bend the rules. Many of these disputes rage on today 30 years later. The program has been hailed a resounding success by EPA advocates even though it brought ruin to many of whom the program was intended to help.

I was only able to find the cost of the farm subsidies for the fifteen years from 1995-2010. In this period, the farm subsidies cost in Iowa was $15.5 billion; in Kansas the cost to the taxpayer was $8.5 billion. The top individual received $5.5 billion for a total of $167 billion for those 15 years. If the totals were available for the life of the program it would probably at least be double the $167 billion for the period of 1995-2010. These figures do not include the satellite programs available from the USDA. Inclusion of these program costs would probably add at least another $100 billion to the cost to the taxpayer. I do not know if these costs are included in what the government call entitlements or if they are carried somewhere else in the budget.

When the original bill expired the government allowed the recipients to renew the contract at a smaller rate since the cost of compliance was covered in the first contract. I don't know if the program has ever been reviewed or not. I recall visiting with   recently retired neighbor who had gone to the Zook School and upon graduation had started farming in Western Kansas. I asked him if his son had taken over his farm. He said no his son didn't like to work that hard so he had enrolled his whole farm in the program. He laughed and said that the program was better even than owning a bank -- they direct deposited his check, once a year, which left him a lot of time to try and spend it all.

The earliest government program that I remember when I started farming in the early fifties was a loan program on crops in the bin after harvest. Your bins were inspected before wheat harvest and if they were approved you could apply for a loan after harvest. The grain had to be leveled in the bin and the grain had to be down 18" from the eve of the bin so an inspector could get in the bin several times a year to inspect the grain. Most of the inspectors were a pain in the ass. They acted like because they were employed by the government they could throw their weight around. The reason I liked the idea of the loan program was the government paid $.25 a bushel storage fees on grain stored on the farm. Once the grain was in the bin, loans applied for, and inspection completed, you were given a loan for whatever the cash price happened to be on the day the loan was approved. The $.25 a bushel was paid after the date the loan had expired and you delivered the grain to the designated delivery point. Usually the delivery date would be in the late spring of the following year. Generally the price of wheat was around $2.00 per bushel so the extra $.25 storage was a significant incentive to store the grain on the farm.

The government inspectors measured the grain in the bin and calculated the number of bushels in the bin by a chart. The local office then issued a check for the grain minus 4% shrinkage. The shrinkage fee covered the cost of inspections and paper work done during the life of the loan. The loan could be terminated at any time by the government if an inspector found the grain was going out of condition. If the grain was below 10% moisture when it went into the bin it would keep well until you redeemed the loan at the time your loan expired the following spring. The only thing that was always a danger was when you had a blizzard and snow would find a way into the bin and melt. When that happened you would get weevils hatching around the wet areas and soon they would infest the whole bin. If the weevil infestation wasn't found early and treated aggressively it wasn't long until the bin of wheat was ruined and had to be sold only for feed.

The only treatment for a weevil infestation was a powerful and dangerous insecticide called Phostoxin. It was sold in tablet form and once it came into contact with the wheat it would start to turn to a deadly gas. I remember several farm deaths of farmers who were treating grain and didn't get out of their bins before the Phostoxin gas killed them.

During WWII, Plum Island, an 840 acre island off of Long Island, New York, was used to study animal diseases that are transferable to humans. The thrust of the research was to identify the animal diseases that could be used by terrorist to disrupt or destroy our meat supply. Hoof And Mouth disease had been eradicated in the U.S. in the twenties but it still existed in much of the third world countries. Plum Island fell to the old axiom of "out of sight, out of mind." The facility suffered from neglect and poor management. When West Nile Virus and Lyme Disease began to show up along the east coast of America, suspicions were that the virus had escaped from Plum Island. Dr. Michael Carroll began investigating rumors of employees who were quitting their jobs on Plum Island because of the fear of some of the pathogens that were being handled haphazardly at Plum Island. He wrote a book called Lab 257 that highlights his findings. The book created a firestorm of charges against the office of Homeland Security who was in charge of the facility. His research left little doubt that both West Nile Virus and Lyme disease had both originated at the lab having escaped from Plum Island on deer that had swam from the facility to the mainland.

The government argued that the research be moved to the mainland because it would be cost prohibitive to bring Plum Island back to the standards of the day. The livestock industry was against the proposal from the start because they felt that Hoof and Mouth Disease may be released by accident and because of its virulent nature it could decimate the whole livestock industry. The only control for the deadly disease is to kill and bury any animal exposed. Since deer can carry the disease eradication of all deer exposed would be nearly impossible.

The government went ahead with plans to move the lab from Plumb Island to the mainland. When it was announced that the new lab was to be built, many towns began lobbying their towns as contenders for the new facility. Among them was Manhattan Kansas. Manhattan quickly moved to the top of the list because of its nearly 100 years of research on cattle and its research facilities. Manhattan was finally chosen but little of the lab work is scheduled to be conducted in Manhattan. A new lab in Olathe, just under three miles from where I live, will now conduct the research on infectious livestock diseases. With Homeland Security's track record at Plum Island and the releases of Lyme and West Nile Virus into the general population, I am apprehensive of the security, safety, and accidental releases of the most deadly diseases known to man. Placing a lab housing such dangerous diseases in the middle of the country is treasonous in my opinion. Where is the Environmental Protection Agency when they are needed?

The Department of Education, formed in 1979 by Jimmy Carter, was the newest member of Department of Government that screwed up the lives of the rural citizens of this country. The reason our education system now ranks #17 in the world can be directly linked to the bumbling Department of Education. Up to that time the school funding was taxes levied in each school district. The schools were run by local boards elected by the patrons of the district. Any complaints were handled by the school board and the principal of the school. This method of funding and control had worked very well until that point. When Washington formed the Department of Education the whole school system as we knew it changed. The taxes for school finance went to Washington. These funds were divided up among all the schools in the state. They instituted a formula based on a per pupil cost. This formula proved to be a disaster for the schools in western Kansas where schools were suffering from falling enrollment and a windfall for the schools in eastern Kansas with high population and large enrollments. Washington allowed each district to maintain the school boards. The boards took care of minor complaints and became the enforcer of the barrage of new rules and regulations that came from the Department of Education in Washington. When a school board complained about a new rule that they felt impacted their school they were threatened with having their share of funds reduced. It proved to be a painful form of blackmail. School boards found their hands tied by Washington blackmail. School boards soon became enforcers of stupid rules of Washington bureaucrats who knew nothing of the needs of the small schools of western Kansas.

AG ENGINEERING INNOVATOR

When Cliff Manry retired in the early eighties, his replacement was Bob Frisbie, a recent graduate from K-State. Bob quickly picked up where Cliff left off. He continued with the unfinished projects that were left due to Cliff's retirement. Bob asked if I cared if he would submit my name to the list of contestants for the Ag Engineering Innovator of the year. I told him I had no problems if he wanted to. The Ag Engineering Innovator of the year contestants were nominated by the County Agents of Kansas sponsored by the K-State School of Engineering and the Kansas Farmer Magazine. By some twist of fate I was the winner of the contest. I suppose my early work with K-State with herbicides and the placement of fertilizer were a couple of the factors that helped me win the award. My family and I received the award at a nice banquet in Kansas City. My duties as the winner were that I help choose the following years' winner of the award. After we had chosen the following years' award winner I never heard from them again. I have always suspected that my lack of a college degree, especially the fact that I hadn't graduated from K-State, may have had much to do that I was no longer on their mailing list. As far as my family and I were concerned, a fine meal, even though we had to go to Kansas City to get it, was recognition enough. I don't know if the program is still active or not.

THE RUSSIAN DIPLOMATS

In the early eighties Harold was asked to host a delegation of Russians diplomats on a tour of Pawnee Beefbuilders and a typical Kansas farm. The soviet group was sponsored by the U.S. State Department and Purina Foods. We never found out what the tour was supposed to accomplish, but I think Purina wanted to develop a relationship with the Soviets so they could sell their products to the Russians. As we talked about it, Harold asked if Jewel and I would serve the group a typical farm meal. When we asked Jewel if she was interested she jumped at the offer.

The group arrived at the PBI mid-morning and the tour began with Harold giving a short history of the feed yard and its operation. The group consisted of the Soviet Minister of Agriculture, another Soviet AG underling, an interpreter, two people from Purina, and two U.S. State department officials. It quickly became obvious that the language difference was going to be problematic. When a statement was given to the interpreter he relayed it to the guests and then interpreted the response back. It was hard to make an idea or thought relevant, but we stumbled through the morning hoping that they understood us. The two Russians converged together and of course we couldn't understand what was being said as they didn't ask the interpreter to relay what they were saying. We stumbled through the morning with our one-sided conversations until it was lunch time.

As news of the use of satellites to broadcast TV programs to rural areas began to be published, the new technology became interesting to me. When TV was introduced in the 50's we had only one channel that we could receive reliably. Another channel could be accessed only sporadically. According to the publications, when using satellite technology, hundreds of channels would be available anywhere in the world. One of the science magazines showed how to build a satellite dish. The article went on to say that all of the required hardware would be available from the major manufacturers in a few months. I decided to build the dish and purchase the rest of the hardware as soon as it was available. We were just finishing the dish when the Soviet delegation arrived. It was hard to miss the 20 foot square dish laying on the shop floor. Through the years I have often wondered what the Russians thought when they found a satellite receiver dish being built at an agricultural manufacturing facility on a farm in the center of Kansas. As I gave a tour of our plant it was necessary to walk around the satellite dish. The interpreter asked what it was and when he relayed to the groups that I had said it was a satellite dish the group seemed shocked that a farm manufacturing plant would be building a satellite receiver. I wonder if they reported to their government that they found a manufacturer of satellite dishes in central Kansas.

We went into the house where Jewel and my cousin Vernon's wife, Mary Ann, had a farm dinner waiting. They had decided the meal should be served family style so all the food was on the table and was passed around to the guests. It was quite obvious that our Soviet guests had not left their appetites back in Europe when they came to the U.S. When we ran out of coffee, the minister turned to me and said in very good English, "Let's go outside and talk." As we left the table I was shocked because we had only talked with him through the interpreter all morning. We went out to the picnic table on our patio and he opened our conversation by thanking me for the delicious meal. His first question was, "Where is your garden where the good food came from?" When I explained that all the food had been purchased at our local grocery store, he got an incredible look on his face and insisted that surely the vegetables had come from a garden. I still think he could not envision that none of it had come from some garden that we had hidden somewhere on the farm.

The minister fit the picture of what I envisioned a Soviet bureaucrat would look like. He was a big man who had a mouthful of gold teeth. His thick black hair was combed straight back. From the hair on the back of his hands and on his chest hinted that his whole body was hairy as well. I suppose that made it easy to survive the brutally cold winters in Russia. He noticed that I had on a pair of Redwing boots. He asked me how much they cost and when I said about $60 he scoffed and said that a similar pair of boots could be purchased in Russia for about $10. They would be made of all leather and none of the rubber that obviously made up the soles of my boots. He said that the Russian boots could easily be repaired if they showed signs of wear. His command of English immediately put me on the defensive as I didn't want to insult him, but I was pissed off because up until now, he had made us think he didn't speak or understand a word of English. As our conversation turned more to the different machinery that stood in our yard, I listened to his criticism of my equipment compared to the farm equipment of the Soviets. I had to choose my rebuttals carefully. After 50 years of being involved in religious and political arguments I had decided it was futile to waste time trying to convince anyone that my opinion was the right one. The correct path was to simply change the subject. Apparently he may have had the same ideas because he next asked how we disposed of our bathroom waste. When I tried explaining our septic tank system to him, it was obvious that he had no idea of what I was talking about. He asked several questions about how the system worked, and questioned the reliability of such a radical idea. He finally said that he thought the European method of collecting the waste and hauling it to the fields as fertilizer was far superior to ours.

Meanwhile, back in the house, the interpreter had spellbound those who remained with his stories of how he had risen to become an interpreter for the Russians. He was born and grew up in Eastern Germany, had joined the Nazi Party, and had become a pilot for the Luftwaffe. Growing up in eastern Germany he had learned all of the Baltic languages plus English. After the war he was recruited as an interpreter and had spent all of his life traveling with the Soviets. Harold was incredulous when I explained that the minister was fluent in English. Their tour of the feed yard would have been much more rewarding had we known that he spoke English.

Because of Harold's work in Washington on behalf of the cattle industry, he had a government security clearance. I did not. A week or so after the tour, a state department official called on Harold and questioned him at length about what the Soviet AG Minister and I talked about while the rest remained in the house. It would be my guess that when the two officials were found to have allowed the Soviet minister out of their hearing, they were probably reassigned to some easier task.

MONKEY WHEEL

Our farm home was built on a hill and I suspect the house was built on the dirt that was excavated for the basement. The ground on the east side of the house was flat for about 25' where it sloped sharply down for about 25'. The ground then gently sloped about fifty yards towards the road. When our kids were small they loved riding their tricycles and wagons down this small hill and the gradual slope to the road. This little hillside was about 50' wide and the kids' favorite place to play. One day as I watched them riding down the hill I got an idea for a playground toy that I thought would take advantage of this little hill. The toy would be built of two 5' wheels. The wheels would each have four spokes, and held apart by four spacers running between the spokes on the wheels. The spacers would be about 10" above the bottom of the wheels. A basket seat made of light rods was suspended between the wheels by collars that slipped over short shafts welded to the wheel centers. The seat would then stay in an upright position while the whole thing rolled down the hill. A safety chain which hooked across the lap of the rider would secure the rider in the seat.

Tony, our oldest child was probably 10 when I built the monkey wheel. That is the name the kids started calling the toy. They would roll it to the top of the hill, one would get in the seat while the rest would push the wheel over the edge of the hill and away it would go with the rider while all of the other kids were racing along behind. When they reached the fence at the edge of the yard they would then push it back up the hill and another would get in the seat and away they would go. In only a few days they found if they hooked their toes on the lower spacer bar and reached up and grabbed the spacer bar above their heads they could rotate head over heels. The safety chain on the seat kept them from falling out. By unhooking their toes and turning loose of the spacer bar they would immediately return to the seated position and continue rolling to the fence. The rider had no control whatsoever of the monkey wheel when it was pushed off of the hill, but the kids racing along behind would most likely stop it before it reached the fence. It seemed it had a magnetism that drew kids to it. When our kids had friends over Jewel could hardly get them to come in and eat. When the kids were small, occasionally one of them would come running into the house crying that the monkey wheel had run over them, but that usually occurred when they tried to stop it while in front of it. They quickly learned that it had to be stopped from the back or sides. I wish I knew how many times it made the trip up and down that hill.

When we retired I was going to cut it up because I felt it was too dangerous to leave it sitting around. If a child was riding it and it was hit by a car, a child would be seriously hurt or killed, or if it was rolled off of a steep hill it would quickly reach a speed that if it hit anything the rider could be seriously injured. Jewel wouldn't let me cut it up so it moved to town with us. When we unloaded it in town I chained it to a tree. The local kids pestered Jewel and I to unchain it but since we lived at the top of a five block long hill we wouldn't let them play with it. When I moved to Olathe I gave the monkey wheel to Gordon who thought he would make a firewood holder out of it. I think if you asked our kids to name their favorite pastime while growing up it would unanimously be the monkey wheel.

PAT TURNER

The idea of dual tires on farm tractors seemed to me a good idea since tractor engines had been increased in size and power. Suddenly we began noticing tire slippage especially under heavy loads. I called Kliesen Tire in Dodge City and discussed it with Gary. He convinced me to try duals on our largest tractor. When he loaded up everything he needed to install them he found there was a critical component missing. Pratt Tire was sending a truck to Larned to service a customer of theirs and said they'd be happy to deliver the missing part for the installation of my dual tires.

Pat Turner had worked for Pratt Tire since his days as a student at Pratt Juco and was slated to run a new tire store in Larned soon to be opened by Pratt Tire. Farm vendors always had their eyes on potential new customers and Pat thought it might be a great opportunity to get his foot in the door and get some of our tire business. When Pat delivered the missing part he introduced himself and it quickly became obvious that he was gregarious, intelligent, and likeable.

Pat's only competitor in Larned would be the local Co-op. I had never been a fan of the Co-ops as I felt they had an unfair advantage over any competitor because of the tax structure they operated under. My philosophy was not shared by most of the farm community as most farmers were fiercely loyal to the Co-ops. The Co-op, run by a general manager whose expertise was grain marketing, treated the tire, feed, and fertilizer divisions as stepchildren who were barely tolerated and therefore the managers of those divisions had no incentives except to show up for work each morning. To me the first priority I expected from my vendors was reliable service. The price of their commodities was way down the list of what I wanted from them. It took me a long time to realize that few of my neighbors shared my values. They thought little of driving all over the state to buy tires that were $10 cheaper, completely ignoring the fact that those same tires were never serviced by the dealer 200 miles away from whom they purchased them. When service was required they took them to the local dealer who did not sell them the tires in the first place and then screamed loudly when he charged a bit more to fix them.

The best example of this conundrum was illustrated to me at our John Deer dealership when a customer came in to get his combine repaired during harvest. He had been coming in every week since early spring trying to beat our manager down on the price of a new combine. After a few months of not getting a lower price quote our manager heard he had bought a new combine in Kiowa, 150 miles

378

away. He felt that the repairs would be under warranty and our service department should fix it right now. Our service manager began filling out a service order which listed where the combine was purchased and its history. After the service order was completed he informed the customer that his appointed time was two weeks from the coming Tuesday. The customer exploded. "I'm just getting started, and you expect me to wait 16 days?" he screamed. Our service manager quietly replied, "I see on the order that you purchased your combine in Kiowa. I'm sure if you would contact them they would be pleased to help a valued customer like you." The customer yelled, "I already have, but they wanted $300 one way to pick it up." That would have cost him $600 in trucking alone. I doubt he was able to save that much over the price our manager had quoted him the first time he checked. I have often wondered if he explained to his friends what he saved by not buying his combine from AVI. As he stomped out our service manager said to him, "If you had bought your combine here I would have a mechanic on the road to get you going!"

Shortly after our first introduction, Pat and his wife Marty and their two kids moved to Larned and were quickly assimilated into the social thread of Larned. Marty was named head of the x-ray department at St. Joseph Hospital while Pat set up his new tire store.

Pat had lost his left eye as a youngster and was paranoid about the health of his right eye as he had some problems with hemorrhaging of blood vessels in that eye. His ophthalmologist had warned him that should he have significant bleeding in his eye he should get to Massachusetts Eye Center in Boston as fast as possible. They had pioneered the use of laser to halt hemorrhaging in the eye.

A couple of years later Pat started having issues with his eye and felt it might be the onset of a hemorrhage. He decided he needed to get to Boston as soon as possible. When news of Pat's Boston trip became known, his friends decided someone should go along in the event he lost his sight while in Boston. He insisted that he was going alone. All of Pat's friends offered to go with him but he wouldn't hear of it. Marty tried to go along but Pat insisted she stay home to care for their newborn twin sons who had been born a short time before.

I knew when he was leaving, so I called the Wichita airport to find out which flight he was taking. I was connected to the Delta desk, but they wouldn't give me the desired information. I told the booking agent that there was a possibility that Pat could be blinded by the procedure he was scheduled to undergo. I must have convinced her of the danger of Pat being alone, blind, and 1,500 miles from home. She finally said, "Why don't you ask me how many flights leave Wichita for Boston?" I asked her that question and she answered, "Just one. Would you like a ticket?" Jewel drove me to Wichita and I boarded the plane shortly before takeoff. Pat nearly fell out of his seat when I boarded the plane.

We got a room next door to the Massachusetts Eye Clinic and were in the waiting room when they opened. Pat's ophthalmologist had called ahead and they were ready to see Pat as soon as we arrived. I settled in the waiting room expecting to wait at least most of the morning for Pat to have the procedure. By this time the huge waiting room had filled with people with eye problems. Because we were the first to arrive I had my pick of the magazines that were in the waiting room and had just got settled in when the door to the waiting room swung open and Pat came charging out. He called over his shoulder, "Come on Schartz, we have things to do!" By now, he was holding the door open for me to follow. I had been relaxed and reading an interesting article when he bolted from the room. I was afraid if I didn't hurry he would abandon me at the clinic. As I took the first step I realized that my leg had fallen asleep and would not respond to my brain's command to move. So I did what any one legged person does when they try to go too fast—I fell down! The look of shock on the waiting room crowd only encouraged me to get out of there as quickly as possible. When I got up, although the leg was trying, it still was not fully awake and I promptly fell again. By this time my two falls had only got me halfway to the door. As Pat watched my progress to the door he said, "Do you usually go to all that trouble to stand up?"

My embarrassment slowly turned to joy as I learned Pat was not going blind, but I knew I might have a hard time keeping up with him. Pat's euphoria nearly got him in trouble a couple of times before we left Boston. The first time was when he decided we would celebrate the great news that he received at the clinic. We had decided that the event called for a Boston lobster dinner. As we boarded the cab Pat told the cabby to take us to the finest lobster restaurant in Boston. We wound up on Boston Harbor at a very swanky restaurant. The dining room was full so we were seated in the bar. Pat ordered each of us a Johnny Walker Black Label Scotch. It is a very expensive scotch which tastes to me like a very cheap scotch. We each had one before we were seated in the dining room. When the bartender came around after we ordered and asked if we wanted another, Pat ordered another round. Pat started saying that he didn't think we were drinking Johnny Walker Black Label. He waved the bartender over and asked him to please bring him a Johnny Walker Black because he was sure that wasn't what he was drinking. The bartender assured him it was Johnny Walker Black but Pat kept insisting it wasn't. The bartender picked up Pat's glass and left. This place was so fancy that the bartender wore a tux. I was not sure what was going to happen. The bartender showed up with a new bottle of Johnny Walker Black laid out on his arm. He asked Pat, "Would you say this is Johnny Walker Black Label?" Pat assured him that it sure looked like it. He then told Pat to open the bottle and with a new glass in his other hand instructed Pat to pour a drink in the clean glass. He sat the glass down in front of Pat and said, "Now would you say that that is a drink of Johnny Walker Black Label?" Pat said, "I sure would," whereupon the bartender said, "Have a good dinner gentlemen," and as he turned away he said, "Oh, by the way, the drinks are on the house." It would be less than 24 hours before I saw Pat speechless again. Pat's dad was a chef in Wichita and he had started working for his dad when he was six years old. Pat chuckled all during his meal at what transpired with our drinks. Before we left Pat waved the bartender over and handed him an obscenely large tip. He told the bartender that he had grown up in the restaurant business and had never seen anyone called a son of a bitch so eloquently in his life. The bartender thanked Pat and wished us a good night.

Our plane left for home the following evening which meant we had the following day to explore the city. We got up early and Pat got all the cab drivers in front of the hotel and told them we wanted to see the city and the one who he chose would be our guide for the morning. The cabdrivers were of all colors and nationalities. The drivers who Pat couldn't understand were quickly eliminated as were those who had to call their bosses for permission to hire out for the morning. One driver stood out among the group. No matter which one Pat was quizzing he would get between Pat and the candidate. He kept pointing out that he owned his own cab and could show us anything and everything in Boston. It quickly became a game between Pat and this guy as to who Pat would choose. I knew instantly that Pat would choose him because he knew that he was the best of the group and all that was left for him to do was convince Pat that he and his cab were the best in Boston. Pat loved these kinds of confrontations and if one wasn't in progress Pat would start one. In a few minutes we found out the driver was from Greece and he made enough to bring his whole family including his father and mother to the U.S. His cab was nearly new and immaculate. He struggled with English but he never left you wondering about what he meant. Pat's family was Irish and apparently the Beacon Hill district of Boston had some significance to those of Irish decent. The driver pointed out the Kennedy homes and the homes of many significant families of Boston's history. We toured the harbor district and the U.S. Constitution, the only sailing ship still carried on the naval roster. It is used to train the midshipman at the Naval Academy at Annapolis.

Our driver insisted that no tour of Boston was complete without a walking tour of Faneal Hall, a kind of farmer's market in downtown Boston. It was located in a huge long building, one of the oldest in Boston. When our guide and we walked into the huge structure Pat said, "We have to have some of the clam chowder. He then started schooling our driver and me on the finer points of how to make clam chowder. We finally found the source of the aroma that had triggered Pat's attention when we walked in. The chowder was in a huge cast iron kettle exactly like the one my mother made soap in when I was growing up on the farm.

Pat and I both wanted to visit the John F. Kennedy Library that had recently opened. Our driver had told us that the street to the library was under construction and the only vehicles that could use it as yet were tour buses, but he could show us how we could get to it by sidewalk from the U Mass campus. He warned us that the sidewalk was very dangerous as gangs had started robbing pedestrians on their way to the library. He told us which student buses to catch to get as near as possible to the library. We finally got to the library and I was very disappointed as Jewel and I had visited the Eisenhower library in Abilene and the Johnson Library in Austin. Everything on display in the Kennedy library was photocopies or reproductions. Very little of the displays were originals as most were owned by the Kennedy family or were in the Library of Congress.

We had to hurry to the airport to catch our flight home. Our half day tour had turned into a whole day as Pat was able to get our cabby friend to extend the tour until our flight time. His timing was perfect as we were able to check in and proceed to our departure gate. The security checks at the gates were just being introduced in the international airports before being introduced in all airports across the country. The lobster restaurant where we had dined the previous evening offered live lobsters at the checkout counter and Pat had bought four to take home to Marty. Being stopped before boarding was new to us. When we were stopped I was quickly passed through. When the inspector got to Pat he said, "Taking some of our lobsters home are you?" The box was about the size of a shoe box and had pictures of lobsters printed all over it. Pat was still on an emotional high from the news that he wasn't going blind. He answered the inspector with, "Dang I didn't hide my bomb very well." Before the word bomb left his mouth a deathly silence fell on the area. At first the inspectors didn't react, but when they realized that they might have a terrorist standing right in front of them their training kicked in. Guards appeared from everywhere and two pinned Pat's arms as they seemed they weren't sure what the next step was. Pat's good eye was huge as he tried to figure out what was going on. I slowly continued to the gate and got on the airplane. I don't have any idea how Pat was able to talk his way out of a problem his mouth got him into. When he finally took the seat next to me he started berating me for abandoning him when it appeared he hadn't a friend in the world. I said, "I came to Boston so I could get you home in case you lost your eyesight which is apparently not going to happen. When you walked out of the Doctor's office not blind my help was no longer needed." He leaned back in his seat and after a minute he said, "Boy I sure got their attention, didn't I?" On the way home every time I thought he was about to go to sleep he would chuckle. I realized that the previous two days had been special to both of us.

Since I have moved to Aberdeen seldom a month goes by that my best friend Pat doesn't call inquiring about my health.

RETIREMENT

Jewel and I realized that our 60th birthdays were nearly upon us and if we were to retire when we had planned many years ago we must begin to start downsizing quickly. Pawnee Beefbuilders had sold a year or so before and AVI had been closed. The small meat processing plant that we had purchased with some friends 10 years previously was sold. That left only the farm and Pickle Creek to dispose of. We sold our share of Pickle Creek to Jay. Since none of our kids wanted to farm, all of our irrigated farm land was sold. The closing of our operations was very hard for Jewel so we kept our one-half section of dryland that we had purchased in the late fifties. Jewel set about finding a home in Larned while I prepared our equipment for auction. Gordon had started farming on his own a couple of years previously and Greg was working as a chemical applicator for a local fertilizer dealer. Getting all of our equipment ready for auction proved to be a bittersweet project for me as each small piece was placed on a trailer where an auctioneer would sell it piece by piece to bidders who had no idea of its significance to me or our family.

Many of the small things I had forgotten about and not handled in years suddenly brought back the memories of the reason I had purchased or built it. One item was a truck that I had bought used several years previously which in its former life had been a fertilizer nurse truck whose cab had nearly been destroyed by the rust where the fertilizer had accumulated while it delivered fertilizer. I patched it up with body putty and gave it a new coat of paint. I repainted my eight row corn head and my eight row crop head. I had found a product called Renuzit, which is a product that made paint that was sun bleached and weather worn to revert back to showroom beauty. My tractors and combine received a coat of Renuzit and again sparkled like new. I had suddenly hid all of my equipment's personality and scars of loyalty beneath paint and Renuzit. I don't remember if this transformation made me sad or proud of these things that had served me so well. I had started in July to be ready for our January auction date. After months of searching Jewel had found us a home that met all of her requirements. She picked the home of Jack and Maimie Stitsworth, a couple who operated a dry cleaner shop we had known all of our married life. Her one requirement that she insisted on was that it had plenty of space for the flower gardens that had been her only reason to retire. She spent the rest of her life trying to outdo the previous year's beautiful gardens. Most of my time was spent on getting underground pipes to her many gardens upon which I had installed drip irrigation systems. The drip systems were controlled by computer timers that performed very well. She also became very active in volunteer work and spent most of her time with the many organizations she felt strongly about.

Our retirement date had been chosen shortly after our marriage when I found that my ability to draw and farming simply could not coexist. When I was drawing time ceased to exist and anything else was a distraction. When I discovered this flaw in my personality and I had chosen farming as my means for our livelihood, we decided that if we retired at 60 Jewel would concentrate on her two great loves, gardening and music, while I painted the things that I had experienced in my life on the farm.

Our retirement home in Larned had a 10x16 garden shed tucked into a corner of our lot and I quickly converted it into a studio. I added a small loft for storage, insulated it, put in good lights, equipped it with a sturdy work bench, converted an old table into an easel and began painting. The only time I wasn't painting was when Jewel needed help on a gardening project or we were travelling. My paintings were getting some recognition around our area, and I was being asked to show my work around the central part of the state.

We grew to share many years of wonderful memories with our friends on "The Hill," including the Reddings, the Heits, the Flints, the Baileys, the Tablers and the Olsons and many other incredible families who welcomed us old farmers into their lives and shared their joy of living day after day, year after year. We enjoyed so many years of morning coffee and long conversations in our backyard full of flowers and hummingbirds, it's hard to even fathom the glory that was our retirement from farming. We had no idea retirement would be so wonderful.

Three of our daughters lived in Olathe and one of them saw an announcement in the local paper that the curator of the National Ag Hall of Fame in Bonner Springs was looking for farm artists to participate in an art show. Susan had called and set up a meeting with the curator. She then called me and told me that I had a meeting the following Monday and I was to bring a sample of my work. The museum was starting a program of monthly shows by farmer artists.

At that time I only had two farm paintings finished. The meeting went well and the following month of August was assigned as when my paintings would be shown. The museum could hang 32 paintings, and they wanted as close to the 32 as possible. One of the requirements of the museum was after the show the museum got to pick their choice of painting which would then be hung in the museum's permanent collection.

Jewel had asked me to do a scene that she remembered from her childhood. She had gone with her father to pick corn. The wagon was pulled by a team of mules. She loved the finished painting. After the show the curator informed us that their choice of my paintings was Jewel's favorite, "The Corn Pickers." We hadn't considered that they might choose it as their favorite. Jewel really hated to leave the painting at the Ag Hall of Fame but I had agreed to let them pick one. 15 years later when Jewel had passed away and I had to choose our headstone I had an image of "The Corn Pickers" etched on the headstone for Jewel. The etching is a poor rendition of the painting but if you squint your eyes you may be able to see her likeness on the seat of the wagon.

Spontaneous healing brought on by unwillingness to imbibe horrible medicine had been my philosophy all through my adult life until I reached the age of 65. It started with strange sensations in my arms. As I waited for spontaneous relief the sensations seemed to intensify. Several weeks after the onset, after we went to bed one night my arms became so uncomfortable that I woke Jewel and told her I wanted to go to the hospital. Upon arrival the nurse on duty quickly shifted into high gear and proved to be very good at multitasking as she started an IV, took blood samples, called my doctor, reassured Jewel, got me into a hospital gown, got me onto a gurney, combed her hair, and did her nails while we waited for my doctor to arrive. The doctor arrived obvious he had been asleep when he got the call from the nurse to come to the hospital. After he administered and examined the EKG and checked the blood sample he told us that I was having a heart attack. They kept me in the Larned Hospital for 10 days to stabilize me before flying me to Wichita for bypass surgery. The medication they administer during the stabilization process was truly a medical marvel. I remained as relaxed as a sack of potatoes for the ten days of stabilization and I barely remember the guys who were recruited at the airport to lift the gurney with me on it into the airplane.

When I awoke the following day I was amazed when I realized they had discovered a new way to administer iodine internally. From my chin to my navel I felt hot enough to cook hamburgers. The fog of my anesthesia was punctuated only by the commands of the masochistic nurses who every couple of hours would rouse me and command me to blow into a device that had no function that I could detect. The only thing that I remember clearly during my stay in the Wichita hospital was when a nurse young enough to have been my great granddaughter came into my room to get a blood sample. She apparently had not read or understood the procedure of how to draw a blood sample from a living patient. After ten minutes of probing, poking, and generally upsetting me I sat up in bed looking for the call button. Fortunately the nurses' station was already aware that all the yelling and cussing coming from my room indicated that there might be a problem.

When the nurse in charge rushed into my room to quiet me down, she explained that the hospital was a teaching hospital and that many of the tasks, including getting blood samples, were performed by nursing students. I told her By God I didn't want my blood drawn by a student who apparently didn't know which end of the device should be inserted into my vein. As the nurses left my room the student nurse was crying. Through the years I have often wondered about that student nurse and if she finished nursing school. Maybe she settled for becoming one of those nurses who wakes people up and commands them to blow into the device after heart surgery.

As I was being prepped for discharge I was visited by a couple of C. Everett Koop missionaries. The esteemed Surgeon General had started waging war against the use of tobacco a year or two previously. I had started smoking when I was seventeen because all the men I knew smoked and I supposed that most of their wives smoked in the privacy of their homes. I asked them if the smoke and fumes from a person's work place was also bad for a person. They agreed that was bad too. I told them to bring Dr. Koop to my shop and after he figured out how to eliminate those problems I would consider stopping smoking. I had long ago decided that living was bad for your health. On the way home I suggested we stop in Yoder at the finest restaurant in the world and get one of their roast beef dinners. When we stopped the line of people waiting was already out the front door. We took our place in line. After about a half hour I began to feel weak and told Jewel we needed to leave. We drove home where I immediately went to bed and slept for 24 hours before I awakened. I got up one morning about six weeks later and could not believe how good I felt. When you start feeling badly very slowly you don't realize how badly you feel until you have recovered from heart surgery. It has now been 20 years since my heart surgery, and I am waiting for the surgical procedure that eliminates the effects of old age.

TRAVELLING

Our family had never travelled while our kids were growing up. Packing enough clothes for eight simply didn't leave enough room for eight passengers. But we promised ourselves that once we retired we would get caught up on travelling. Jewel was on one of the local boards and heard of a travel agency located in the Amish town of Yoder. The agency was operated by a very professional Amish lady named Vi who would be our escort on many trips in the ensuing 10 years. The first thing we learned on our own driving trips after we retired was how stressful it was for the both of us when we had to drive in cities.

One trip in particular causes me to break out in a sweat as I write about it. We were on our way to Dallas to visit with Jim and his wife Lisa. We hit Oklahoma City just at lunch hour. Highways I-44 and I-35 intersect in downtown Oklahoma City and they were upgrading that intersection. They had squeezed eight lanes of traffic down to one lane and had funneled several side streets into the one lane as well. By the time we were through the worst of the congestion we were like two cats in a bag. Jewel was trying to figure out how to navigate the maze while I was dodging drivers who honked and gave us one finger salutes while they yelled at me. After we had survived the worst of the congestion we pulled into a drive-in for a coke and tried to give thanks that we had gotten through Oklahoma City without a scratch or loss of blood. While in the McDonald's parking lot we made a pact that we would never let ourselves get caught in anything like that again.

Out of the blue we would decide it was time for another trip, so we would pack our bags and take off. A few of our trips took us to visit Jewel's brother and sisters who were scattered from Montana to New Jersey. In our earlier travels we had found the month of October was our favorite time to travel. The kids were all back in school, the weather was always good, and the days were long enough for sightseeing. When we visited Jewel's families in the east we always flew so we didn't have to drive in the cities. They always drove us to the local sights and showed us around. We quickly became aware that if we bypassed the cities we would be going through the small communities where the original settlers and their families still lived. Many of these communities had built museums that depicted the community's life-style from their earliest days and were always a delight for us when we found them. Jewel had always wanted to travel along the Mississippi River and on one of our trips we were going to drive from St. Louis to the gulf. This trip was memorable because she was a dedicated fan of Elvis Presley and wanted to see Beal Street in Memphis and Elvis' birthplace in Tupelo. We made an exception to driving in cities on this trip. We had few problems in Memphis and we found everything she wanted to see. She was disappointed in the things she had read about such as the music area in Memphis as it was all a tourist trap and not a shrine to Elvis that she thought it would be. The same was true in Tupelo where it was very commercialized. We were very disappointed that the only time you could see the Mississippi River was when you crossed it on a bridge as the levees were 50 feet high and you couldn't drive on them. So we would cross the river on every bridge we came to. When we reached Greenville, Mississippi and crossed the bridge we saw a Bunge elevator right on the river. We had delivered our soybean crops to a Bunge elevator in Macksville earlier that fall and we decided it would be fun to visit that elevator in Mississippi. We finally found the road to the elevator and drove in the parking lot. We walked into the office, introduced ourselves and asked to speak to the manager.

There were several ladies who were obviously bookkeepers and secretaries and when we said we were from Kansas and wanted to see what they did at an elevator on the Mississippi River they all stopped what they were doing and surrounded us and began questioning us. The manager who was on the phone when we went in, came out to see what all the commotion was about. He joined in with questions and comments. He invited us into his office where we spent the next two hours learning how they handled soybeans and shipped them by barge to New Orleans or Minneapolis, Minnesota. It proved to be one of four great stops in Greenville, Mississippi. While we were searching for the road to the elevator we passed a barge building factory. While visiting with the elevator manager I asked if he knew anyone at the barge company who might show us around. He said the owner of the barge company was a friend of his and he would set it up for us to visit the facility.

A secretary ushered us into the office and introduced us to the owner of the barge building company. He was a large red headed man whose office walls were covered with pictures of the many tug boats and barges his firm had built. He gave us an overview of the history of his firm and suggested we go to the floor of his business and see his latest project. We knew nothing of tug boats but when he showed us the two G.E. locomotive engines that would furnish the power for his latest build we were impressed. Two 8 foot stainless steel propellers were waiting to be installed after the engines and the 24 inch diameter drive shafts were installed. It was nearly impossible for us to comprehend the power and capacity he was telling us about. This tugboat would push a string of barges a quarter of a mile long up and down the Mississippi for the next 25 years. The tonnage it would move in one trip was incomprehensible to us two Kansas wheat farmers.

After our tour of the barge factory I asked if there was anything else we should see in Greensville and he suggested we might enjoy a small cotton museum that an aunt of his volunteered at. The Cottonlandia Museum was easy to find following his instructions. The museum was housed in an old building in downtown Greenville. It chronicled the town's history from its first days as the nation's cotton growing center during the slavery days up to the present. There were six elderly ladies who answered any and all questions we threw at them. These six ladies were perfect examples of southern hospitality. The two older ladies of the group were in their late 80's and had lived in the Mississippi delta all their lives. They shared their stories of their lives and the delta when cotton was king and most of the people were black. When we were ready to leave we asked the ladies if there was anything else to see in the area. One of the ladies suggested we might enjoy a tour of the recently finished lock on the Tom Bigbee River just outside of Greenville. She said her son-in-law was the lock master and would give us a tour. We found the lock headquarters and were impressed by the facilities that the area offered to visitors. There was a huge trailer park with a beautiful campground, shelters, and recreation facilities all new and no one that we could see using any of it. We found the office of the lock master and were met by a middle aged gentleman who assured us we were among the first visitors to the facility. He started the tour at a huge map that covered one wall of his large office. The Tom Bigbee River started in eastern Pennsylvania and ran generally to the southwest eventually emptying into the Mississippi at Greenville. The Corps of Engineers had been studying the feasibility of making the river navigable for barges for over 100 years, but had only started construction in the previous 25 years. The last lock was just finished at Greenville. With the finishing of the lock, the entire northeast of the country had access to barge traffic up and down the Mississippi River. It was hard not to get excited about what this would mean to industrial cities in the eastern part of the nation. Starting in his office we saw how a barge could be lowered to the Mississippi in the lock. When I mention that I hadn't seen a single barge or tug on the river he laughed and said it would probably be at least 25 years before the system would show a profit, because it would take that long for the industrial east to recognize what it offered. When we commented on the recreational facilities he replied that every lock on the system contained the same facilities because they hoped it would draw people to the area that would eventually cause towns to spring up along the length of the river.

We continued down the Mississippi with stops at many of the historical battlefields of the civil war. The battlefield at Vicksburg was very interesting. It had a huge memorial that contained the names of all the men who fought for the south in the Civil War. We toured several of the great plantation homes that dotted the Mississippi delta from Vicksburg to New Orleans. Two of these plantations still had small populations of blacks who still lived on the plantations who kept the homes and grounds up.

We always marveled that no matter where we traveled everyone involved in agriculture were faced with the same problems. It seemed that as parents insisted that their children have a better education than they, the more reluctant the kids were to come back home and continue the parents' way of life. Some of the reluctance was caused by the globalization of trade among the nations of the world. In the south where cotton was king for generations, it was cheaper to ship cotton from the Mediterranean cotton producing countries than it was to grow it in Mississippi. Cotton production was replaced by soybeans and plantations of pulp wood trees used in the manufacturing of paper. The livestock industry was facing challenges from beef imported from South America and Australia. Auto manufacturers suddenly found manufacturers in Europe and Japan to be formidable opponents for customers who had been their exclusive customers for generations.

Global trade was real, and everyone was scrambling to survive. It is a gut wrenching experience to wake up one morning and realize that what you and all the generations before you did is no longer relevant. I think this was illustrated best by our visit with a farmer in Central Montana who we saw in his yard working on his combine. From the looks of the wheat stubble it was a very good year for him. When we got out of the car and introduced ourselves as wheat growers from Kansas he immediately invited us into his home to meet his wife and share a cup of coffee. In less than fifteen minutes we were visiting as if we were long lost relatives. When his wife asked where we were from and we answered, Larned, she said, "Do you know a custom cutter by the name of Don Nolde? He has cut wheat for us many times." I had known Don all my life and I had always envied his nomadic way of life as a custom cutter. We visited the morning away and joined them for dinner at a nearby restaurant. As we were finishing dinner he suddenly asked "How do you feel about the reintroduction of wolves into Yellowstone?" My only knowledge of the subject was I had read that the Department of Interior had decided to reintroduce a small pack of wolves into Yellowstone above a strong outcry from the ranchers in Wyoming and Montana.

When I admitted I knew very little on the subject he proceeded to educate us on the idea of the reintroduction of wolves into the lower 48.He told us how his grandfather had homesteaded in Montana as a rancher and had to leave his homestead and move to the open country further east to escape the wolves who preyed on his livestock. He told of how in his father's lifetime the ranchers were able to eradicate the wolves and make cattle and sheep ranching again possible in the mountains of Montana. We left them not knowing which side of the issue was the correct one. Our sympathies lay with the ranchers, simply because we knew how hard it is to fight anything that you have no control over.

We had planned to drive home through the Dakotas as we had never been in North Dakota. We had left Great Falls, Montana that morning headed for North Dakota when we stopped at the farm described earlier. We had planned on getting through most of North Dakota that day. But by mid afternoon we still had half of Montana to cross. The map showed the road ran straight through eastern Montana with few towns to slow us down. We stopped to get gas because a sign said the next service station was 120 miles ahead. The map showed that there was probably not much to see until North Dakota, so we decided to drive into the night on this highway. We had always been amazed at the expanses of the wheat fields of Northern Wyoming. Eastern Montana proved to be much of the same. On this highway there were no side roads. Occasionally a turnoff would be passed. A sign would say a ranch or farm would lay behind the sign a number of miles reached by a path that ran out of sight over the next rise. We met very few cars headed west to the mountains and cities of central and western Montana. Montana had no speed limits so we cruised along at 75 to 80 miles per hour. We were enjoying the huge expanse of wheat fields and grasslands as the sun set at our backs.

Suddenly a huge explosion jerked us to attention. I saw hooves and antlers sail over our heads and land on the road behind us. When I finally got stopped and got out to check for damage the grill was smashed in and a horn or hoof had punched a hole in the radiator. Antifreeze was dribbling out of the radiator at a rate that I knew we would never let us get help. Jewel quickly estimated our location to be 75 miles from Jordan, Montana and about the same back to Twin Falls. We decided to drive on until the engine got hot and then try to figure out what our options were. We drove perhaps 10 miles before the red light indicated that we had lost all of our coolant. We coasted to a stop. I got out and raised the hood. As I was getting back into the car I saw a semi about a half a mile behind us and I could hear him downshifting, so I was pretty sure he would stop. As he climbed down out of his cab he said, "You made it a lot further than I thought you would. I saw the deer and the antifreeze so I knew you would have to stop pretty soon."

There were two semis and the drivers were delivering groceries to the small grocery stores in eastern Montana. The drivers said they always convoyed on this stretch of road because the deer were so bad. The drivers said to lock the car and they would take us into Jordan which was about 70 miles east. Jewel rode in one of the trucks and I rode in the other. The driver said they made this run every other day and it was seldom when they didn't pick up someone who had hit a deer. They dropped us off at a service station that had tow service. The manager said he would call the highway patrol so we could make out an accident report and then he would get the car.

While we made out the accident report the trooper asked if I had deer alerts on my car. I said no but the first chance I got I was going to buy one. He laughed and said don't bother I'll take you to our impound area tomorrow and you can take one off one of our cruisers that have been wrecked when they hit a deer. I said "Don't they work?" and he said if you ask anyone who has a deer alert and hasn't hit a deer they will swear by them. But if you ask someone who has an alert and hit a deer he will swear he hit the only deaf deer in Montana. When we went to the service station the following morning the mechanic was just finishing repairing the hole in the radiator and wished use a safe trip home. We were vigilant as we went across the Dakotas. The following day as we drove across

Nebraska we decided to go ahead and drive on home that day. We figured we would be home before midnight. We drove into Kansas just after sunset. We stopped in a small town and ate a sandwich before heading on home. Jewel wanted to drive so I told her to go ahead and take us home. We had talked all day about how relaxing it was to drive in Montana and the Dakota's as the roads were very good, but the best part was the lack of traffic. Traffic had increased considerably in Nebraska and in northern Kansas. We were driving about 60 miles per hour and meeting several oncoming cars when I noticed a movement in the right ditch. Before I could warn her she had hit a deer. The deer slid down the road ahead of us into the oncoming traffic. We saw the deer's body disappear under the oncoming car. When everyone finally got stopped and was able to check for damage a trooper had arrived and got a statement from us. Our car was not drivable as the radiator was ruined and the hood would not close. The trooper called a tow truck in Stockton to tow our car into town and take us to a motel. I had recently purchased a salvage engine for a backup irrigation engine. The engine had a radiator with it and had been removed from a car like ours. Once we had calmed down from excitement I called Greg and asked if he and Gordon could bring the radiator the 100 miles to Stockton. When they arrived the following morning we replaced the radiator, tied the hood down, and proceeded home. As we drove home we talked about all the wonderful people we met and how if you showed the least interest in their lives and livelihood they would treat you as family.

We also decided that any more traveling would be done by touring with Vi at Heritage Tours of Yoder. This decision began a 10 year adventure of travel with Vi. Our first trip with Vi was a 14 day bus tour of Alaska. The tour began with a flight to Juneau where Keith, our bus driver, met us at the airport. He'd driven the empty bus to Juneau so unlike the ship cruises we would tour all of inland Alaska by bus. I had just finished reading James Michener's book Alaska and we saw most of the things that Michener had written about. Jewel was going to celebrate her birthday when we were in Alaska and Vi wanted to have a surprise birthday party for her. We were staying in a motel in Anchorage and Vi had made arrangements with the manager to hold the party. Vi had arranged a short walking tour for the women and told me to not get alarmed at what might be going on while Keith our driver and a few of the women might be doing while she got Jewel out of the motel. I was amazed at how quickly they put up banners, balloons, and other things like punch bowls and hors d'oeuvre plates. All this was set up in a large meeting room at the motel. Apparently motels that had tour groups as customers value the groups very highly because they transformed the room into a very nice party room. When the women returned from the walking tour Jewel could not believe what greeted her. Many years later she still talked about the wonderful party that Vi had arranged for her.

We took about two tours a year with Vi and Keith. The Alaska tour was always our favorite with the Panama Canal cruise a close second. We visited every state in the lower 48 and many of the Canadian Provinces as well. We went to the Rose Parade in California and saw the fall foliage in New Hampshire. We visited the Florida Keys and several of the northern towns in Northern Old Mexico. Vi's daughter teaches in Barrow, Alaska and she was our guide when we visited Point Barrow, Alaska. There were always people on our tours who had been on previous tours with us. Many of them became good friends as well.

Our halcyon days of long vacations would eventually come to an end when Jewel had cataract surgery resulting in a detached retina which was followed by nine surgeries as the doctors attempted to save her eye. Trips to the doctor or hospital replaced our travelling as time continued to march on and our general health succumbed to the vagaries of old age.

THE REDDINGS, THE PORTERS AND JACK MANION

About the middle of each June excitement started to build among our Hill Gang as Clark and Judy Redding, our next door neighbors and great friends, began to plan for their annual 4th of July fish fry and party. Clark and Judy had come of age during the mid sixties in the midst of the flower children era. Judy was teaching in Aspen and Clark was working construction in Breckenridge. Aspen, next to Woodstock, became the mecca to many of the flower children of the day.

As a recent college graduate with a teaching job, Judy, drawn to the party scene, took an afterhours job in a jewelry store in Aspen hoping to meet some of the partying crowd who came to Aspen to ski. When the lights came on it was party time. Everyone in the clubs would head for the favorite party site which was a hot springs in the mountains behind Aspen. One of her favorite friends was a folk singer who worked the supper clubs in and around Aspen. His name was John Denver. She recalled that John performed his latest song he had written. The song was Rocky Mountain High which would later become his signature song. While working at the jewelry store one evening a tall striking lady came in and wanted some earrings. Judy showed her all of the earrings they had in stock, but the

410

lady said she wanted something like Judy was wearing. So Judy removed her earrings and gave then to her. Any time Cher was in town she would stop by and visit with Judy.

Judy's grandmother was still living in Larned and as she got older she became more feeble. Judy's mother passed away before Judy graduated from high school and since her belief in family was very strong Judy moved back to Larned and became her grandmother's primary caregiver.

Clark came back to Larned on vacation to visit some of his high school classmates who had remained in Larned after graduation. When told that Judy was in town he looked her up. They married shortly after and settled in her grandmother's home on the hill in Larned.

When Clark and Judy married Clark got into the agricultural insurance business. At this time the Federal Government was offering ag insurance to farmers as a stabilizer to take some of the weather risks incurred during farm production. Clark quickly became known as the expert in the nuances of ag insurance. Most insurance agents didn't particularly like having to learn all that was required to offer this new insurance to their farm customers. Since Clark had gotten into ag insurance from the start he was being offered jobs with established agents all over the country. He finally went to work with Rabobank, a huge Dutch bank who had opened agencies all over the United States. He set up agents and trained their sales forces in the finer points of the ag business.

Clark's job required him to be on the road constantly as he called on agents in southern Nebraska, western Kansas, eastern Colorado, and northwest Oklahoma. Weekends found him back in Larned or in Alma, Nebraska, visiting his father Crump and fishing on Harlan Reservoir. It was these trips to the lake that supplied the fish for Clark and Judy's annual 4th of July celebrations that Jewel and I loved attending.

At Clark and Judy's 2006 July 4th party I found myself visiting with an English gentleman, Eric Porter. Eric was visiting Larned with his friend Jack Manion, who had family in Larned. Eric and I had an interesting conversation and exchanged e-mail addresses, promising to stay in touch. I only had the opportunity to enjoy a quick introduction to his friend Jack.

Buddy Tabler, owner of the furniture store downtown and a brother-in-law to Jack Manion, loaned me a copy of Jack's autobiography that some of our friends on The Hill had read. I found Jack's book to be fascinating as we shared many commonalities. Jack and I were each born in 1931 and both of us raised by strong Catholic families. As young men, we had both begun to question our catholic upbringing and had finally renounced our shared religion, Jack a few years after I had. I wish I could write and explain my descent from the religion I was born into as eloquently as Jack did in his wonderful book "The Wind at My Back."

Jack was born into a coal mining family in the coal mining area of Pennsylvania. He believed his father when he told Jack that if he became a miner, he would personally break both of Jack's legs. Jack left the mines after graduating from high school and his skills at organizing and speaking became apparent. He quickly rose to become one of the leading lay persons in the U.S. in the Catholic Church. He knew most of the bishops and archbishops in the U. S. who were involved in church politics.

His organizational skills were soon put to use working for the U.S. government. Eventually he was appointed to an international water board that the developing countries of the world had organized to study and implement clean drinking water for Third World countries. It was through his activities on the international water board that Jack met Eric Porter who represented the U.K. and they became good friends. They visited each other several times each year. It was on one of these visits that I met both Jack and Eric and since they were guests of the Tablers that weekend they showed up at Clark and Judy's 4th of July party.

After reading Jack's book, I asked Buddy to express to Jack how much I enjoyed his book. Buddy said, "Why don't you email him and tell him personally?" I told Buddy that I had only shaken hands with him and I would feel a bit forward in writing to him. Buddy said, "Jack would be pleased to hear from you." I left Buddy's store with Jack's e-mail address and that was the beginning of a barrage of e-mails between Jack and me. The e-mails morphed into telephone calls between us and I always looked forward to hearing from him. He never tired of telling me how much he and Eric enjoyed their trip to Larned in spite of the fact that there was nothing to see but flat land between Denver and Larned. Later that year he began talking about how Eric and his wife Yvonne were thinking of coming back to the states the next summer and was wondering if Clark and Judy would be hosting another 4th of July party. When I told Clark and Judy that Jack had asked about another 4th of July party they were thrilled and fired off invitations to Jack, Eric and Yvonne to be their guests at the next party.

At our first visit I learned that Eric along with his work on the water board was also a Toastmaster General for the British government. He explained that there were forty some Toastmaster Generals in Britain. The Toastmaster Generals were in charge of planning all of the festivities when visiting dignitaries from around the world visited England on official business, along with planning and supervising any festivities hosted by the English Royalty. He explained that it was their job to find out what

414

each guests' favorite foods, drinks, dinner companions and anything else that would insure that the visiting guest had an enjoyable time at the festivities. They were in charge of the seating arrangements, liquors served and any festivities during the dignitaries' visit. He explained that the time spent researching the invited guest was unbelievable and that, depending where in the world the guests were from, some of the things they knew about world leaders would have made great books. They were present at all times trying to make sure everyone was having a good time, and if the party started to sag the General in charge would tell jokes to liven up the party. Eric had hosted many events for the English royalty and knew most of the world leaders. When Eric and Yvonne received their invitation from Judy, Eric called Judy and asked if he could bring his uniform that he wore while serving as Toastmaster. Judy was thrilled at his offer.

I had learned that Eric's wife, Yvonne, was a bird watcher and lined up a day or two of birding with a friend of mine, Scott Seltman, who is a world famous bird expert. Scott is a farmer who lives north of town and offered to be a bird-watching guide for Yvonne when they next came to Larned for a visit. With Scott, birding was not a hobby but rather a passion. The first morning when I was introduced to Yvonne, my spirits soared as she was a lovely, gregarious person who was looking forward to spending a couple of days birding in Kansas. Scott and Yvonne spent two full days exploring the myriad species of bird that dwell in the region of Central Kansas.

The following day was the Fourth and time to party. The middle of the afternoon found Clark busy getting set up to deep fry this year's catch of fish from Harlan Reservoir. Judy and the early arrivals were busy decorating tables and preparing for the delicious foods that their guests always brought to the party. As the number of guests continued to arrive their number increased until it had swelled to nearly one hundred. It was a perfect afternoon as it was sunny with only enough wind to discourage the flies and mosquitoes. There was enough beer and liquor on hand to whet everyone's appetite. As the evening progressed and the tables were cleared Eric appeared uniformed in something never before seen in Larned. He was wearing a kilt, a fancy shirt, knee length socks, and patent leather shoes. A gold chain around his neck held a huge medallion identifying him as a Toastmaster General for the Royal Court of England. From the heft of the chain and medallion I would have bet that all the gold in Larned could not have matched the gold in those items. It seemed to me that he must have had a lot of trust and love for these simple farm people of Kansas to allow us to pass around his priceless regalia. He was kept busy answering the questions that all of us asked him and continued speaking until the first aerial bomb exploded above the city calling everyone to Moffett Stadium for the annual fireworks display.

Jewel and my home lay on the same block as Clark and Judy and only a block east of the stadium. From our front yard we could see the stadium and all of the Independence Day treasures it held. Our front yard was the perfect place to view the fireworks while not having to fight the crowds around the stadium. Those who had not left the party would all grab a chair and wind up in our front yard to celebrate another 4th of July while watching the fireworks.

I had taken Jack and Eric to Hutchinson to visit the Cosmosphere while Scott and Yvonne birded the first day. The Cosmosphere houses some of the finest artifact collections in the world, from late World War II up until the moon landing. Part of the display is a map showing where the rockets from the Nazis landed in England. Neither had ever seen such a map and Eric quickly pointed out where friends and family had lived during those perilous times.

I had learned in Jack's book how much he loved old churches and loved visiting them. Some of the unknown gems in Kansas are the old Catholic churches that dot the landscape south and east of Hays. So on July 3rd I took Jack and Eric on a tour of those old churches. I think that some of them rival the finest examples of church architecture anywhere in Europe. They are not as large but they rival their European sisters in beauty and grace. The stone that was used was all quarried by the immigrant farmers who settled in the region, while the building and finishing was done by church builders brought over from Italy and France. These churches are about eight miles apart and are the only things that remain of those towns that once surrounded them. The churches are no longer used except when reopened for weddings and funerals. The rest of the time they sit empty, just waiting for vandals who won't take the time to appreciate the beauty of these old churches. The rural population continues to shrink and there are few keepers of these masterpieces.

It was only a week or so after the big party that Jewel's health began to fail. I notified Jack and Eric of my concern and they both began to help and support me and our kids. Their constant emails and letters helped me immensely through that terrible time.

When I first met Jack it was obvious he was not well. He suffered from diabetes and a bad heart, but he never complained. On February 4, 2009 he passed away. He had told me that when he died he wanted Eric to conduct his Celebration of Life. He said his family was aware of his wishes and had agreed with him. My kids knew how badly I wanted to attend his funeral so Susan and Mike drove me to Denver. It was a bittersweet reunion for Eric and me. As I watched Eric conduct Jack's celebration I knew that Jack had made the correct choice in having Eric in charge of his last party.

Jewel's Health, A New Phase Begins

After nearly ten years of touring Jewel was beginning to feel poorly. After many visits to doctors she was diagnosed as having Rheumatoid arthritis. She was devastated by the diagnosis as she feared she would lose the use of her hands and would no longer be able to play her beloved piano and organ. As the disease progressed her knees and ankles became more bothersome along with her fingers and wrists. The doctors told her to keep using her hands as long as she could or they might become so rigid as to be useless. Her hours at the piano increased to the point where the first thing I heard in the morning was her at the piano and the last thing I would hear at night. Her rheumatologist had been giving her steroid injections in her knees every six weeks for a couple of years. Cortisone worked very well for her. When it was time for her next injection she could hardly get out of the car. After her injection she would dance to the car. It was unbelievable. As the effects started to wear off after a couple of weeks she would begin reverting back to the severe limitations similar to the painful weeks prior to the cortisone injection.

We had a new neighbor move in next door. Shadia was an Egyptian doctor who worked at the state hospital west of town. She too suffered from R.A. and only in her forties had been inflicted about as long as Jewel. Shadia had been employed in New York State before transferring to Kansas so she could pick up some requirements she felt she needed to add to her resume. Of course since they had a common affliction they became friends. Every couple of months Shadia would fly back to New York for what we thought was a family visit as her brother and sister lived in New York. Jewel and I were amazed at how her health always improved after she spent a week with her family. Over a cup of coffee Jewel mentioned her improved health after her latest trip to New York. We thought it was her visit with her family that seemed to work so well with her wellbeing.

It seems that her frequent trips to N.Y.C. were to receive her Remicade treatments from her rheumatologist. Shadia immediately began trying to get Jewel on Remicade. Remicade had only recently been released for use by the public for arthritics. She warned us that it had some potential side effects. She gave us the label for Remicade and told us to read it before we decided to try it. Remicade works by suppressing the immune system. The user is then at risk of contracting many ailments that the body's immune system would normally fight off. One of the risks the label warned of was the risk of potential blood disorders. Any questions we had we would ask Shadia as she was a licensed M.D. as well as a psychiatrist. As

Jewel's disease progressed her quality of life was becoming an important issue for her. One of our close neighbors had been diagnosed with R. A. ten years before so we knew what was in store for Jewel. Our neighbor had nearly all her joints replaced and the disease had progressed to her spine. Her doctors had suggested a complete fusion of her spine but she declined and was bed-ridden the rest of her life.

We talked with Jewel's doctor about starting her on Remicade. He informed us that he had a few patients on it but because it was so new he felt it would be several years before enough data was available before he could recommend it. His current patients were on it as a last resort to stop any further joint damage. Because she had lost the sight in her left eye due to a detached retina and the sight in her right eye degraded by a cataract she was concerned about her sight as well as being crippled by arthritis. She decided to proceed with the Remicade treatment. Her rheumatologist's office was in Pratt so every six weeks when she needed another infusion we found ourselves in Pratt. We didn't know what to expect when she started on the Remicade regimen. Her doctor had a small suite in his office where he infused his patients and we made some new friends whose infusions fell on the same date as Jewel's. Everyone has read of the miracles of modern medicine I am sure. But when it happens to you it is truly a marvel. Jewel's pain would be gone as soon as the

Remicade entered her bloodstream and much of the stiffness would disappear by the time the infusion was finished. Its effects lasted for about three weeks when the stiffness and pain would start to show up again. By the end of the six weeks she would revert back to suffering from the crippling arthritis, looking forward to her next treatment.

One morning after about 18 months on Remicade she awoke and complained of being short of breath. We immediately left for her doctor's office in Great Bend. After examining her, the GP said she could find nothing that would cause her shortness of breath. She told us to go home and call if her symptoms worsened. On our drive home we decided to call her rheumatologist. He told us to come to his office so he could check her. He ran several tests but it would be several days before he would have the results from the lab. Her condition continued to worsen. We decided to call our kids and tell them. She spent an uncomfortable night trying to sleep in a chair. Early the following morning Susan called and told us to pack as she was leaving to come get us and take mom to the doctors in Kansas City. I told Susan to wait because I had decided that we were going to drive to Kansas City today to try to find out what was wrong with their mother. Cindy's husband, Mike, had worked at Shawnee Mission Medical Center for nearly 30 years as a registered nurse. He knew the entire medical staff and had made all the arrangements for her admission to the hospital.

Our drive to K.C. was a sobering trip as her health seemed to be worsening and she was very uncomfortable. The previous two days, the trip to KC, and the next few days are now a blurred memory for me and I am sure some of the details will contain errors of fact. I can only now, five years later, bear to write about what I think I remember of that time. When my cousin Vernon died while he napped on their sofa and was found dead by his wife, did we understand what an unexpected death can do to a family. Vernon and I had grown up only ½ mile apart and separated by four months in age so our relationship was as close to being brothers as possible. His widow told Jewel and I that they had never discussed the possibility that one of them might die before the other. She wished they would have talked of that possibility as she felt that it might have made her loss more bearable. I am sure couples who discuss this probability find it very hard because you must face your mortality face to face and no matter how much you talk it is a sobering fact that you are going to die. Jewel and I talked many times of what our wishes were if one or the other should suddenly die. We found it much easier to face this fact after we had retired because it seemed with retirement we had taken the first step to the inevitable.

Jewel was checked by a cardiologist who couldn't find anything wrong and told her to come to the hospital the following morning to be admitted and checked by other doctors and try to find out what was wrong with her. We stayed with Cindy and Mike and by 10 o'clock she became so uncomfortable that Cindy and Mike thought she should be in the hospital. We took her to the E.R. and she was admitted. When we went to the hospital the following morning she was sitting up in bed and obviously feeling better. They had put her on oxygen the night before and that had eased her breathing difficulty. Four doctors conducted tests all day. In the evening her cardiologist said it would probably be two days before all the lab work would be done before they could give us a diagnosis. The following day we found Jewel sitting up in bed and feeling much better. The oxygen was obviously helping, but I am sure we both were relieved to have her in a good hospital, with a great group of competent doctors looking after her. Sharon and Ron had driven up from Rogers, Arkansas and Mom was enjoying being surrounded by our daughters. We spent the day visiting while we tried to be positive about the diagnosis we would hear tomorrow morning. We all went to the hospital around nine and found Mom sitting up in bed and seemingly in good spirits. Shortly her four doctors came in the room. A fifth doctor had been added to the four who had handled her since she was admitted. He was introduced to us as the oncologist who had been added to her team of doctors. I can't begin to describe how I felt when I heard the word oncologist. Suddenly the time we had discussed many times had arrived and we were starting on a new uncharted journey. He was the one who gave us her diagnosis.

He started by saying that all of the tests had shown that Jewel was suffering from acute leukemia. He went on to say that it could be treated but that the treatment was so aggressive that she might not survive the treatment and if she survived her remission would probably be very short because of her age. Jewel immediately said she didn't want any treatment to prolong her life with no hope of recovery. The doctor then introduced a young social worker who described the hospice program and said she would contact our local social worker who would contact us when we returned home. After this presentation Jewel said, "Let's go home, I've got a lot of things I must do!" She immediately started a list of things to do once she got home. The girls and she went in our car, and I rode with Ron. It seemed like a long ride as I in was still in a fog as I tried to comprehend what we had just learned of her diagnosis.

Jewel quickly set up meetings with our accountant and attorney. Her greatest concern was how I would master all of our finances since she had been in charge of it for 55 years. Since we had changed accountants after we had retired nearly 20 years before, our accountant was very familiar with our operation and he tried to reassure her that between the two of us we would get along just fine. She would continue calling him in the coming weeks to discuss things she felt we had not discussed in our first meeting. Sharon, Susan, Cindy and Carolyn were with us and would make mad dashes home as they tried to maintain their family life as best they could. Cindy took a leave of absence from her teaching job so that she could become Mom's primary caregiver and rarely returned to Olathe during the entire ordeal.

The first thing Jewel did when she got home was to resign from the many boards that she was involved in and e-mail everyone on her e-mail list of her illness and prognosis. Our home was soon filled with her friends and delicious food from well-wishers. She especially wanted to see our many grandchildren one more time. She gave many of her favorite trinkets to them and enjoyed their visits. Our daughters and she decided that we should have a big party while she could still enjoy the experience and she enjoyed a party that evening attended by our friends on the hill, and many of our children, their spouses, and quite a few grandchildren. By this time she spent most of her time in a wheelchair so she could have her oxygen close by. The girls had arranged for hospice to bring an oxygen machine and hospital bed for her. Hospice is a wonderful organization and is staffed by many dedicated people. When a problem or question arose they quietly resolved the problem. They made sure we had all the medication on hand and frequently visited to be sure that she didn't want or need anything. They quickly became part of our family of caregivers. Jewel had reached the point where she seldom left her hospital bed and had need of painkillers.

Cindy administered her medication at night. If any proof of the value of a large family is needed one only has to experience the terminal illness of a family member to be aware of their value. There was no way I could have cared for Jewel in the last couple of weeks by myself. It was only with Cindy and her siblings' dedication and love that Jewel's wish to die at home was able to happen. For me it is futile to describe the last weeks leading up to and the weeks following her death. I vaguely remember her Celebration of Life which she wanted in lieu of a traditional funeral. Only snippets of memories remain of the burial of her ashes. I am sure Jewel and I had tried to prepare ourselves for the inevitable but it is impossible to prepare oneself for the indescribable sense of loss and deep grief you feel when it is all over. Only the memories of good times can sustain you.

After it was all over Cindy remained to get the dishes and plates that held all of the food back to their owners and put the house back in order. I began trying to get Cindy to return home. When she finally agreed to leave and the door closed behind her did my sense of loss really hit me.

Since I had started painting when we retired I often found myself lost in my painting. I decided rather than feeling sorry for myself maybe I could lose myself in painting again. I had no time table that I had to stick to or anything else that would dictate a schedule when painting. I soon found the wonder of putting paint on canvas was not as satisfying as it had once been. I am really not sure what I thought or did for the next two years. In the spring of the second year my kids informed me that they planned to come home and get Mom's gardens back in shape for the coming summer. All of our kids plus most of our grandkids showed up on a Friday night. On Saturday morning they all started in on her gardens and yard. Although I never counted, there were at least 15 or 20 people involved. As I watched them scurry about I realized how selfish it was of me to allow them to do all of this work. When they finished and we sat down to eat I told them that I felt it was time for me to sell our home and move closer to where they lived. I asked my daughters to check into rentals in Olathe and if I liked what they found I would move. It was with a lot of enthusiasm that they left the following morning.

I have often wondered if they even unpacked their bags before they started their search for a new home for me. That evening I got a call from my daughters asking how soon I could come and look at what they found. I left for Olathe the following morning. As I drove I had no idea that I was about to begin a new chapter and perhaps the final episode of my life. When I arrived in Olathe all four of my girls met me. Sharon and Ron had postponed their trip home so they could help in search for my new home. My original thought was perhaps to purchase or rent a home was what I needed when in fact all that would accomplish would have moved most of my problems from Larned to Olathe. A lawn and grounds would need tending. Snow would have to be removed. Trees would need trimming and upkeep of a house would all be required. My kids had totally dismissed the rental or purchase of a home for me and had instead focused on a retirement home environment for me.

My kids had chosen two retirement homes for me to visit. Their criterion was that it first and foremost had to be close by their homes and must meet their requirements. They had booked tours in their two final choices. The first one that we visited was my introduction to retirement homes and was a real eye opener to me. When we retired and moved to Larned our home was situated in a nice residential neighborhood and all our neighbors were young professionals. We were quickly accepted and were introduced to their lifestyle. Although we assumed the elder mantle that our age bestowed on us, we considered ourselves to be young enough to become the party animals alongside the Hill Gang. Although Jewel and I were nearly 70, we thought, felt, and acted like we were 45.

When we visited the community I was shocked at how old all of the residents were. It appeared that a large group of old people had gathered and were simply waiting for their turn to die. This perception took a long time to dissipate as our previous role as the patriarchs of the Hill Gang had been quite pleasing and enjoyable. We then went to visit the second facility the girls had found. The shock of the old residents had begun to wear off a bit by this time as I tried to prepare myself for more of the same.

The girls had arranged a tour of Aberdeen Village. The head of the marketing department was a pleasing young lady named Suzanne Wiley, and it didn't take long before it became evident why she was head of marketing. She explained the philosophy of the retirement home and what their goals were. The physical building consisted of two three story parts, an independent living wing and an assisted living wing which also has a state of the art rehab center. Each wing has a population of around 100 residents. In the independent living wing the population is about 80% women to 20% men with about 10 to 15% married couples. I believe that since it is so close to Cindy and Mike's home which is only a few blocks away and Susan and Mike's home is about 15 minutes away that this fact alone made Aberdeen Village very attractive to us all.

After we finished the tour of Aberdeen Village it was apparent that it was the choice of my daughters. It seemed the only thing left was to decide on the apartment size. We had been shown several apartment models ranging from a small one bedroom to a large two bedroom model. The girls favored the two bedrooms and had argued that I could use the second bedroom as my painting studio. I felt that the small single bedroom would give me all the space I needed to be comfortable and to paint as well. I had built an adjustable easel on a 3 by 5 foot table when I set up my studio in the small garden shed in Larned and it had served me well for nearly 20 years. The following morning we told Suzanne that I would buy the one bedroom apartment. She said it would take a couple of weeks to get the apartment cleaned and painted. This fit my plans perfectly as I had to prepare my move from Larned to Olathe.

Before my plans to move I had contacted Tom Seltman to auction off most of Jewel's and my 65 years of accumulated stuff. It had proven to be painful for me at every turn to find another reminder of Jewel. Tom had come in and had everything sorted and priced. Tom suggested that I have the family come in and take anything they wanted and then he would sell the rest. When the kids came home to get what they wanted of our stuff it gave us the chance to choose what I could take with me to Olathe. We chose to take three chairs, a desk, our computer, some lamps, two chests, and my painting table and easel. Tom sold everything else. I listed my house with the same broker Jewel and I had purchased it from when we had retired from the farm. Two days later it had sold. I called the kids and told them that my home had sold. The girls said they would come on the weekend and would move me to Olathe. They had been shopping and had bought everything I would need that wasn't being brought from home.

Mike and Susan hooked their 12' trailer behind Ron and Sharon's SUV and when they arrived they quickly loaded the furniture in the trailer. The smaller stuff and clothing all went into the trunks of our cars. Mike and Ron had left as soon as we had the SUV and trailer packed with the furniture so that they could start unloading as soon as they got to Olathe. It was hard to leave everything that I had ever known and loved and just drive away. I was however looking forward to being closer to my daughters and their families.

We were nearly halfway to Olathe when my car suddenly stopped. I had never been a fan of cell phones but our kids all felt that they were indispensible. Before we had quit rolling everyone was aware that we were having car trouble. Carolyn's brother-in-law in Ellsworth was contacted and he recommended a good mechanic in Ellsworth. He then arranged for the mechanic to send a tow truck to get the car and repair it. Mike Potter had decided to visit his parents in Great Bend on his way back to Olathe. So Mike was behind us an hour or so. We sat along I-70 for about an hour before the tow truck arrived and Mike was close behind. We jammed all of our necessary luggage in Mike's car and watched the tow truck leave with my car for Ellsworth. When we got to Olathe Mike and Ron had all of the furniture in my apartment along with all of the stuff that the girls had purchased to make my new apartment livable. A couple of trips to the cars soon had everything in my new home.

Aberdeen Village is one of 16 retirement homes operated by the Presbyterian Church. Most of the homes are in Kansas with a few in western Missouri. Their primary goal is to make the residents feel at home as much as possible. I was concerned that it would be hard to have any privacy in a building that housed some 200 + residents. That fear was unfounded. When I walk into my apartment and close the door I might just as well be in Siberia. The building is very well insulated and sound proof, and the residents respect everyone's privacy.

One of the first people I met was a retired preacher who grew up on a ranch in eastern Colorado. Bill Walters is a self appointed ambassador for Aberdeen Village. He seems to be the first person to greet newcomers and to offer help in meeting the established residents. He quickly found out that I painted. He had taken up painting when he and his wife retired to Aberdeen Village. He was instrumental in promoting a yearly art contest at the villages in Kansas and Missouri. The winners of the many different categories are then judged and the winner's work is used to make a calendar for all the Aberdeen Villages. My work has been chosen for the calendar a couple of times. After my first win I was asked to represent Aberdeen Village to be the representative for the Governor's Senior Art Council and since the requirements of this lofty position was only that I attend the Governor's reception in Topeka, I accepted.

Another resident, a civil engineer, was surveying the street outside of the pentagon on the fateful morning of 9-11. His reactions of that terrible incident are unbelievable. His hobby is building museum quality model sailing ships. In a lifetime of building he has completed two models. He has amassed a library of drawings and information on each of the ships he has completed.

An occasional dinner partner was married to a top General Electric executive. I knew that Ronald Reagan had worked for G.E. as well. I asked if she had ever met him and she said, "Oh yes." When he had a promotional meeting or tour of the G.E. dealers in the central part of the country her husband always accompanied him and they both knew him well. She left me with the impression that he hadn't impressed her or her husband all that much.

Another dinner partner who described herself as being an adventurous type informed me that after graduating from college with a teaching degree, decided she wanted to see the world and had gone to work for a contractor who ferried military aircraft to Europe during World War II. She had flown every imaginable plane across the Atlantic during the war. I found it amusing when I asked about her job her first reply was about all the fabulous parties she attended in England. I suppose because of their religious affiliation many of the women residents here at Aberdeen had been teaching missionaries who had served their churches all over the world. Most still retain their love of kids and teaching and would not trade their experiences for anything in the world.

Residents have a choice of meals, either the noon lunch, or the evening dinner. Because the noon meal was always the main meal on the farm I always eat the lunch meal. Generally about 12 women and I and another man eat at lunch. Early on the women let me know that they preferred us men to eat with a table of women. One day while I was trying to do as they wished I found myself at a table with two older ladies who always seemed to sit at the same table and who seldom had any dinner partners. I introduced myself and asked if I could join them. They seemed pleased. I asked them their names and found myself with Mary and Miriam. Both had poor eyesight and hearing. Of the two, Miriam had the poorest eyesight and for all purposed was blind. Mary was only slightly better but her hearing was worse than Miriam. Conversing with them was rather embarrassing as it seemed I was shouting to make myself heard. At first my shouting made all the other residents look at our table, but soon went back to their gossiping while stealing glances at our noisy table. Miriam was 100 years old and Mary was in her early 90's. It became obvious that other than being old they were probably the loneliest people at Aberdeen. Their poor eyesight kept them from reading or watching TV so they only knew what someone told them. Mary was a missionary teacher who taught on the Indian Reservations in the southwest all her life. Miriam and her husband were in the lumber business and at the time of his death, owned twenty-four lumber yards in northern Kansas and southern Nebraska. Miriam's husband died when he was 60 and Miriam managed the yards for the next twenty years and sold them when she retired at 80.

As a resident of Aberdeen you are offered one meal per day. The diner fills out a meal ticket at mealtime. Because neither of them could see, filling out the tickets were a real chore for them. Once I offered to fill out their tickets for them I signed my fate. I was soon reading the menu and helping them decide what to order. This led to cutting up most of their food into bite size pieces. Both of them were constantly falling in their apartments and always had bruises. Mary stayed in the independent wing only a month or so until she moved to the assisted wing. A few months later she passed away. Miriam however seemed to be thriving. She had a lady who came in twice a week and helped with her letter writing, chose her clothing, and helping with finances. She looked forward to the days when Georgia was scheduled to arrive. Miriam has a daughter who lives in Houston and generally comes to visit several times year. These occasions are the highlights of Miriam's year. She had Georgia rearrange the apartment, make meal arrangements, and is constantly worrying if she forgot something. When Mary Lou, her daughter, leaves after a visit Miriam is despondent for a month. Miriam's 104th birthday is approaching and she is trying to decide how big a party she wants.

Miriam is an exceptional woman. She clearly remembers her mother's problems with the Indians who roamed northern Kansas when she was small. Her mind is clear, and she has a wonderful sense of humor.

The loneliness and sense of loss after Jewel's death still persists even though I am surrounded by many people who must feel exactly as I. One of the things that I find very enjoyable is when I can get a resident to tell me of their life before Aberdeen. The stories are absolutely unbelievable. I was coaxing the life stories out of a Rhodes Scholar who, during WWII, worked for the intelligence division of the U.S. government and later taught at Oxford. He died before I was able to get the rest of his story. It is a wonderful place to live with every resident brimming with fascinating stories.